International Governance and Law

International Governance and Law

State Regulation and Non-state Law

Edited by

Hanneke van Schooten

and

Jonathan Verschuuren

Centre for Legislative Studies, Tilburg University, the Netherlands

Edward Elgar

Cheltenham, UK • Northampton, MA, USA

Published by
Edward Elgar Publishing Limited
The Lypiatts
15 Lansdown Road
Cheltenham
Glos GL50 2JA
UK

Edward Elgar Publishing, Inc.
William Pratt House
9 Dewey Court
Northampton
Massachussetts 01060
USA

A catalogue record for this book
is available from the British Library

Library of Congress Control Number: 2008932906

ISBN 978 1 84720 727 2

Printed and bound in Great Britain by MPG Books Ltd, Bodmin, Cornwall

Contents

Contributors

Marloes van Amerom finished a PhD in political geography at the University of Durham, researching the governance of transboundary eco-tourism parks in Southern Africa. Today, she is a post doc researcher on nanotechnology, risk scenarios and governance at the University of Twente, the Netherlands.

Francesca Dominello teaches law in the Division of Law, Macquarie University, Sydney, Australia. Her current research interests include legal history, law and social justice issues, and cultural studies and law.

Bärbel Dorbeck-Jung is Associate Professor of Legal Governance at the Faculty of Management and Public Administration, University of Twente, the Netherlands. She holds a Master's degree in German law (University of München) and a PhD from the University of Twente. She teaches bachelor and masters courses on law and governance and legal governance in health care. Her current research activities focus on multi-level legal governance (medical technologies and nanotechnological regulation) and the legitimacy of alternatives to state regulation.

Neil Gunningham is an interdisciplinary social scientist who is currently Professor in the Regulatory Institutions Network, Research School of Social Sciences, and in the Fenner School for Environment and Society at the Australian National University. His principal focus has been environmental policy, institutional and regulatory design, and on developing integrated policy instruments to achieve efficient and effective environmental policy outcomes. His current projects concern global environmental governance and climate change.

Marc Hertogh is Professor of Socio-Legal Studies at the University of Groningen, the Netherlands. His theoretical and empirical work focuses on the role of law in everyday life. His research interests include studies of legal consciousness, legal pluralism and legal alienation.

Jenny Job completed her PhD in 2007 at the Australian National University, where she is currently a Visiting Fellow at the Regulatory Institutions Network. Her research interests include the sources of trust in government, how social and legal systems work together in government, social capital, regulation and ethical behaviour in government. Her work as a Commonwealth public (civil) servant has included adapting responsive regulation for taxation administration, and research and policy roles in transport security and occupational health and safety regulation.

Bart van Klink is Associate Professor of Jurisprudence at the Department of Jurisprudence and Legal History at the Faculty of Law in Tilburg, the Netherlands. His research topics include the relationship between law and politics, especially in the field of security issues. In 2002, he wrote, at the request of the Netherlands Scientific Council for Government Policy, a study on law and power in the Dutch *Rechtsstaat*. In his current research, he focuses on the role of the state in protecting the common good.

Martin Krygier is Professor of Law at the University of New South Wales, Australia. His work spans a number of fields, including legal, political and social philosophy; communist and post-communist studies; sociology of law; and the history of ideas. Apart from academic publications, he also writes for journals of public debate. His writings are generally concerned to explore the moral characters and consequences of large institutions, among them law, state and bureaucracy.

Oliver W. Lembcke is Associate Professor of Political Science at Friedrich Schiller University Jena, Germany. His main fields of research are political theory and jurisprudence. He has recently finished a study on the German Constitutional Court (*Hüter der Verfassung*, Tübingen: Mohr, 2007), and is now working on a critical assumption of theories on human dignity.

Hans Peters is an Associate Professor of Administrative Law at Tilburg University, Faculty of Law, the Netherlands. In addition to general administrative law, he is interested in the interaction between public law and private law, both from a substantive perspective (private law aspects of government activities, two-way doctrine) and from an institutional one (government enterprises, government participation).

Hanneke van Schooten is Associate Professor of Constitutional Law at the Faculty of Law, Tilburg University, the Netherlands. She teaches bachelor and masters courses on constitutional law. In her current research, she focuses on the role of the Constitution in the Dutch *Rechtsstaat* and semiotic processes of meaning construction from an institutional perspective.

Sanne Taekema is Associate Professor of Jurisprudence at Tilburg University, the Netherlands. Her main research interests are contemporary legal theory, especially legal pragmatism and the role of values and morality in law, and law and literature. She is currently researching different aspects of a citizen's perspective on the concept of law.

Olga Tellegen-Couperus is Associate Professor for Legal History at Tilburg University, the Netherlands. She has specialized in Roman law, and particularly in the connection between Roman law and rhetoric.

Jonathan Verschuuren is Professor of International and European Environmental Law at Tilburg University, the Netherlands. His research focuses on the interplay between the various sources of law that apply to any given environmental topic at the same time. He has been leading the Centre for Legislative Studies since 1999.

Preface

This is an important book. It focuses on a question that has been put since statehood emerged: what is to be regulated by the state? The subject has great actuality, too. In a world of interdependency, in which, for example, economic, social and environmental problems are of a growing international character, in which national borders are disappearing and international non-state actors play important roles, the question remains: what is to be regulated by the state? Nowadays this question must be extended to the many international legal bodies, the international institutional framework.

The answer or answers to that question are influenced by points of view from at least two dimensions: a theoretical dimension and a practical one. The theoretical dimension, which contains ideological elements, implies a view on the role of the state, on what is the '*bonum commune*', on the relation between state and society, on the role and responsibilities of individuals within a polity. It implies judgements about the role of law and the rule of law. It is about Justice and its meaning for contemporary and future relations.

The practical point of view concerns effectiveness and efficiency. Once a certain policy has been considered necessary, it may be effective to stimulate self-regulation in one of its manifestations. That may lead to non-intervention by the state or by another official legal body; it may lead to a combined strategy of state law and non-state regulation.

Non-state regulation can be seen as a matter of principle and as a matter of practice, in that order. In fact, the latter is probably the result of a development in state regulation. In the period in which the rule of law started as a leading orientation for the organization of a polity, particularly the national state, there was not much room for non-state regulation next to state regulation. Non-state law was only valid when recognized by law-creating bodies of the state. But the lesson has been that non-state regulation *de facto* exists and that it may be important to use it as a tool for ordering society and societal relations. Although it is tempting for states and their governments to assume that they can 'rule' their countries, the idea of a manipulable society has been abandoned. Besides, state law itself needs the cooperation of the citizens concerned. Here we enter the area of 'governance'.

In this connection I would like to add the notion of 'trust'. States and other legal bodies should trust their citizens, their people; this implies that their officials operate in a way that people can trust government and state officials.

It is challenging to transfer this issue to the international level of (non-) regulation.

This book arrives at a good moment. Many governments are confronted with the boundaries of their possibilities because of, for example, internationalization, societal complexity, new challenges. Nevertheless, they have to be concerned about the well-being of their people and have the task to order society thereto. In this respect, I would like to mention that deregulation doesn't necessarily mean fewer rules. Rules may be very necessary to make it possible for people to live together peacefully. The question is particularly who will make the rules and how specific rules have to be; how much room they leave.

In this book, both aspects – the theory and practice of state regulation and non-state law – are discussed in a broad perspective. I welcome it with pleasure. It will contribute to the essential discussion about a major problem of our time and times to come, as mentioned here before. I hope it will stimulate many people, citizens and officials, to reflect on government, governance and law. And on Justice.

Dr Ernst M.H. Hirsch Ballin
Minister of Justice of the Netherlands

Editors' foreword and acknowledgements

The idea for this book emerged in discussions we had within the Centre for Legislative Studies at Tilburg University, the Netherlands. For more than a decade, this research centre has focused its attention on the relationship between legislation and all kinds of law originating from sources other than the legislature. The Centre's main focus is particularly on the relationship between legislation and sources of law outside the sphere of government, i.e., non-state law, in the light of effectiveness and legitimacy. We wondered whether there were other research groups that researched this theme from a similarly broad perspective. The most important characteristic of the research by the Centre for Legislative Studies is its multidisciplinary approach, including various areas of positive law, legal sociology, legal theory and legal history. We came to the conclusion that a similar group did not exist, and there was not much relevant academic literature that takes a similarly multidisciplinary perspective, either. However, since various academics from around the world do study the same subject, we decided to invite these researchers to come to Tilburg University to further discuss the topic and to write a book on it together with several of the Centre's researchers.

We are very grateful to these authors for embarking on this project. The results of the project are important as well as topical. Many legislatures and regulators around the world struggle with the question of what should be done with non-state law. We believe that, with this book, we have made considerable headway in the ongoing discussions on this issue.

We are honoured that the Minister of Justice of the Netherlands, His Excellency Ernst Hirsch Ballin, devoted his precious time to reading the book and writing the preface. We are very grateful to Edward Elgar Publishers for believing in our project from the start and for their continuous interest and support. Also many thanks to those who contributed to the editing process, especially Ineke Sijtsma and Truus Verhoeven (both from Tilburg University).

The contributions are current as of 1 December 2007. We sincerely hope that this book will further enhance the relationship between non-state law and state regulation. The book shows that, in some instances, the legislature should refrain from intertwining regulation and non-state law, yet it can also be concluded that there are cases in which such a relationship may lead to better regulation.

21 January 2008

Hanneke van Schooten
Jonathan Verschuuren
(Tilburg University, the Netherlands)

1. Introduction

Jonathan Verschuuren

In most western societies, the role of the legislature was originally based upon the principle of the separation of powers, as 'developed' by Montesquieu in his *De l'esprit des lois* (Montesquieu [1748] 1979), and upon the principle of the rule of law. Elected representatives in parliament adopt the law, the executive applies the law and is limited in its powers by the law, and courts test the executive's decisions against the law and thus interpret the law. In modern states, the principle of the separation of powers does not fully apply. In particular the role of the executive in the law-making process has changed. As indicated by Türk, modern governments have broad legislative competence, leading to a decrease in the role of parliaments in the adoption of legislation. Modern bureaucratic administrations are better suited to generate the necessary laws, especially in times when state intervention covers many fields (Türk 2006, p. 8). The theoretical responsibility of the state for everything has resulted in the practical presence of the state in every aspect of life, thus causing a flood of laws (Karpen 1996, p. 55).

Today, this is generally seen as one of the major weaknesses of the legislature. There are too many laws, sometimes they contradict each other, or they are inaccessible. In general, legislatures are criticized for the phenomenon of 'overregulation' and for producing poor-quality legislation which ignores input from citizens and stifles private initiative. Already since the late 1980s, many countries have adopted deregulation programmes, today usually referred to as 'better regulation' (Wiener 2006).

It was probably not a coincidence that the same period saw the global rise of non-state law, i.e., all kinds of self-regulation and soft law (guidelines, handbooks, etc.), aimed at issues of public interest that, undoubtedly, are issues that normally are or can be governed by 'official' law as well. Such 'non-state law' is generated by a whole range of very different non-state actors such as business organizations, groups of individual companies, non govermental organizations or other non-profit organizations, or combinations of these, sometimes even with some government involvement (usually referred to as 'co-regulation'). The rapid growth of non-state law can be observed not only at the national level, but also at the regional (for instance, European) level and the international level. The latter is not only relevant for international institutions, including institutions of the EU, but also for the national state legislature, both directly and indirectly (through its involvement in international and EU law). In many policy fields, the international or regional level cannot be clearly distinguished from the national level.

Non-state law has several advantages over traditional state law. Most importantly, since the people who develop, apply and enforce the rules are the same as those bound by them, these people are probably more committed to them than to state rules. In addition, they are better known to the regulated, easier to understand, more flexible (in the sense that they can be changed more easily than official state rules), and so, in general are more effective (Baldwin and Cave 1999, p. 40). Therefore, non-state law is considered to be an alternative to state law. In addition to reducing the shortcomings of state law, non-state law could also be better suited to address problems connected to globalization, as non-state law is not necessarily restrained by national borders (Bastmeijer and Verschuuren 2005, p. 317).

These developments, i.e., the growing role of the executive and the diminishing role of parliament in the law-making process, and at the same time the rise of non-state law, have many fundamental as well as practical implications for legislatures around the world. The rule of law ideally reserves a monopoly position for democratically legitimized legislatures to act decisively in order to solve societal problems by way of legislation. What does the decreasing role of the legislature mean for the concept of the rule of law and, vice versa, what does the rule of law mean for non-state law? Practical questions arise as to the relationship between laws and regulations by the state and non-state law. Should legislatures keep an eye on the development of non-state law in a certain policy field, should they take it into account when drafting new legislation, or should they even integrate non-state law into statutes and regulations?

This particularly topical and complex problem is the leading theme of this book. The focus is on the interaction between state legislatures and state regulators on the one hand, and regulations and other regulatory activity by non-state actors on the other. We take a broad perspective not only by looking at statutory and regulatory law, but also by including in our scope the process of implementation and enforcement of laws and regulations, as well as application of laws and regulations by the judiciary.

The central question of the book is thus the following:

To what extent does non-state law currently influence state regulation, and what should be the consequences of non-state law for state regulation?

The two parts of the question can be understood as follows. The first part of the question involves clarification of the different phenomena that can be grouped under the heading of non-state law. What different forms of regulation by non-state actors is the legislator confronted with and how do these interact with state law? Codes of conduct, rule-making by private organizations, trade customs – they are all examples of law of which the primary author is not the state legislature. Does the legislature take such phenomena into account, either explicitly or implicitly?

The second part of the question concerns the consequences for the role of state regulation. Should legislation be adapted to make room for non-state law? If the state legislature is not the only producer of rules, its primary task may change. The legislature may have to focus its attention on more specific tasks, such as protecting weak interests, and safeguarding rule of law values, legal certainty and democracy. Or can non-state law serve these interests just as well?

In this book, scholars in various fields of law, as well as socio-legal studies, from around the world address the central question in a cross-disciplinary manner. The book comprises two parts: a theoretical part and an empirical part.

In the theoretical part, non-state law is defined: its goals and functions, its legitimacy and its relationship to state law. From several theoretical starting points, conclusions will be drawn as to the consequences of non-state law for today's national legislature. In Chapter 2, the various attempts in international socio-legal literature to construct a general theory of non-state law are examined through concepts such as 'living law' (Ehrlich), 'emergent law' (Selznick), 'implicit law' (Fuller), 'intuitive law' (Petrazycki) and 'law as whatever people recognize as law' (Tamanaha). Analysing these concepts, Hertogh focuses on two dimensions: the distinction between 'subjective' and 'objective' approaches to non-state law, and the question of whether non-state law is something which will eventually develop into state law. In this chapter, a broad overview is given of the legal theory on non-state law, focusing on the main question of the book, i.e., the relationship between non-state and state law.

The next three chapters are closely related, focusing on the theoretical core of law and non-state law. First, Krygier goes into the relationship between state and non-state law through a critical analysis of the work of Philip Selznick, who can be seen as the most influential author on this topic. Because of the dominance of Selznick's work, this book would have been incomplete without such an analysis. Since the book mainly deals with the question of what still is or should be the role of state law, given the growing role of non-state law, the author focuses his analysis on this question.

Then, Taekema further defines state and non-state law along the lines of its functions, taking a legal theory perspective (i.e., based on legal theory literature). The chapter is interesting because it goes into more detail regarding the various functions of the law in general and may offer better insight into the part to be played by the state legislature, and how big a part that could be, and probably also into what exactly has to be regulated by the government. The exciting question that remains is whether such an approach really leads to concrete indications as to the future role of regulators.

Finally, van Klink goes into the differences between state and non-state law starting from the discussion between legal sociology and positivist legal science on what law is. In that discussion, the conceptual and political question of what norms can be legitimately enforced is important. Originally this debate focused on the recognition of (for instance) tribal law, but more recently sociologists have tended to include all kinds of non-state law. The main argument seems to be based on the concept of democracy: non-state law is preferred over state law because it is supposed to originate directly from 'the people' themselves. Van Klink criticizes this point of view and defends a positivist conception of law instead, without neglecting the emancipative goals of non-state law. This chapter confronts a legal vision on non-state law with sociological and political views, especially focusing on the position of the legislature within this debate, since the legislature, as one of the three state powers, has a special position within the concept of democracy.

Although these four chapters already set out a fairly complete and substantive theoretical basis for providing answers to the research questions formulated above, a legal history perspective is still required. In the last chapter of the theoretical part of the book, Tellegen-Couperus tests Ehrlich's statement that, under Roman law, non-state law was the most important source of law, used by jurists to interpret the law, including state law. In his influential work, this legal sociologist uses the example of Roman law to show that public law laid down in statutes and judge-made law are not the prime sources of law, and should only be applied and understood in the light of norms that originated from institutions and structures in society. This legal history perspective on the book is interesting because it refutes Ehrlich's statement which has consequences for the theoretical basis of non-state law.

In the empirical part of the book, examples of non-state law in the field of, among other things, international and national environmental law, law with regard to nanotechnology, tax law and health care law are discussed, again especially focusing on the consequences of these alternative sources of law for the state legislature, both on an international and a national level.

In the first of these empirical chapters, Gunningham shows how government regulators have lost (at least part of) their power to regulate businesses, and how other forms of regulation have taken over (again part of) the role of government regulation. Then he goes into the regulatory reform that has been or is taking place as a consequence. Since we aim to focus the book on what (still) is, or should be the role of government regulation, in the light of the growing role of non-state law, the second part is the central focus of this chapter. In other words: what are the broader lessons for the future? Gunningham illustrates his chapter with empirical data and concrete examples from the field of environmental law.

The emergence of nanotechnologies creates huge governance challenges which, for instance in the UK and the US, are mainly tackled through self-regulation. The state legislature appears to view such self-regulation as a preparation for hard law. For example, the UK and US self-reporting schemes are expected to deliver information about nanotechnological properties and risks on the basis of which the applicability of existing legislation can be tested. Dorbeck-Jung and Van Amerom describe the UK soft law and self-regulation activities and their interaction with regulatory activities of other countries, the EU, the OECD and the ISO. Then they discuss the influence of these regulatory activities on UK legislation. In their analysis, they also pay attention to the various public interests involved in nanotechnological development and the conflicts between them. In this respect, the question arises how governmental support for nanotechnological innovation is balanced against protective measures that call for legislation. Does the UK government focus on soft law and self-regulation because it regards legislation as an impediment to desirable technological development? What insights does the UK case provide on the 'hardness' of soft law and self-regulation in nanotechnological governance?

The next chapter deals with tax law. Job goes into the issue of compliance with state law in Australia through programmes run by the tax office to achieve better compliance. Within these programmes, several private actors, such as the New South Wales Bar Association and large accounting companies, were very active, resulting in a close cooperation between state and non-state actors, towards self-regulation and new state tax law. Focusing on this part of the process generates answers to such questions as: Was the government indeed able to have private actors create non-state law? How did government regulators subsequently react to that non-state law? What were the consequences as far as compliance was concerned?

The next empirical chapter deals with the judiciary and the oldest category of non-state law: native law. How do judges deal with non-state law, in this case, with Australian aboriginal law? Dominello answers this question by going into case law on native title to land.

Subsequently, Lembcke focuses on the role of the state legislature in questions that are primarily dealt with in a non-state environment, in this case the relationship between a patient and his doctor in an end of life situation. While the topic of euthanasia has already been discussed quite extensively in legal ethics literature, focusing on the role of the state legislature adds an interesting new perspective. This perspective is interesting for the book in cases where there actually is non-state law, for instance, agreements between a right-to-die association and the medical profession, or, on an individual level, an agreement between the doctor and his patient. In addition, the case of euthanasia is an interesting one because the role of the state in such personal, ethical questions clearly differs from issues such as environmental protection or the raising of taxes, where the state more naturally has a firm position. Lembcke proposes an integrative framework combining legislation and non-state law agreements.

After these five chapters, the final chapter of the empirical part takes a more general perspective, focusing specifically on the 'official state law' environment in which non-state law is applied. The question that arises is whether private organizations that, in one way or another, are involved in public policy are subject to (general) administrative law norms. Under Dutch law, various courts of law have approached this question differently. In this chapter, Peters looks into administrative (state) law that applies to non-state law made by private organizations, thus possibly limiting the opportunities non-state law has to offer. On the other hand, these limitations can also be viewed as a rightful intervention of the state legislature to bring non-state law into the public realm. For the book, this chapter is important because it offers an answer to the question of how the state legislature can and should intervene in non-state law.

In the concluding chapter, the results from the theoretical and the empirical approaches to the central question will be further analysed and appraised in order to give a convincing answer to the research questions formulated above. By doing so, we hope to be able to give directions to national legislators in a time where norms regulating societal problems stem from a wide range of actors.

REFERENCES

Baldwin, R. and M. Cave (1999), *Understanding Regulation: Theory, Strategy, and Practice*, Oxford: Oxford University Press.

Bastmeijer, K. and J. Verschuuren (2005), 'NGO–Business Collaborations and the Law. Sustainability, Limitations of Law, and the Changing Relationship between Companies and NGOs', in I. Demirag (ed.), *Corporate Social Responsibility, Accountability and Governance*, Sheffield: Greenleaf Publishing.

Karpen, U. (1996), *Legislation in European Countries*, Baden-Baden: Nomos.

Montesquieu, C. [1748] (1979), *De l'esprit des lois*, ed. V. Goldschmidt, Paris: Garnier-Flammarion.
Türk, A.H. (2006), *The Concept of Legislation in European Community Law: A Comparative Perspective*, Alphen aan den Rijn: Kluwer Law International.
Wiener, J.B. (2006), 'Better Regulation in Europe', *Current Legal Problems Yearbook*, Vol. 59, available at http://papers.ssrn.com/sol3/papers.cfm?abstract_id=937927, accessed 30 September 2007.

PART 1

Non-state law in theory

2. What is non-state law? Mapping the other hemisphere of the legal world

Marc Hertogh

> By confining the attention of the investigator to the state, to tribunals, to statutes, and to procedure, this concept of law has condemned the science of law to the poverty under which it has been suffering most terribly down to the present day. Its further development presupposes liberation from these shackles and a study of the legal norm not only in its connection with the state but also in its social connection. (Ehrlich [1936] 2002, p. 164)

1. INTRODUCTION: NON-STATE LAW OR NONSENSE LAW?

In recent years, the number of references to 'non-state law' has increased dramatically, from less than 1500 in 1985–1995 to well over 15,000 in 1995–2005.[1] All these publications, on subjects ranging from customary law and indigenous rights to the rules of the world wide web, struggle with the same fundamental question: What *is* non-state law? This is not an issue for the faint-hearted. Over the years, it has led to many 'emotionally loaded debates' (von Benda-Beckmann 2002, p. 37), it has been at the centre of 'ideological combat' (Woodman 1998, p. 21) and it has even sparked the occasional 'war of faith' (Teubner 1997, p. 8). For some legal anthropologists and sociologists, non-state law is equally as important as official law. In their opinion, only those lawyers with a similar view should be considered true 'enlightened jurists' (Allott and Woodman 1985) and those who hold a different opinion are guilty of promoting an 'ideology of legal centralism' (J. Griffiths 1978). Some lawyers and legal theorists, on the other hand, argue that non-state law is no law at all. In their view, a wider perspective on law represents 'the height of curiosity' (Kelsen 1915) and will eventually lead to some sort of 'megalomaniac jurisprudence' (Allen 1964, p. 32).

This ferocious debate has undoubtedly contributed to our present understanding of law and society. Yet, because of its strong normative focus, many important conceptual and empirical questions are left unanswered. This chapter is an attempt to fill this gap. It is not a critique of the previous work by lawyers, social scientists and legal theorists in this field. Neither does this chapter set out its own theory of non-state law. Instead, my goal is more modest: to review the socio-legal literature on non-state law and to draw a tentative conceptual map of this 'other hemisphere of the legal world' (Galanter 1981, p. 15). Rather than following one particular route, this mapping exercise is aimed at locating and organizing important trails in the international literature.

The first half of this chapter discusses three waves of attention for non-state law in the socio-legal literature. In the second half, this material will be used to draw a conceptual map of non-state law. The chapter concludes with some critical reflections, both on the quality of the map and on important empirical questions related to non-state law.

2. FIRST WAVE: COLONIALISM

In this chapter, non-state law will be tentatively defined as 'a body of norms produced and enforced by non-state actors'. In the international socio-legal literature the focus on non-state law is part of a wider focus on 'legal pluralism' (A. Griffiths 2002; J. Griffiths 1978). Legal pluralism is based on two ideas. One idea is that two or more legal orders can exist side by side within the same territory; the other is that 'legal systems derive from sources other than the state and exist as independent fields of law' (Galligan 2007, p. 162). Generally speaking, the literature is characterized by three consecutive and partly overlapping waves of attention for non-state law, which will be referred to as: 'colonialism', 'legal pluralism at home' and 'globalization'. Each of these waves corresponds to a different type of legal pluralism.

The first wave of attention for non-state law is set against the background of colonialism. In Africa, Asia, the Pacific and elsewhere, the colonizer was confronted with a situation of local rules and customs without the presence of a Western-style central state. 'Social scientists (primarily anthropologists) were interested in how these peoples maintained social order without European law' (Merry 1988, p. 869). This focus on non-state law is associated with 'classic legal pluralism' and typically looks at the intersections of indigenous and European law (Merry 1988, p. 872). Although there was some information available on customary and religious laws in law reports and administrative minutes of the colonial powers, studies specifically conducted on the laws and cultures of pre-industrial societies did not generally appear much before the early years of the twentieth century (Hooker 1975, p. 8).

One of the pioneers in this field was Bronislaw Malinowski. His classic study *Crime and Custom in Savage Society* (1926) is based on an anthropological field study among the Melanesian community who lived in the Tobriand Archipelago, a group of coral islands situated to the north-east of New Guinea. In his study, Malinowski rejects the early school 'anthropological jurisprudence' of his time, which claimed that there was no law in primitive societies. According to these studies, the inhabitants of primitive communities were subject to some sort of automatic, spontaneous submission to custom based on 'mental inertia' or 'group instinct'. Malinowski, on the other hand, set out to study 'all the rules conceived and acted upon as binding obligations, to find out the nature of the binding forces, and to classify the rules according to the manner in which they are made valid' (Malinowski [1926] 1972, p. 15).

In his study, he closely observes a group of fishermen and he discovers that only a small portion of their catch remains with the villagers. Most of the fish is used in a food barter system between inland and coastal villages. People from inland villages visit the coast and supply the fishermen with vegetables. In return, the coastal community repays them with fish. According to Malinowski, this relationship has important economic and ceremonial elements. Yet it also has a distinct legal side; it is in effect 'a system of mutual obligations which forces the fisherman to repay whenever he has received a gift from his inland partner, and vice versa' (Malinowski [1926] 1972, p. 22). Both villages are mutually dependent on each other and this provides them with a strong weapon for the enforcement of their rights.

Malinowski claims that this type of relationship is not limited to the exchange of fish for vegetables, but includes other forms of trading and many other mutual services as well. Moreover, similar relationships are present between husbands and wives, between parents and their children, and so forth. From this he concludes that, although the Tobriand Islands lack a 'definite machinery of enactment, administration, and enforcement of law' (Malinowski [1926] 1972, p. 14) (typically associated with the state), law is an important aspect of tribal life:

> The whole structure of Tobriand society is founded on the principle of *legal status*. By this I mean that the claims of chief over commoners, husband over wife, parent over child, and vice versa, are not exercised arbitrarily and one-sidedly, but according to definite rules, and arranged into well-balanced chains of reciprocal services. (Malinowski [1926] 1972, p. 46)

According to Malinowski, the rules of this 'primitive law' of the Tobriand Islanders stand out from other customs in that 'they are felt and regarded as the obligation of one person and the rightful claims of the other' (Malinowski [1926] 1972, p. 55).

This type of anthropological knowledge about the 'primitive' law (or: 'tribal', 'customary' and 'religious' law) of indigenous peoples was not only discussed among social scientists, but also became integrated within different systems of colonial law. In Africa, for instance, 'the British and the French superimposed their law onto indigenous law, incorporating customary law as long as it was not "repugnant to natural justice, equity, and good conscience . . ."' (Merry 1988, p. 870). In his book, Hooker (1975) provides a comprehensive review of 'colonial and post-colonial law' in Asia, Africa and the Middle East. To give but one example, his paper on French colonial law includes the following sections: 'Colonial Policy and Islam in Algeria', 'French Civil Law and Hindu Law', 'French Civil Law and African Laws' and 'French Civil Law and the Laws of Indo-China'.

In more recent times, the use of different types of non-state law in colonial legal systems has been severely criticized. It is now argued that many rules which were originally presented by the colonizer as 'customary law' were in fact not *found* but *created* by the colonizers themselves. For instance, in his study of law in Malawi and Zambia, Chanock (1985, p. 4) argues: 'The law was at the cutting edge of colonialism, an instrument of the power of an alien state and part of the process of coercion.' This criticism, which is also reflected in recent studies about the 'myth of adat' in Indonesia (Burns 1989), means an important break with traditions of legal scholarship that saw in customary law the ancient or original law of indigenous peoples (Merry 2003b, p. 572).

3. SECOND WAVE: LEGAL PLURALISM AT HOME

Beginning in the late 1970s, a new wave of attention for non-state law has developed as well. Typical for this second wave is that more and more socio-legal scholars have become interested in applying the concept of legal pluralism to non-colonized societies, particularly to the advanced industrial countries of Europe and the United States. This development is sometimes referred to as 'new legal pluralism' or 'legal pluralism at home' (Merry 1988, p. 874). This change of focus in the literature is symbolized by the fact that during this period one of the leading journals in the field, *African Law Studies*, changed its name to *Journal of Legal Pluralism and Unofficial Law*:

> [T]he new journal will address phenomena of legal pluralism and unofficial law wherever they are found . . . This new and distinctive focus is upon all those circumstances in which more than one normative order is present within a single social group, and upon the normative orders themselves ('customary law', 'unofficial law', 'folk law', 'indigenous law', 'traditional law', or whatever other name they may be known by). (J. Griffiths 1980, p. i)

This constitutes an important shift in the study of non-state law. It means that in contexts in which the dominance of a central legal system is unambiguous, 'this [approach] worries about missing what else is going on; the extent to which other forms of regulation outside law constitute law' (Merry 1988, p. 874).

Although most empirical studies of this 'new' approach only started to emerge in the 1970s, its foundations had been laid out in the early twentieth century by Eugen Ehrlich and his study of the 'living law'. Ehrlich (1862–1922) was a professor of Roman law in the city of Czernowitz, in an area called the Bukowina, on the outskirts of the Austro-Hungarian Empire. In this part of south-eastern Europe, many different ethno-cultural groups lived side by side, including Armenians, Germans, Jews, Romanians, Russians, Ruthenians, Slovaks, Hungarians and Gypsies. Based on observation and through empirical study of the habits and customs of these and other groups, Ehrlich developed an alternative perspective on law.

Ehrlich focuses on the rules of conduct that people in actual fact obey and concludes that most people do not follow the official Austrian law, but rather live according to their own social norms. One of his many examples looks at the German peasantry. In the part of the Austrian code that deals with matrimonial agreements there are only four sections that deal with the matrimonial regime of community of goods. Yet, Ehrlich claims, anyone who has had an opportunity of coming into contact with the German peasantry of Austria realizes that this is not representative of their situation:

> [They] live, almost exclusively, under a matrimonial regime of community goods. But this matrimonial community of goods, which is the prevailing, freely chosen property regime of the German peasantry in Austria, has nothing in common with the community of goods provided for in the Austrian Civil Code, and the provisions of the Civil Code are never being applied . . . (Ehrlich 2002, p. 489)

Ehrlich calls the German peasants, as well as other formal and informal groups, 'social associations'. This is a plurality of human beings 'who, in their relations with one another, recognize certain rules of conduct as binding, and, generally at least, actually regulate their conduct according to them' (Ehrlich 2002, p. 39). According to Ehrlich, these organizational norms should be considered 'living law'. This is 'the law which dominates life itself even though it has not been posited in legal propositions' (Ehrlich 2002, p. 493).

A similar focus can be found in Pospisil's work. He rejects the idea of law as 'the property of a society as a whole' (Pospisil 1971, p. 99). Instead, he argues, society consists of many different subgroups, or 'legal levels':

> Society, be it a tribe or a 'modern' nation, is not an undifferentiated amalgam of people. It is rather a patterned mosaic of subgroups that belong to certain, usually well-defined (or definable) types with different memberships, composition, and degree of inclusiveness. Every such subgroup owes its existence in a large degree to a legal system that is its own and that regulates the behaviour of its members . . . (Pospisil 1971, p. 125)

According to Galanter (1981), people experience justice (and injustice) not only in forums sponsored by the state but at 'the primary institutional locations of their activity': home, neighbourhood, workplace, business deal, and so on. Just as health is not found primarily in hospitals or knowledge in schools, 'so justice is not primarily to be found in official justice-dispensing institutions' (Galanter 1981, p. 14). He therefore calls attention to different types of 'indigenous law': 'concrete patterns of social ordering to be found in a variety of institutional settings in American society' (Galanter 1981, p. 14).

Most studies during this new wave of attention for non-state law focus on two fields: (i) the diverse laws of immigrant groups and religious, ethnic and cultural minorities in industrialized societies; and (ii) unofficial forms of ordering located in social networks or institutions.

3.1 Immigrant Groups and Cultural Minorities

One example of a study which looks at non-state law among immigrant groups and cultural minorities is an anthropological study of the 'internal law' or 'folk law' of the Moluccan (Indonesian) community in the Netherlands (Strijbosch 1985). This group consists of ex-soldiers of the Dutch colonial army who moved to the Netherlands in the aftermath of the decolonization of Indonesia in 1951, and their families and offspring. Many of them live in distinct neighbourhoods of Dutch towns and villages. This particular study focuses on the role of 'pela' in one such community; an institutional bond of friendship or brotherhood between all native residents of two or more villages. More specifically, it studies an important element of 'pela' according to which persons mutually engaged in the same alliance are not allowed to intermarry.

The study gives a detailed account of the 'indigenous legal system' in this Moluccan community. Using observation, case studies and interviews, it demonstrates that within the Moluccan community in the Netherlands there is a tendency to interpret the pela intermarriage taboo in a strict, 'traditional' way. Moreover, these rules are enforced by a variety of social sanctions, ranging from pressure and persuasion to permanent exclusion from the Moluccan community.

Similar studies have been conducted in many different communities, ranging from American Indian tribes in the United States (Forer 1979) to, for instance, a Quaker community in central England (Bradney & Cownie 2000).

3.2 Social Networks and Institutions

Inspired by Malinowski, Stewart Macaulay set out to study business practices in Wisconsin (cf. Macaulay 1963, 1995). He found that a significant amount of business exchanges are done on a non-contractual basis. First, business agreements are frequently made without knowledge of the relevant rules of contract law. Moreover, disputes are frequently settled without reference to the contract or potential legal sanctions and lawsuits for breach of contract are rare. Macaulay argues that the key in understanding this practice is the long-standing relationship between businessmen.

In most cases, a detailed contract is not needed because its functions are served by other devices. According to Macaulay, 'customs of their industry' are such that both parties will exercise care to see both understand the primary obligation on each side. Moreover, in disputes businessmen can fall back on many non-legal sanctions. Two norms are widely accepted within the business community: commitments are to be honoured in all situations and one ought to produce a good product and stand behind it. As in Malinowski's study, the business community in Wisconsin is built on an elaborate system of exchange relationships and, for instance, salesmen and purchasing agents take each other out for dinner and exchange Christmas gifts. Anyone who does not follow the local norms and rules of the business community runs the risk of being excluded from future business deals. In his later work, Macaulay (1986) generalizes these findings about non-state law in the business community to other social sectors as well. He refers to this as 'private government':

> If governing involves making rules, interpreting them, applying them to specific cases, and sanctioning violations, some or all of this is done by such different clusters of people as the Mafia, the National Collegiate Athletic Association, the American Arbitration Association, those who run large shopping centers, neighborhood associations, and even the regulars at Smokey's tavern. (Macaulay 1986, p. 445)

This position is similar to Sally Falk Moore's (1973) analysis of 'semi-autonomous social fields'. In her view, it is well established that between the body politic and the individual, there are various smaller, organized social fields. 'These social fields have their own customs and rules and the means of coercing or inducing compliance. They have what Weber called "legal order"' (Moore 1973, p. 721). Moore builds her argument on the findings of her fieldwork among the Chagga people of Mount Kilimanjaro (Tanzania) and a case study of the dress industry in New York City.

The work in the fashion industry is subject to detailed contracts, which are closely monitored by a union representative. However, business is such that it would be impossible to make a profit unless the precise terms of these contracts are regularly broken. As a result, in busy times, workers put in many more hours of work than union contracts permit. And in quieter times, workers must be paid even when they are in fact not working. According to a set of 'binding rules and customs' (Moore 1973, p. 728) generated in this social field, the union representative accepts these breaches of contract and, in return for his 'reasonableness', he receives various favours and gifts from the contractor (like an expensive dress for his wife).

Many of Macaulay's and Moore's findings are also reflected in Ellickson's (1994) more recent study of how residents of rural Shasta County, California, resolve a variety of disputes that arise from wayward cattle. His overall conclusion is that in Shasta County neighbours apply informal norms, rather than formal legal rules, to resolve most of the issues that arise among them. For instance, in resolving trespass conflicts, 'most rural residents are consciously committed to an overarching norm of cooperation among neighbors' (Ellickson 1994, p. 53). In their view, an owner of livestock is responsible for the acts of his animals. Based on empirical research, Ellickson paints a detailed picture of an elaborate system of informal norms. The enforcement of these norms is primarily based on reciprocity. Rural residents deal with each other on many different occasions and expect those relationships to continue in the future. 'Thus any trespass dispute with a neighbor is almost certain to be but one thread in the rich fabric of a continuing relationship' (Ellickson 1994, p. 55).

4. THIRD WAVE: GLOBALIZATION

The third, and most recent, wave of attention for non-state law is related to globalization. In general terms, this refers to the 'movement, diffusion, and expansion [of trade, culture and consumption] from a local level and with local implications, to levels and implications that are worldwide, or, more usually, that transcend national borders in some way' (Friedman 2001, p. 347). A growing number of authors claim that these developments also have profound legal implications:

> Globalization reminds us that the state is constrained not only by other states and supranational organizations but also by non-state organizations (e.g. NGOs), communities (e.g. religious groups), and powerful private players

> (e.g. multinational corporations). All these actors, in one way or another, play roles in the globalizing world that were traditionally reserved to the state. One of these roles might be the role of lawmaker. (Michaels 2005, p. 1211)

It is argued that, after 'classic' and 'new legal pluralism', these developments should be interpreted in terms of 'global legal pluralism' (Snyder 1999; Berman 2005, 2007). Similar to the Austro-Hungarian Empire of the early twentieth century, in which Eugen Ehrlich identified many different social associations with their own legal order, the present social and legal context can be understood as a 'Global Bukowina' (Teubner 1997). The study of this 'global law without a state' (Teubner 1997) or 'post-Westphalian conception of law' (Twining 2003) focuses primarily on two fields: (i) the development of international merchant law, and (ii) human rights law.

4.1 *Lex Mercatoria*

There is a considerable body of literature on what some scholars describe as the 'new' *lex mercatoria*. The 'old' *lex mercatoria* refers to the mercantile custom or non-national law of international commerce in the Middle Ages, created not by the authority of states but rather by and within international commerce itself. This non-state law was recognized not only in several treaties but also in decisions by judges of the state (Michaels 2005, p. 1219). Starting in the 1980s and 1990s, several scholars claim that we are now witnessing a similar development of a new, transnational, non-state law: 'The idea is that the transnational [lawyers and businesses] of today have their own customs, norms, and practices, and a sort of merchant law is emerging, without benefit of legislation, from their patterns of behavior' (Friedman 2001, p. 356). Like the old *lex mercatoria*, the new version is said to be 'an autonomous non-state legal order with special rules and special adjudicating [and in particular arbitral] bodies' (Michaels 2005, p. 1219). Multinational corporations use standard contract forms and conditions which are recognized by business organizations and (non-state) institutions such as the International Law Association, the International Chamber of Commerce and the International Maritime Commission Group. Their international contracts often contain elaborate and detailed provisions to prevent the application of national law. Moreover, international commercial arbitration has long been the superior institution for resolving international legal disputes compared with national courts and has developed well-organized arbitral systems of high procedural quality (Mertens 1997). Similarly, in the world of sports, people are discussing the emergence of a *lex sportiva internationalis* (Simon 1990; Nafziger 1996). Schultz (2006), for example, refers to the handling of two doping cases during the Olympic Games in Turin. In his view, these cases illustrate the pre-eminence of a special type of non-state law (*Olympic lex sportiva*) over the public legal system (Italian criminal law).

A special element of this new type of non-state law is associated with the Internet. According to Johnson & Post (1996, p. 1389): 'Cyberspace is anything but anarchic; its distinct rule sets are becoming more robust every day.' These and other authors consider Cyberspace as a 'self-governance system' with its own set of 'rules and customs' and its own means of enforcement, disconnected from national states. It is argued that, for example, the current domain name system evolved from decisions made by engineers and the practices of Internet service providers (Rutkowski 1995, cited in Johnson & Post 1996, p. 1388). Similarly, widespread agreement is said to exist about core principles of 'netiquette' in mailing lists and discussion groups (Goode & Johnson 1991, cited in Johnson & Post 1996, p. 1389).

4.2 Human Rights Law

The second element of an emerging global legal order without a state is connected with the development of human rights law. 'It is not only the hamburger, pizza, and rock and roll that have internationalized,' Friedman (2001, p. 364) argues, 'so too have concepts like the rule of law or basic human rights.' It is noted that in the last few decades 'non-state actors [especially NGOs] have started playing an increasing role in the shaping of international human rights doctrine, deeply infringing on the once indisputable prerogatives of the nation-states' (Bianchi 1997, p. 179).

Merry (2003a) has, for example, conducted an ethnographic analysis of the Convention on the Elimination of All Forms of Discrimination against Women. Its implementation relies on a complex process of periodic reporting to a global body meeting in New York and 'a symbiotic if sometimes contentious relationship between government representatives and international and domestic NGOs'. She concludes that, despite a lack of formal legal sanctions, this convention can be considered 'part of an emerging global system of law' with its own 'law-like documents' and 'quasi-legislative processes' (Merry 2003a, pp. 943, 974).

5. TOWARDS A CONCEPTUAL MAP OF NON-STATE LAW

These three waves of attention have produced a vast and complex landscape of literature on many different kinds of non-state law. In order to navigate through this terrain, we need some sort of conceptual map. The primary step in drawing such a map is to take a closer look at what scholars actually mean when they refer to 'non-state law'. We can break down this concept into two separate components, which will later serve as the two axes of our map.

5.1 First Dimension: Within or Without the State?

First, what do the words *non-state* in 'non-state law' refer to? The literature in this chapter focuses on different types of norms, rules and regulations that are produced by various non-state actors. However, the position of the state in relation to these actors varies. Whereas in some cases there are non-state actors *within* the context of a national state, in other cases these actors operate *without* the unambiguous presence of a central state. This dimension of the literature on non-state law will be referred to as *the geographical axis* of our conceptual map.

The early studies during the first wave of attention for non-state law focused on pre-state societies. How do these indigenous peoples maintain social order without the presence of a Western-style central state? This is also the focus of Malinowski's study of the Tobriand Islanders. In this category of studies, different varieties of 'primitive law', 'tribal law' and 'folk law' take central stage. In later studies on colonial law, however, these and other types of non-state law are studied against the background of the colonizing force, which now effectively acts as a central state. These studies look at different types of 'customary law', 'adat' and 'religious law'.

During the second wave of attention for non-state law, a number of central ideas of the previous wave are applied to industrialized societies such as Western Europe and the United States. Here the presence of a central state is undisputed. These studies look, for instance, at different types of 'living law' or 'indigenous law'. Within the boundaries of the state, there are studies of folk law and religious law in different ethnic and cultural communities, but there are also studies about the 'private government' and 'self-regulation' of businessmen and in different types of industry. During the third wave, the presence of national states (or perhaps one global state) is less obvious. Most discussions about the new *lex mercatoria* and Internet law focus on non-state law *beyond* the national state. The same holds true for studies about global human rights law.

5.2 Second Dimension: Rules of Conduct or Norms for Decision?

Second, what does the word *law* in 'non-state law' refer to? This element is, of course, responsible for most of the 'emotionally loaded debates' and 'ideological combat'. The literature on non-state law covers a great variety of academic disciplines, which include studies in anthropology, sociology, jurisprudence and international relations. Although all these studies, in one way or another, look at non-state law, the underlying goal and the methodological focus of these studies vary. An anthropological analysis will most likely serve a different analytical purpose from a study in international law. In both cases, the use of the word (non-state) 'law' refers to something different as well.

Following a distinction which was first introduced by Ehrlich ([1936] 2002), it is important to note the difference between *rules of conduct* and *norms for decision*. A historian, Ehrlich argues, conceives of law as a rule of human conduct; he states the rules according to which, in antiquity or in the Middle Ages, marriages were entered into or husband and wife lived together. Similarly, a 'traveler returning from foreign lands' will tell about marriage customs or family life. Yet, according to Ehrlich ([1936] 2002, p. 11), he will have little to say about 'the rules according to which law-suits are being decided'. This is what he refers to as the norms for decision; 'that which is of importance as law in the administration of justice' (Ehrlich [1936] 2002, p. 10). It is essential to recognize the 'ontological divide' between both categories (Tamanaha 1993, p. 206). The rules of conduct refer to 'concrete patterns of social ordering' (Galanter 1981, p. 14). They refer to 'what people [in a social group] actually do, accompanied by a felt sense of obligation' (Tamanaha 1993, p. 215, n. 71). So, in this sense, they are much closer to *conduct* than to *rules*. By contrast, the norms for decision refer to those rules that are identified and applied by state or non-state 'legal' institutions and which are used to justify their decisions. This dimension of the literature on non-state law will be referred to as *the methodological axis* of our conceptual map.

During all three waves of attention, there are many examples in which non-state law primarily refers to patterns of social ordering (or: rules of conduct). Malinowski ([1926] 1972, p. 125), for example, describes his own fieldwork as 'the study by direct observation of the rules of custom as they function in actual life'. Rather than focusing on a 'bald enumeration of rules', he concentrates on 'the ways and means by which these are carried out'. Similarly, Ehrlich has repeatedly argued that he is not interested in making normative claims about what should count as law (for instance, in a court of law). Instead, he argues, his work is aimed at describing and analysing what people actually do and what they themselves consider 'living law'. '[T]he question itself how law should be, goes beyond the reach of sociology' (Ehrlich 1986, p. 179).

A similar approach is used in many of the other studies discussed earlier, including the study of Moluccan folk law in the Netherlands, the business community in Wisconsin, the garment industry in New York and various examples of emerging global law. All these studies focus on what rules and customs people observe in their everyday lives. They are not addressed to legal institutions and are not meant to tell them how they should decide individual cases before them.

By contrast, all three waves of attention for non-state law in the literature also contain examples in which specific norms for decision are extracted from these concrete patterns of social ordering. The most obvious example is, of course, where elements of indigenous law were incorporated into colonial law. A more recent example is the landmark Australian court decision *Mabo v Queensland* (1992). In 1982 three inhabitants of the Murray Islands brought an action in the High Court of Australia against the State of Queensland. They claimed that, based upon local custom and traditional title, Queensland's sovereignty over the Murray Islands was subject to the land rights of the Murray Islanders (also known as the Meriam people). On 3 June 1992, the High Court supported this claim and ruled that the Meriam people are entitled to possess, occupy and enjoy the Murray Islands (cf. Butt and Eagleson 1996). Similarly, much of the literature on the new *lex mercatoria* focuses on the normative debate whether various types of non-state law should or should not be recognized as norms for decision.

Combining the geographical dimension on the horizontal axis and the methodological dimension on the vertical axis, we can now draw a tentative, conceptual map of non-state law (Figure 2.1). This map is intended as a heuristic device only; its purpose is no other than to organize the existing literature. In this literature, it locates four fields of non-state law. The list of examples in each field is meant as an illustration only and is by no means exhaustive.[2]

The first thing this map illustrates is why a discussion about non-state law between lawyers and social scientists often ends up in a dialogue of the deaf. Although both of them use the label of 'non-state law', they are in fact talking about two different things: while lawyers are usually talking about Fields C and D, most social scientists are referring to Fields A and B. We may also look at each individual field in greater detail.

Field A: rules of conduct, within the state

Of all four fields, this area is the most documented. For many years, 'rules of conduct, within the state' have been the object of numerous empirical studies in anthropology, sociology and criminology. These include different studies of 'living law' and 'indigenous law' in immigrant groups and cultural minorities, but also examples of customs and self-regulation in social networks and institutions, such as a business community, a group of

	Within the State	Without the State
Rules of Conduct	Field A Folk law Living law Customary law 1 Unofficial law Indigenous law Traditional law Private government Code of the street Religious law 1 Informal law	Field B Primitive law Tribal law *Lex sportiva* New *lex mercatoria* 1 Internet law 1 Human rights law 1
Norms for Decision	Field C Colonial law Adat Customary law 2 Native title Religious law 2 Indigenous rights	Field D Old *lex mercatoria* New *lex mercatoria* 2 Internet law 2 Human rights law 2

Figure 2.1 Four fields of non-state law

ranchers in Shasta County or the 'code of the street' in the ghettos of Philadelphia (Anderson 1999).

Field B: rules of conduct, without the state

This field combines both some of the earliest and some of the latest literature on non-state law. It includes pioneering anthropological studies on different types of 'primitive law' and 'tribal law' in pre-state societies. But it also covers areas beyond the national state in which empirical studies have only just started to emerge, such as the new *lex mercatoria* (including different types of *lex sportiva*) and the rules of the Internet.

Field C: norms for decision, within the state

This field illustrates that, in order to move from the upper to the lower half of the map, it is necessary to cross the previously mentioned 'ontological divide' between actions and rules. Many of the examples in Field C are the mirror-image of the examples in Field A. The major difference between both categories is that (in Field C) specific norms are extracted from concrete patterns of social ordering (or 'rules of conduct', to use Ehrlich's terms) and are recognized as 'norms for decision' by legal institutions (both of the state and non-state kind). Hart (1961) explained this process through his combination of primary and secondary rules. Pursuant to the secondary rules, legal actors (in his case only those related to the state) make certain lived norms into primary rules, thereby bestowing upon them 'legal' status (cf. Tamanaha 1993, p. 208). In this way, 'customs' become 'customary law' and some forms of 'indigenous law' are recognized as 'colonial law'.

Field D: norms for decision, without the state

This field is the exact opposite of Field A. It is the most uncharted terrain of non-state law (*terra incognita*). First, most of the research done in this area is primarily doctrinal research. There are still very few empirical studies in this field. Second, in theory Field D could be the mirror-image of Field B (just as Field C is, to some extent, the mirror-image of Field A). However, unlike the situation in Field C with the undisputed presence of a national state, in Field D it is often not clear which state or non-state 'legal' institution should recognize some of the examples from Field B as norms for decision. This also makes it the most controversial field of non-state law.

6. ELEGANT MAPS, EMPIRICAL PICTURES AND THE COMPLEXITIES OF NON-STATE LAW[3]

An analytical map of non-state law is a useful tool for understanding the existing literature. Yet, as other authors have demonstrated, the use of maps to enhance our understanding of law and society is not without its problems (cf. Santos 1987; Tamanaha 1995). While in the previous paragraphs our mapping exercise was aimed at reducing the complexities of non-state law, in this section it will be argued that it is also important not to oversimplify things too much. Our conceptual map raises at least three important issues; the first two are of a conceptual nature, while the third issue looks at non-state law from an empirical perspective.

In some cases, the first (geographical) dimension of our map is less straightforward than it looks. In the early years of colonialism, there were many communities in Africa, Asia, the Pacific and elsewhere without the presence of a clear, Western-style central state. Here, the dominance of the colonizer led to the establishment of such a state. The second wave of attention also took place against the undisputed presence of a central state in the advanced industrial countries of Europe and the United States. This picture, however, has become much more complicated during the final wave of attention for non-state law in the era of globalization. Take, for instance, the Internet or the global legal order of human rights. Whether these practices take place within or without the national state is subject to debate. Here, the issue often is not simply a matter of (empirical) observation, but a matter of (legal and political) evaluation.

The application of the second (methodological) dimension of our conceptual map can be complicated as well. This is because sometimes non-state law is considered *both* a rule of conduct *and* a norm for decision. Some anthropologists, for instance, not only describe the norms and rules of an indigenous community. They also argue that policymakers and state courts ought to base their decisions on these local rules. Likewise, some students of the new *lex mercatoria* are not only interested in analysing the use of international contracts, but they also claim that these contracts should be considered superior to national legislation (cf. Teubner 1997, p. 9). A second complication is related to the move from the upper to the lower half of our map, after a (state or non-state) 'legal' institution has recognized certain lived norms as norms for decision. In those cases in which a lived norm receives an official stamp of approval from the national *state*, it may no longer be self-evident that this particular norm for decision should remain on our map of *non-state* law. Whether a particular norm still deserves a place on the map is a matter of degree. Does the (now officially approved) provision of non-state law retain its own character and identity with, for instance, its own separate legal regime or has it been completely remodelled into a norm of state law?

Finally, our conceptual map of non-state law also invokes several empirical questions. It is often suggested that, in recent years, there has been a strong proliferation of non-state law. If this means that nowadays there are more publications on this subject than before, then it is unmistakably true. Insofar as it is meant to indicate anything other than this, however, this is a highly problematic empirical statement. First, our conceptual map illustrates that the phrase 'non-state law' covers a great variety of different things. Despite the shared label 'non-state law', however, these are diverse phenomena, not variations of a single phenomenon. Second, our map emphasizes that, in trying to measure the empirical significance of non-state law, it is important to look at the purpose of our study. Clearly, a study which focuses on various 'rules of conduct' will produce a different empirical picture from an inventory of various 'norms for decision'. Moreover, it should be noted that (non-state) law has many existences (von Benda-Beckmann 2002, p. 65). Empirical research aimed at 'measuring' non-state law may be directed towards one or more of the following dimensions: (i) written and spoken texts, (ii) non-state law in the knowledge of people, (iii) the extent to which non-state law is referred to in disputes, and (iv) the extent to which non-state law is referred to in (other) social processes and interaction. Statements about 'more' or 'less' non-state law are further complicated by the fact that, in most cases, there are no historical data available that can serve as a reliable baseline for comparison.

7. CONCLUSION

The socio-legal literature is characterized by three waves of attention for non-state law, which highlight important changes in law and in society. First and foremost, however, they illustrate the changing role of the state. One of the most significant characteristics of colonialism was the powerful presence of the (foreign) national state. This undisputed presence of the state continued during the second wave of attention, albeit – of course – with important legal, political and social differences. The third wave of globalization is, however, significantly different from its two predecessors. Here, as illustrated by the examples of the new *lex mercatoria*, Internet law and human rights law, the national state plays only a minor role or has disappeared altogether. Moreover, these latest examples of non-state law are no longer connected with marginalized tribal societies, immigrant groups or cultural minorities, but with large multinational businesses and powerful non-governmental organizations.

This raises all sorts of important questions about law and about the role of the state legislature, but also about the future of legal studies. Writing in the early twentieth century, Ehrlich argued that the legal scholars of his day seriously impoverished the science of law because they confined their attention to the national state. Today, in the rapidly changing 'Global Bukowina' of the twenty-first century, Ehrlich's plea for a decoupling of law from the state has lost little of its relevance and a 'liberation from these shackles' seems more appropriate than ever.

NOTES

1. In Google-Scholar, the number of hits associated with the term 'non-state law' has increased from 1350 (1985–1995) to 15,800 (1995–2005).
2. Sometimes the same term is used twice, but in different fields. For example, 'customary law' appears both in Field A and in Field C. This illustrates that a norm for decision may have the same content (and the same label) as a rule of conduct, but their criteria of existence are different. A norm for decision remains a norm for decision regardless of whether

it actually relates to concrete patterns of social ordering. But a rule of conduct ceases to exist when it is no longer part of the social life of the group (cf. Tamanaha 1993, p. 209). To highlight the difference between both categories, they are marked as 'customary law 1' and 'customary law 2', and so on.

3. See Macaulay (1977).

REFERENCES

Allen, C.K. (1964), *Law in the Making*, Oxford: Oxford University Press.

Allott, A. and G. Woodman (1985), *People's Law and State Law: The Bellagio Papers*, Dordrecht: Foris Publications.

Anderson, E. (1999), *Code of the Street: Decency, Violence, and the Moral Life of the Inner City*, New York: W.W. Norton.

Berman, P. Schiff (2005), 'From International Law to Law and Globalization', *Columbia Journal of Transnational Law*, **43**, 485–556.

Berman, P. Schiff (2007), 'Global Legal Pluralism', *Southern California Law Review*, **80**, available at SSRN: http://ssrn.com/abstract=985340.

Bianchi, A. (1997), 'Globalization of Human Rights: The Role of Non-State Actors', in G. Teubner (ed.), *Global Law Without a State*, Aldershot: Ashgate/Dartmouth, pp. 179–212.

Bradney, A. and F. Cownie (2000), *Living without Law: An Ethnography of Quaker Decision-Making, Dispute Avoidance and Dispute Resolution*, Aldershot: Ashgate.

Burns, P. (1989), 'The Myth of Adat', *Journal of Legal Pluralism*, **28**, 1–127.

Butt, P. and R. Eagleson (1996), *MABO: What the High Court Said and What the Government Did*, Sydney: The Federation Press.

Chanock, M. (1985), *Law, Custom, and Social Order: The Colonial Experience in Malawi and Zambia*, New York: Cambridge University Press.

Ehrlich, E. (1986), 'Soziologie des Rechts', in M. Rehbinder (ed.), *Eugen Ehrlich: Gesetz und Lebendes Recht*, Berlin: Duncker & Humblott, pp. 179–194.

Ehrlich, E. [1936] (2002), *Fundamental Principles of the Sociology of Law*, New Brunswick: Transaction Publishers.

Ellickson, R. (1994), *Order Without Law: How Neighbours Settle Disputes*, Cambridge, MA: Harvard University Press.

Forer, N. (1979), 'The Imposed Wardship of American Indian Tribes: A Case Study of the Prairi Band Potawatomi', in S.B. Burman and B.E. Harrell-Bond (eds), *The Imposition of Law*, New York: Academic Press, pp. 89–114.

Friedman, L.M. (2001), 'Erewhon: The Coming Legal Order', *Stanford Journal of International Law*, **2** (37), 347–364.

Galanter, M. (1981), 'Justice in Many Rooms: Courts, Private Ordering, and Indigenous Law', *Journal of Legal Pluralism*, **19**, 1–47.

Galligan, D.J. (2007), *Law in Modern Society*, Oxford: Oxford University Press.

Griffiths, A. (2002), 'Legal Pluralism', in R. Banakar and M. Travers (eds), *An Introduction to Law and Social Theory*, Oxford: Hart Publishing, pp. 289–310.

Griffiths, J. (1978), 'What is Legal Pluralism?', *Journal of Legal Pluralism*, **24**, 1–55.

Griffiths, J. (1980), 'From the Editor', *African Law Studies*, **18**, i–ii.

Hart, H.L.A. (1961), *The Concept of Law*, Oxford: Clarendon Press.

Hooker, M. (1975), *Legal Pluralism: An Introduction to Colonial and Neo-Colonial Laws*, Oxford: Clarendon Press.

Johnson, D.R. and D. Post (1996), 'Law and Borders: The Rise of Law in Cyberspace', *Stanford Law Review*, **5** (48), 1367–1402.
Kelsen, H. (1915), 'Eine Grundlegung der Rechtssoziologie', *Archiv für Socialwissenschaft und Socialpolitik*, **39**, 839–876.
Macaulay, S. (1963), 'Non-Contractual Relations in Business: A Preliminary Study', *American Sociological Review*, **28**, 55–67.
Macaulay, S. (1977), 'Elegant Models, Empirical Pictures, and the Complexities of Contract', *Law & Society Review*, **3** (11), 507–528.
Macaulay, S. (1986), 'Private Government', in L. Lipson and S. Wheeler (eds), *Law and the Social Sciences*, New York: Russell Sage Foundation, pp. 445–518.
Macaulay, S. (1995), 'Crime and Custom in Business Society', *Journal of Law and Society*, **2** (22), 248–258.
Malinowski, B. [1926] (1972), *Crime and Custom in Savage Society*, Totowa, NJ: Littlefield, Adams & Company.
Merry, S.E. (1988), 'Legal Pluralism', *Law & Society Review*, **5** (22), 869–896.
Merry, S.E. (2003a), 'Constructing a Global Law – Violence against Women and the Human Rights System', *Law & Social Inquiry*, **4** (28), 941–977.
Merry, S.E. (2003b), 'From Law and Colonialism to Law and Globalisation', *Law and Social Inquiry*, **2** (28), 569–590.
Mertens, H.-J. (1997), 'Lex Mercatoria: A Self-Applying System Beyond National Law?', in G. Teubner (ed.), *Global Law Without a State*, Aldershot: Ashgate/Dartmouth, pp. 31–43.
Michaels, R. (2005), 'The Re-Statement of Non-State Law: The State, Choice of Law, and the Challenge from Global Legal Pluralism', *Wayne Law Review*, **51**, 1209–1259.
Moore, S.F. (1973), 'Law and Social Change: The Semi-Autonomous Social Field as an Appropriate Subject of Study', *Law & Society Review*, **4** (7), 719–746.
Nafziger, J.R. (1996), 'International Sports Law as a Process for Resolving Disputes', *International and Comparative Law Quarterly*, **45**, 130–149.
Pospisil, L. (1971), *Anthropology of Law: A Comparative Theory*, New York: Harper & Row.
Santos, B. de Sousa (1987), 'Law: A Map of Misreading. Toward a Postmodern Conception of Law', *Journal of Law and Society*, **3** (14), 279–302.
Schultz, T. (2006), 'The Lex Sportiva Turns Up at the Turin Olympics: Surpremacy of Non-State Law and Strange Loops', available at SSRN: http://ssrn.com/abstract=896673.
Simon, G. (1990), *Puissance sportive et ordre juridique étatique.* Paris: Librairie générale de droit et de jurisprudence.
Snyder, F. (1999), 'Governing Economic Globalisation: Global Legal Pluralism and European Law', *European Law Journal*, **4** (5), 334–374.
Strijbosch, F. (1985), 'The Concept of Pela and its Social Significance in the Community of Moluccan Immigrants in the Netherlands', *Journal of Legal Pluralism*, **23**, 177–208.
Tamanaha, B. (1993), 'The Folly of the "Social Scientific" Concept of Legal Pluralism', *Journal of Law and Society*, **2** (20), 192–217.
Tamanaha, B.Z. (1995), 'An Analytical Map of Social Scientific Approaches to the Concept of Law', *Oxford Journal of Legal Studies*, **4** (15), 501–535.
Teubner, G. (1997), 'Global Bukowina: Legal Pluralism in the World Society', in G. Teubner (ed.), *Global Law Without a State*, Aldershot: Ashgate/Dartmouth, pp. 3–28.

Twining, W. (2003), 'A Post-Westphalian Conception of Law (Review Essay)', *Law & Society Review*, **1** (37), 199–257.
Von Benda-Beckmann, F. (2002), 'Who's Afraid of Legal Pluralism?', *Journal of Legal Pluralism*, **47**, 37–82.
Woodman, G. (1998), 'Ideological Combat and Social Observation: Recent Debates about Legal Pluralism', *Journal of Legal Pluralism*, **42**, 21–59.

3. Philip Selznick: incipient law, state law and the rule of law

Martin Krygier*

1. INTRODUCTION

If celebratory rhetoric is to be believed, or money devoted to a cause regarded as a sign of its success, ours is the era of the rule of law. No one will be heard to denounce it, leaders of countries all round the world claim to have it, vast sums are spent to spread it. But how is that to be done? Typically, programmes of rule-of-law promotion focus on state agencies, particularly legislatures and courts. Laws are enacted, judges trained, computers bought, libraries stacked with books, and still, far from atypically, the results are disappointing (see, for example, Carothers 2006; Jensen and Heller 2003; Krygier 2006, 2007).

This identification of the rule of law with state law is not news, nor should it be surprising. Lawyers, legal philosophers and political theorists, not to mention ordinary folk looking to find law (or evade it), typically start with official emanations of state agencies, primarily legislatures and courts. They consider links between law and state to be intimate, unseverable, uncontroversial and exhaustive of the law. Lively questions might remain about the *point* of law, whether these are descriptive questions – what does law do? – or normative ones – what *should* it do? – but rarely about its proper location or source. These, it is assumed, are in centralized and legally co-ordinated offices of state. Lawyers know that law affects society and some are aware that reciprocal effects also occur, but their expertise rarely extends that far. For them society lies at the end of the road, not the beginning. If the question is whether the rule of law might be extended to non-official institutions, their starting point will be with the official agencies of state and if they move anywhere they will move outwards from there. On views such as these, talk of non-state law is simply a category mistake.

And yet the difficulty of establishing the rule of law wherever one wants to, by the state-centric means commonly resorted to, might give one pause. For even when legislation is at the centre of things, which it often is not, the rule of law has indispensable social conditions and elements that are arguably as important as, or more important than, any legislative contribution, or indeed the contribution of state institutions of any kind. The law has to *count* in the society, and whether it does so depends on social facts of many sorts. For the rule of law to exist, still more to flourish and be secure, many things beside state law matter, and since societies differ in many ways, so will those things (see Krygier 2004, 2006, 2008).

These observations are perhaps all truisms, but they are often ignored. We still await a sociology of the rule of law, while in the meantime we pour huge sums of money into inadequately grounded, if well meant, attempts to deliver it. Were we to seek such a sociology we would not have a huge number of sources. One place to start is the work of Philip Selznick. That recommendation is at large, and even in relation to this subject could refer to much of Selznick's work. In this chapter, however, I will focus primarily on one book that raises these issues most centrally: *Law, Society, and Industrial Justice* (*LSIJ*) (Selznick 1969). It has nothing specific to say about how to implant the rule of law in societies that lack it and have been little acquainted with it. However, those with such ambitions might well pause to attend to the sociological complexities this work reveals in a relatively modest proposal: to generate the rule of law in a well-regulated domain of life, industrial relations, in one of the most rule-of-law-rich countries in the world, the United States. Their reliance on state law, and ignorance of non-state law, might then come to acquire some recalibration.

2. SELZNICK, SOCIOLOGY AND THE RULE OF LAW

Imagine someone were to suggest that the rule of law should be extended to industry. What should that be taken to mean? Perhaps that protective legislation should be applied to factories? That it should be clearly drafted, publicly promulgated, free of contradictions, stable? Perhaps, more adventurously, that it should provide workers in industry with particular legal rights? None of these would be implausible renditions of the claim, but none of them captures what is distinctive of Selznick's argument. And, whatever their chances of success, what they advocate is rather simple. His understanding of the suggestion, for it is his suggestion, starts at the other end, and is anything but simple.

The central questions with which the book is concerned are whether the rule of law might be extended to relations between employers and employees and, if so, whether it should be. His answers, put briefly, are 'yes' and 'yes'. He also has something to say about how this might come about. That may be all a reader in a hurry wants to hear. But it isn't as simple as that. For Selznick's life work is of a piece, and he revisits several of its central elements. From his first writings, we have a focus on the inner life of organizations; and the significance of 'the embodiment of ideals in institutions', 'the infusion of group life with . . . aspirations and constraints', the 'enlargement of institutional competence'. From his essays on law we have 'a special ideal – the rule of law' and the claim that it is a value apt to be immanent and at least latent where, as Fuller put it, humans are subjected to the governance of rules. We learn, too, that an analyst must 'look closely at the values themselves, at the characteristic ways they are elaborated and extended' and 'at the social circumstances that invite or resist them' (all passages come from Selznick 1969, p. 1). But how do all these themes come together in the particular context of management–labour relations?

How, in other words, do all these macro-themes arise in this micro-context? Perhaps microcosm would be a better word, since so many of the major lines of Selznick's thought come together in the particular enquiry that gives the book its title. Why all this heavy metal, in what can be read, plausibly and at one level, as a work of advocacy with a simple message: organizations should respond better to, better protect and better fulfil, the interests of labour? But why should they? Why now? Can they? Are they likely to? How might they? Can they be made to? How deep will any recommended or legislated ideal penetrate? What sources of resistance can be expected? What are the chances that it will last as a governing ideal? What sorts of slippage might we expect between ideal and real?

A legislator who shared Selznick's convictions might ignore all these questions and simply legislate or decree what he sought. Selznick, however, had spent almost thirty years pondering the recalcitrance of people, practices and institutions, the precariousness of the finest ideals, the complexity and delicacy of attempts at institutional transformation, the ease with which fine motives are refracted in unexpected directions. At the same time, at least since his book on *Leadership in Administration* (1984), it had become clear to him that, while wisdom might begin in recognition of obstacles, neither it nor virtue ends there. Interested above all in the fate of ideals in the world, his life's work has been devoted to exploring 'the conditions and processes that frustrate ideals or, instead, give them life and hope' (Selznick 1992, p. x). That might, for example, involve seeking out latent values in social arrangements that may, in the right conditions, develop and even be helped to develop. The time of such values might have come, or be coming. Then again, the time might not be ripe, circumstances might be unfavourable, opportunities of development minimal or less. How to tell? Institutional analysis is needed to recognize and clarify relevant values. It will also examine the extent to which particular historical and institutional conditions favour their development. From the analysis might come diagnosis, prognosis and prescription.

3. LAW AND ASSOCIATION

The problem *LSIJ* addresses, put bluntly, is what law might offer to improve one pervasive consequence of relatively recent social transformations: 'the condition of Administered Man' (Selznick 1969, p. 37). Most of us in Western societies spend much of our time today in large governmental and non-governmental bureaucratic organizations. As these organizations and their significance have grown, so too has the importance of relationships within them, prominent among them power relationships, and 'new modes of belonging and dependency' (Selznick 1969, p. 36). The importance of 'freedom *of* association' has long been recognized in Western law; concern for 'freedom *in* associations' is more recent. Yet the large modern organization has become '*a generic phenomenon*, a locus of authority, commitment, dependency and power. It is the reality of this nexus . . . that poses problems of freedom and civic participation' (Selznick 1969, p. 41). Life in organizations generates sets of in-practice compulsory relationships within which most of us are enmeshed for our whole working lives, and by which we are, in one way or another, affected for all our lives. Such forms of association are not intermittent or self-chosen, as they once might have been, but systematic, enduring, unavoidable. That leads to strains and opportunities.

According to Selznick, the state law regulating modern non-governmental organizations – primarily the law of corporations, contract and property – was increasingly ill-suited to transformations in the 'condition of Administered Man'. Traditional concepts of the corporation, for example focusing on consequences of formal legal status, have difficulty dealing with the social realities of institutionalization in modern organizations.

In one of his most distinctive contributions to organization theory, Selznick argued that institutionalization is a key transformative process to which organizations are commonly subject. Organizations are institutionalized to the extent that they become '*infuse*[*d*] *with value* beyond the technical requirements at hand' (Selznick 1984, p. 17). He later came to regret the single focus of that definition, for there are other elements besides infusion with value that distinguish institutionalization (see Selznick 1992, p. 234; 1996, p. 271), but he never doubted that it captured the central, key, component of the process. As an organization becomes institutionalized, members come to treat it as more than a neutral instrument, develop group and institutional attachments, loyalties and rivalries, adopt and promote institutional values, create and adapt to an 'internal social world' (Selznick

1984, p. 7). Institutionalization also develops as a result of institutions' dealings with their external environment, particularly where they develop stable clienteles there (Selznick 1984, p. 7).

However it takes place, whether deliberately as a result of leaders' initiatives or spontaneously over time, institutionalization often occurs in large and enduring organizations, whether formally recognized as corporations or not, and it 'sets problems for the legal system' (Selznick 1969, p. 46). Where an organization becomes institutionalized, as Selznick's organizational writings showed, it 'takes on a distinctive character, competence, or function, and becomes charged with meaning as a vehicle of group identity or a receptacle of vested interests' (Selznick 1969, p. 44). This, in turn, has law-related significance of various sorts. Rights are claimed for the system (rather than merely for the individuals within it); there is a demand 'for legal cognition of the nature of the institution', where that nature is not merely a result of legal definition but 'is known by its mission and competence, its commitment and capacity to perform a social function'. That in turn is tied up with 'the social structure of the agency – the roles and relationships, the norms and values, that comprise an operating social system. Types of institutions have characteristic structural attributes and requirements, and the law of associations is continually pressed to develop ideas that fit these realities' (Selznick 1969, p. 45). Finally, there is a

> strain toward public accountability . . . What may have begun as a purely private effort to mobilize resources for particular ends becomes in time a captive of the broader interests that have become implicated in its existence. Sociologically, if not legally, there is a movement from private to public responsibility whenever leadership loses full freedom to manipulate resources and becomes accountable to the interests of others and to the enterprise as a continuing system. (Selznick 1969, p. 45)

Selznick is well aware that any such trends do and must encounter resistance; indeed,

> a great deal of managerial effort is devoted to blocking and overcoming the drift toward institutionalization, with its attendant broadening of responsibility and dilution of power. But the more enduring the organization, and the larger the scale and scope of its activities, the more likely is it that the strain toward public accountability will be manifest. (Selznick 1969, p. 45)

Selznick approaches the two other key relevant areas of state law – contract and property – with similar sociological and diagnostic attention. Voluntaristic, individualistic contract law expresses a social imaginary inhabited by roughly equal, independent right-and-duty-bearing individuals, engaging with each other at arm's length, in specific, self-chosen transactions which are bounded and limited in scope by the participants' choice. Participants pursue their individual projects, co-operating when they choose to; outsiders to contractual bargains are truly, or at least in the contractual imagination, outside. But the modern bureaucratized, *institutionalized* world puts all these assumptions in question, for classical contract law is unable 'to grasp the reality of association' (Selznick 1969, p. 63).

Property law, too, is alert to possession, domination and subordination; deaf to association, stewardship and authority. It has difficulties with collective ownership, that 'invites scrutiny of the inner order of the enterprise, especially the way power over persons is generated and used', as it does with concentrations of wealth and power in large and complex organizations 'that are immortal and know no boundaries' (Selznick 1969, p. 67). All these accumulated changes 'create a demand for restraint and accountability, for countervailing institutions, and for a conception of the organization that yields a theory of authority' (Selznick 1969, p. 67).

Together, corporation, contract, property all 'fail to grasp the reality of association' (Selznick 1969, p. 63) and in so failing they fail, too, to ground authority. For authority in institutions will wane unless reinscribed in altered terms that do justice to the social realities of the modern work-and-life-space. The search for those terms, Selznick suggests, might be cast as a

> quest for the corporate conscience: its origins, its locale, its sustaining forces, its legal implications, its troubles and limits. . . . What is at stake is the capacity of the institution to do justice. That competence is located in the attributes of a social system, conceived as an arena within which authority is exercised and rights are asserted. To grasp the nature of that system, and to draw the legal conclusions, is the major task of a law of associations. (Selznick 1969, p. 72)

4. LAW IN SOCIETY

In a review of Fuller's *Morality of Law* (1969), Selznick praised Fuller's capsule definition of law – 'the enterprise of subjecting human conduct to the governance of rules' – on several grounds, among them that it was 'remarkably congenial to the sociological perspective' in that it did not limit the subject of inquiry to the state. Instead, Fuller had recognized that law was 'endemic in all institutions that rely for social control on formal authority and rule-making. That legal experience occurs in the "private" associations of religious, educational, or industrial life is a postulate of legal sociology, a precondition of much significant inquiry' (Selznick 1965, p. 947). That observation lends particular significance to the recommendation that we 'grasp the nature' of a social system 'where authority is exercised and rights are asserted' and 'to draw the legal conclusions'. For it has not been everyone's view of where law might be sought or found.

However, within sociology of law, there is a broad stream with many tributaries, according to which such law is all around us (see Krygier 2007). The tributary to which Selznick contributed, and indeed that he might be said to have been one of the first in the United States to carve, is that called by Marc Hertogh in Chapter 2 of this volume, 'rules of conduct within the state'. In 'Sociology and Natural Law' (Selznick 1961), one of his first and most important articles on law, Selznick had already referred to the sociological truism that 'education, politics, religion, and other social activities are found outside of the specialized institutions established to deal with them. Sociology has located these phenomena "in society", that is, in more informal and spontaneous groupings and processes' (Selznick 1961, p. 84). He believed the same was true of law. Like Fuller, whose opinion he shared in this as in many things,[1] Selznick conceived of law as a particular sort of practice or enterprise, and like Fuller too he was more concerned to explore the character, imperatives, purposes and requirements of that enterprise than to identify it with one highly visible source.

So formal provenance is not definitive; law can develop in many sorts of non-official locations. Thus, Selznick explains that

> legality does have a central place, for our concern is with the capacity of special-purpose organizations to 'establish justice.' At the same time, we recognize that the legal potential, if it exists, is to be found in the social dynamics of the institutions themselves. We can therefore accept the dictum of Ehrlich that 'the center of gravity of legal development lies not in legislation, nor in juristic science, nor in judicial decision, but in society itself'. (Selznick 1969, pp. 33–34, quoting Ehrlich 1936, p. xv)

What might this mean?

Eugen Ehrlich himself, one of the earliest and most intriguing contributors to sociological jurisprudence and the sociology of law, had in mind at least two things. The first is that the sources of the law by which we live, 'living law', as he called it, come not primarily from where it has become conventional to locate them – official legal structures – but from the normative arrangements that govern everyday social life. That can just sound like a sociological platitude, often of little weight since so unspecific, but in Ehrlich's work it amounted to considerably more. For the 'society' to which he referred is not some featureless black box in which everything happens, but a web of the 'associations' in which we participate, the 'inner orders' of which are *normative* for us. A sociology of law has to attend to those inner orders, rather than merely to the pronouncements of jurists or even, as Pound famously (mis-)interpreted Ehrlich, to the 'law in action'. For Pound's 'law in action' is really the 'law-in-books-in-action', that is, what happens to the law-in-books when manifested (or not) in the actual operations of legal officials in the world. But Ehrlich had something different in mind (see esp. Nelken 1984). 'Living law' was not in the first instance official state law even 'in action', though it influenced it and in turn was affected by it. The 'inner order of associations' remained for Ehrlich still the primary source of normative regularities and problem-solving by which people oriented their lives. Official law was a response to that, sometimes more adequate, sometimes less, not the unmoved mover of the social world.[2]

Selznick cites Ehrlich with approval in several writings, but it is not clear to what extent he was influenced by what he had read (as Chester Barnard, who *did* influence Selznick, had been[3]) as distinct from agreeing with it.[4] There were other sources of the points Selznick makes, and those points flow naturally from his earlier organizational writings.

Nevertheless, *Law, Society, and Industrial Justice*, of all his writings on law, shares a number of themes with Ehrlich. First is his insistence that law is 'generic'. Law is 'found in many settings; it is not uniquely associated with the state' (Selznick 1969, p. 4). A key task for sociology of law is to attend to the law of such settings in those settings. Selznick accepts this, though he does not follow Ehrlich in according *priority* to the non-official. His ambition is, rather, to extend our understanding of law to encompass both official and non-official settings; indeed, 'all institutions *that rely for social control on formal authority and rule-making*' (Selznick 1969, p. 7). As so often, when confronted with easy, apparently clear dichotomies, Selznick's tendency is to be suspicious of the choices they demand. Law often can be found outside the state,[5] but inside it too. To rule that out, or establish *a priori* some universal order of priorities, is to blind oneself to complexities and to sources of useful guidance wherever they can be found. In classic pragmatist fashion, Selznick advocates drawing upon experience wherever it is useful and has been subject to test, and so he writes:

> [t]o equate law and the state impoverishes sociological analysis, because the concept of law should be available for study of any setting in which human conduct is subject to explicit rule-making; and when we deny the place of law in specialized institutions *we withhold from the private setting the funded experience of the political community in matters of governance*. (Selznick 1969, p. 8)

A second theme is the importance of attending to the 'inner order of associations', a phrase that Selznick adopts and parses as 'the natural settings and adaptive outcomes of group life' (Selznick 1961, p. 84); that is, associations rather than either society-as-a-whole, on the one hand, or atomic individuals, on the other, and with an emphasis on their *inner order*.

Ehrlich and Selznick are sociologists through and through: the 'living law' they are concerned with is generated from within the associations that set the particular normative frameworks in which we conduct many of the most important interactions of our lives. These associations are *ordered*, organized in some ways rather than others, and such particular modes of organization matter for how we think, how we act, and how we think about how we and others think and act. For Selznick, this was all the more true, and all the more important, in a world dominated by large-scale organizations, the significance of which he had spent most of his life exploring, with their particular and complex hierarchies, internal orderings, modes of institutionalization, and the attendant centrality of association and membership in the lives of their members.

Thirdly, even within official domains, law should not be conceived narrowly. Understood as a generic phenomenon, it 'extends to administration as well as adjudication' (Selznick 1969, p. 14), 'applies to public participation as well as to the conduct of officials' (Selznick 1969, p. 17), and so is expansive in its reach through all sorts of activities subject to 'formal authority and rule-making' (Selznick 1969, p. 7).

Finally, stressing, as Ehrlich had, that law might grow up gradually out of people's associations rather than descend peremptorily from official imposition, Selznick suggested sociologists must be alert to the possibility of finding within associations what he called 'incipient', 'inchoate', 'emergent' forms of law (see Selznick 1969, pp. 32–4), generated in response to internal pressures, dynamics and demands.

In an essay written at the same time as *LSIJ*, Selznick explained that the sociologist seeking sources of the rule of law should be aware that they will not always be found full blown and ready to go, nor where lawyers are accustomed to look. On the contrary, sociologists, used to ferreting around in 'the problem-solving practices and spontaneous orderings of business or family life', should be alert for patterns of 'incipient law . . . implicit in the way in which public sentiment develops or in any increasingly stabilized pattern of organization; . . . a compelling claim of right or a practice so viable and so important to a functioning institution as to make legal recognition in due course highly probable' (Selznick 1968, p. 55). Among these he mentions 'some of the private arrangements worked out in collective bargaining agreements, especially seniority rights and protection against arbitrary dismissal'. These were to figure centrally in his exploration of *LSIJ*. Incipient law was important socially, and conceptually too, since it connects social behaviour and legal constraint, inseminated by the former and, in appropriate circumstances, giving birth to the latter. Or, in a less strained metaphor, a focus on incipient law:

> bridges the concepts of law and social order without confounding the two; it assumes that law does indeed have its distinctive nature, however much it may rely on social support or be responsible [*sic*] to social change. On the other hand, some law is seen as *latent* in the evolving social and economic order. For example . . . the growing importance of large-scale organizations carries with it the likelihood that new claims of right will emerge, based upon a new perception of organizational membership as a protectable status. (Selznick 1968, p. 56)

What Selznick is looking for is latent, liminal signs of legal growth and development out of the pressures and changes that occur in social life. Incipient law is one such sign. As it develops, *if* it develops, it can generate in turn 'inchoate' law, that is:

> Unordered and unsystematic, often based on *ad hoc* but convergent pronouncements. Instead of a clearly enunciated authoritative principle, there may be many diverse evidences, coming from a variety of official voices, that new claims are being recognized, new powers or expectations affirmed. Thus inchoate law is something more than incipient law. The latter is mainly an attribute of social practice and belief; the former is an attribute of law itself. (Selznick 1969, p. 33)

Incipient, emergent, inchoate, these legal seeds are potential starting points and stages in legal evolution, of a sort that might both develop legal characteristics within the social settings from which they derive, and then infiltrate official state law itself. Both these unofficial and official developments were important, *legally* important, within a suitably expansive concept of law.

For Selznick also believed that incipient law might – as Ehrlich thought it did and needed to – come to influence and be absorbed into the official legal order. Rather than always start with official legal institutions and end up with individual recipients of legal directives, law spurred by sociological realities within human associations will often come to be taken up by official legal organs; 'Incipient law is emergent *positive* law, responsive to, and made possible by, particular social circumstances' (Selznick 1969, p. 8).

5. THE RULE OF LAW

What, then, does it mean to extend the rule of law so conceived? Against a conception of science, which would expel such a question as 'unscientific', Selznick had long argued that a central job for sociology was to seek out the latent values, the 'master ideals', immanent in social practices. Law, like many fundamental social institutions and practices, has immanent sources of 'envaluation', normative tendencies provoked and stimulated by the nature of the practices themselves, expectations generated within them and by them, and of them. The relevant values of legal orders, as explained in 'Sociology and Natural Law' (Selznick 1961) and repeated here, are summed up in the concept of the rule of law, defined by Selznick as the 'progressive' reduction of arbitrariness in law and its administration. So, 'to infuse' the 'mode of governance [of an organization] with the aspirations and constraints of a legal order' (Selznick 1969, p. 8) is to extend the rule of law to and within it, where that means 'to build it into the life of society, to make the master ideal of legality a true governor of official conduct' (Selznick 1969, p. 35). However little any particular legal arrangement exhibits it, 'the restraint of official power by rational principles of civic order' (Selznick 1969, p. 11) has salience to law-governed settings, and to the extent that industrial settings are or might be law-governed in the extended sense under discussion, it has salience to them. The argument of the book, then, is that the 'condition of Administered Man' can be improved by an infusion of legality and a consequent reduction in arbitrary exercise of power, and that his circumstances include forces that strain in that direction. What cannot be assumed, and what only investigation and theorization can determine, is how strong at any time are these strains to the rule of law, how strong are forces that pull in other directions and what are the relative weights of force and counter forces. Outcomes are rarely pre-determined.

Selznick admits that the concept of arbitrariness is not a simple one, and he never explicates it in great detail.[6] Like most who write about the rule of law, he associates arbitrariness with traits such as capriciousness, wilfulness and, most of all, with the absence of reasoned justification. The role of reason as a governor of action varies, and so then does the extent to which action is arbitrary. The task of partisans of the rule of law wherever it occurs, and the task of those who seek to better 'Administered Man's' condition, is to seek 'progressively' to make it less so. This is no small task, for while it 'begins as a principle of constraint . . . [it] promises more than a way of moderating the uses of power' (Selznick 1969, p. 18). It must never slight the former, and importantly so, since '[t]he assumption is that no man, no group of men, is to be trusted with unlimited power'. On the other hand, it should stretch to the latter too, for:

> The 'progressive reduction of arbitrariness' knows no near stopping-place. The closer we look at that process, the more we realize that it calls for an affirmative view of what it means to participate in a legal order, whether as citizen, judge, or executive. In its richest connotation, legality evokes the Greek view of a social order founded in reason, whose constitutive principle is reason. (Selznick 1969, p. 18)

6. LEGAL EVOLUTION

There is no doubt that Selznick favoured extension of rule-of-law values in the industrial domain. But he did not believe or suggest that they would be extended simply because that would be a nice idea. The argument that they might be so developed is based on quite other, sociological, premises. In this argument is a strong suggestion of movement and direction over time. This is not inadvertent. He believed as a matter of general theory and specific observation that forces were at work which pressed – not in any sense inexorably, but really, 'objectively' – in the direction of legal transformations in the industrial field. The job of institutional assessment was to discern their weight, direction and prospects.

It was, of course, possible that these prospects would turn out to be nil. Societies are littered with legislative dead letters that went nowhere but seemed good ideas at the time, because someone thought them smart in principle and/or because they thought they suited the times. How to tell, and what to do?

Even though, as we have seen, Selznick had enumerated vulnerabilities to which members of organizations were exposed and holes in legal protection of them, it was not from these difficulties by themselves that he thought change would be generated. Nor would it be enough for some benevolent legislator to take heed of the vulnerabilities and legal gaps that Selznick had exposed and pass laws to deal with them. For Selznick understood that you cannot expect to legislate successfully to an unreceptive society. He had long assimilated from Chester Barnard notions of the interplay of authority and consent. His experience of the university turmoil of the 1960s highlighted the ways that law needed to be *responsive* to social realities and demands, both because that would be a good way to behave and because commands are impotent if people ignore them. Indeed the (complex and uncertain) virtues of responsive institutions became a central question of his next book (Nonet and Selznick 1978).

On the other hand, there were trends, moments, opportunities, possibilities in the world that one could seek to understand, at times exploit and sometimes further and fashion. He believed that normative theory needs to be alert to such developments. Where they were favourable:

> The rise of new centers of potential oppression may be less important than (1) the changing aspirations of the community and (2) the opportunity to do something about them. Subordinate and dependent men have always been treated badly by their masters. The contemporary situation is different in this, that new expectations are penetrating areas hitherto closed to scrutiny or immune to challenge; and modern organizational settings make possible new ways of asserting claims and institutionalizing victories. (Selznick 1969, p. 39)

Selznick emphasizes, then, that ideals cannot be grafted onto institutions simply because *we* would like it. All his institutional investigations told against that, and it goes very deep in his thought. But Selznick's evolutionism has a positive aspect, too. While 'progress' is never inevitable, it is also not simply random, accidental. For the logic of institutional development often produces the *strain* he has often written about, to realize immanent values. Such logic is never inexorable, it competes with other forces, values, tendencies; it will often be defeated. There are no guarantees of success, either metaphysical or empirical. And yet, such a logic can be discerned in many contexts, and theoretically explained. And, then, it might be supported. There is nothing inevitable about an acorn becoming an oak tree, still less a thriving one, but there is a disposition which, in appropriate conditions, might flourish. And a poppy seed needn't try. Horticulturalists identify such conditions and seek to furnish them, or at least support and nurture them. Less expertly, perhaps, and often with more fervent hope than deep understanding, so too do many parents. Failure is not unknown in either endeavour. Nor, however, is success.

Normative systems are driven to develop in part by internal tensions, the resolution of which provides pressures apt to propel the system to higher stages. Moreover, when certain things occur, whether as a result of conflict or other sources of development, others can be contemplated, people do contemplate them, and often something can be done about them. Sometimes that is a matter of new possibilities, as is common in the evolution of technological systems, but also in human and other ways of maturing. Sometimes, and also common in institutional development, new dissatisfactions arise at particular stages of development in the light of possibilities revealed that were earlier unconceived, indeed inconceivable. Tensions are generated by new demands and criticisms made by participants angry that previously unheard-of values are ignored or traduced. Maturity may not occur, dissatisfactions may simply be ignored or suppressed, but a new disposition is available which was not there before. It creates a strain to and, in congenial circumstances can lead to, novelty.

In the specific case of law, a key source of development lies in the dynamics of legitimacy. Legitimacy can be claimed on all sorts of grounds, only some of them connected with legality. Yet:

> legitimacy carries the lively seed of legality, implanted by the principle that the exercise of power must be justified. From this it is but a step to the view that reasons must be given to defend official acts. Reasons invite evaluation, and evaluation requires the development of public standards. At the same time, implicit in the fundamental norm that reasons should be given is the conclusion that where reasons are defective, authority is to that extent weakened and even invalidated. (Selznick 1969, p. 30)

Selznick emphasizes that nothing inevitably propels a legitimate order to the rule of law. Notwithstanding the sources of itchiness immanent in the very idea of legitimation, not every sort of legitimacy is as itchy as every other; 'If power is justified on the basis of hereditary succession, for example, it is difficult to find the leverage for calling officials to account' (Selznick 1969, p. 30). Normative social theory does not pretend that tradition leads necessarily to the rule of law, just as Weber did not think it necessary that 'patrimonial administration' led to bureaucracy. However, there was what might be called a social logic of values at work in both cases, and in particular circumstances that is how things worked out. Again, there are plenty of legal orders where rule-of-law values are scarcely recognized, plenty where they are outweighed by competing values. The claim is just that there are immanent tendencies in the 'enterprise of subjecting human conduct to the governance of rules' which, given congenial conditions, will incline towards the values of legality and that a legal order is more successfully developed to the extent that those values are manifest in its operations.

Attributes of existing practices, then, as well as expectations and frustrations engendered by them, produce that 'strain' towards more elaborated developments of the ideals of which Selznick had earlier written. He refers to Durkheim's theory of social development, Piaget's and Mead's of individual moral development, Weber's of the development of society and institutions, and that of Mary Parker Follett and Chester Barnard of developments within organizations. In each he discerns a story of moral development 'understood as a natural process, a kind of maturation' (Selznick 1969, p. 19). Each in their own context and way postulated development, whether over the life course of individuals or over generations in societies and institutions, towards a 'morality of cooperation . . . a morality of rational rules, interdependent activities, and autonomous individuals' (Selznick 1969, p. 21). Even Weber, so notoriously ambivalent about the 'rationalization' he saw sweeping the world (as indeed is Selznick himself) and so determined to keep evaluations and science apart, 'nevertheless . . . did trace a pattern of change in which a received morality of constraint – traditional norms and forms of authority – was replaced by a new morality founded in the requirements of rational action. A basic feature of that morality was the reduction of arbitrariness in official conduct' (Selznick 1969, p. 23). A morality of co-operation emphasizes personal autonomy and competence; norms rooted in experience (rather than, say, deference to authority figures or traditions); dialogue and problem-solving, rather than demands for conformity. The *strain*, in other words, is towards 'an ethos of problem-solving . . . [and] . . . strongly opposed to a morality of constraint, which imposes solutions and limits alternatives' (Selznick 1969, p. 25).

That ethos and that evolved morality, Selznick believes, fit closely with the rule of law insofar as each 'abhors arbitrary judgment and constraint, presses for justifications, invokes the authority of agreed-upon purpose, and values the competent participant' (Selznick 1969, p. 25). These features of morality and legality add up to a constellation that is not merely what Selznick values (though pretty clearly it is that too), but rests 'on a natural foundation and has objective worth. It may lose out in competition with other values, or be blocked by the absence of congenial conditions, but the legal ethic finds its warrant in the contribution it can make to human growth and self-realization' (Selznick 1969, p. 25). A disposition in this direction is likely 'where rational forms of social organization prevail', and these forms themselves militate against arbitrariness. Directed movement occurs because '[w]hen the ethic of cooperation makes sense historically as the preferred way of organizing human relations, a dynamic toward legality is created. For this reason, we see legalization as a peculiarly salient issue for the modern special-purpose organization' (Selznick 1969, p. 28).

Notwithstanding these fairly abstract and apparently idealistic formulations, Selznick has concrete social processes in mind. As even in his earliest academic writings, but obviously freshened by the 'Berkeley events' of the 1960s,[7] Selznick takes an example from the modern university. Demands are increasingly made for legalization, and restriction of the arbitrary power of university officials. Where this is successful, the rules are formalized to specify rights and obligations, reduce administrative discretion and spell out the rules of the game; 'Having made what they conceive to be a transition to rule-governed administration, the university officials congratulate themselves – and await obedience' (Selznick 1969, p. 29). But that is not how things turn out, for:

> Unfortunately for the administrators' peace of mind, the quest for law generates new aspirations and more comprehensive goals. Once the rules become problematic, authority is in disarray. There is a demand that the rules be legitimate, not only in emanating from establishing authority, but also in the manner of their formulation, in the way they are applied, and in their fidelity to agreed-upon institutional purposes. The idea spreads that the obligation to obey has some relation to the quality of the rules and the integrity of their administration. A critical spirit emerges which insists that decisions be justified and that channels be available for effective review and the hearing of grievances. When discipline is imposed, it is demanded that due process be protected . . ..
>
> As awareness expands and the dialogue is pressed, issues of academic 'law and order' merge into larger questions of governance. Attention turns to the distinctive nature of the academic polity . . . law is the servant of polity not its master. It follows that legal procedures and rules are not self-justifying, even if they are offered as extrapolations from the ideal of legality. The contributions they make, and the costs they exact, must be assessed in the light of substantive ends. (Selznick 1969, p. 30)

There is no train that takes you direct from latent to manifest, no guarantees, no certainties. There are just dispositions and circumstances. Whether the dispositions have formed, how far they have emerged, whether they are being deflected or redirected, are questions to be answered in part empirically, by evidence of 'incipient' and 'inchoate' signs in the development of the persons, institutions or societies under scrutiny. One looks for signs of emergence, and then one asks questions directed by theory:

> First, the social viability of the practice is in question – its functional significance for group life and especially for new institutional forms – must be considered. Second, the contemporary evolution of relevant legal principles must be assessed to see whether the new norm can be absorbed within the received but changing legal tradition. Thus incipient law is not based on abstract postulates; nor does it reflect the moral preferences of the observer. Incipient law is emergent *positive* law, responsive to, and made possible by, particular social circumstances. (Selznick 1969, p. 33)

7. INCIPIENT LAW

Much of the book is therefore a search for 'incipient', 'emerging', even if yet 'inchoate' signs of legality in the life and law of modern industrial organizations. Selznick finds many, particularly in tranformations in organizational management, the impact of collective bargaining on the organization, expectations of employees, and in the relationship of public policy to once 'private' institutions.

He draws upon Weber's theory of bureaucratization, and rationalization more broadly, to characterize the social and organizational transformations from social orderings dominated by 'kinship, fealty, and contract' to ones where 'the principle of *rational coordination* dominates the scene' (Selznick 1969, p. 75). He is aware of Weber's complex and ambivalent appraisals of rationality, and of the latter's many-layered consequences. Nevertheless, Selznick agrees with Weber that bureaucratic forms of organization contain seeds of legality. Whether the seeds will grow or not cannot be determined with certainty, but bureaucracy contains them in a way that other forms of organization do not. For Selznick emphasizes 'one striking feature of the bureaucratic model, with its stress on objectivity and impersonality. *In theory, bureaucratic administration is the antithesis of arbitrary rule*. Bureaucracy formalizes every facet of decision-making and in doing so sets an ideal of limited discretion' (Selznick 1969, p. 80). This is central to Weber's account of bureaucratic authority as 'legal–rational', a feature of modern bureaucracies, whether or not they are offices of state; 'the "legality" of bureaucratic authority does not necessarily derive from the public status of the agency or enterprise . . . *The source of these attributes is internal; the dynamic they create calls forth the ideals of legality*' (Selznick 1969, p. 81).

Selznick sees similar developments, 'a strain toward internal legality' (Selznick 1969, p. 82), with the decline of family-based firms in American industry: '[p]re-bureaucratic management was typically one-man rule . . . The pre-bureaucratic business leader was impatient with formal rules and procedures. He liked to keep his accounts in his hat and to run the organization from day to day without clear-cut policies . . . The bureaucratic way is directly contrary' (Selznick 1969, p. 83). This should systematically push towards managerial self-restraint. So too the 'flowering of "personnel policy" and a concomitant elaboration of rules and procedures . . . [that] limit the arbitrary exercise of managerial prerogative' (Selznick 1969, p. 84), spread of seniority as a criterion of decision, formalization of disciplinary procedures. Bureaucratization is no sufficient condition for the rule of law, still less for democracy. On the other hand, for all their differences in form and purpose, Weber was right to see that both bureaucracy and modern law were part of the same larger historical story, and had affinities which did not exist between legality and, say, charismatic or traditional ways of running organizations. And development does not stop there. Post-bureaucratic tendencies are generated that seek to temper bureaucratic rigidities with flexibility, and such developments too have their own logic. That logic applies broadly.

This is not just preaching, but diagnosis and prognosis, according to Selznick. He finds contract law pressed by the changes in the social and organizational environment. It is subject to transformative pressures in industrial settings, with the development of new forms of labour law, including collective bargaining, which no longer is envisaged as a creature of 'the intentions or expectations of the founders' but 'creates new and continuing institutions, new and irreversible commitments . . . creates a system of government' (Selznick 1969, pp. 151–152). That in turn generates rule-making for the continuing administration of the agreement, and so '"creates" a system of government . . . by helping to reconstruct the managerial process. Management becomes more conscious of rules, more conscious of rights, *and more capable of building that consciousness into the routines of institutional life*. The administration of "things" becomes the governance of men as this reconstruction proceeds' (Selznick 1969, p. 154).

Other straws in the wind abound. 'Human relations' teaching has brought a 'new image' of the worker, and 'new ideas that are reconstructing the premises of management' (Selznick 1969, p. 100). Grievance arbitration 'and the legal evolution to which it has contributed, lend much support to the governmental analogy. For in this institution we see a response to the need for lawfulness in the day-to-day administration of the large enterprise' (Selznick 1969, p. 155). Creative arbitration, many of the principles of which Selznick seeks to review, 'adapts generic legal experience to the industrial setting' (Selznick 1969, p. 178). All of this contributes to a development from the 'master's' prerogative to something far more directed and constrained:

> Once it is accepted that reasons and justifications are to be offered, prerogative must give way to policy. The idea that management can do as it pleases simply because of historic privilege loses credibility and therefore weakens in authority. For such an idea cannot meet the test of dialogue. It is a conversation-stopper, inviting an early test of power and a retreat from reason. (Selznick 1969, p. 182)

Selznick draws on other pieces of evidence as well, to show the existence of a '*receptive institutional setting* within which further legal change may take place' (Selznick 1969, p. 243) and in the last chapter of the book he sketches what he calls 'the emergent law', whose substance is a 'law of governance'. And this connects to an old theme in his work, at least since *Leadership in Administration*: just as law does not stop with the state, nor does politics, nor indeed is it inappropriate to conceive of a non-state *polity*. In relation to that, the state polity and its laws have a crucial role, however, partly as exemplar and partly as instrument; *not* as the sole locus of legality but rather as a source and inspiration for building the rule of law 'into the life of society', infusing group life 'with the aspirations and constraints of a legal order' (Selznick 1969, p. 3).

8. TRANSITION TO POLITY

What, then, is governance and where is it to be found? Here there are broad analogies with Selznick's approach to law: seek out function, don't obsess about location. Selznick sees a number of sources of convergence between what are conventionally understood as 'public' and 'private' domains. Central among these is the decline of the persuasiveness and symbolic power of 'sovereignty' of the putatively public institutions. Again, the enormous growth of large-scale institutions, in private as much as in public spheres, has eroded the distinctive state-orientation of public law. Similarities come to blur differences, both in the sense that 'governmental' powers can be found and that 'nongovernmental' activities occur, in both state and non-state organizations. Governance is not simply a product of what we call 'government': state-relatedness is neither necessary nor sufficient for it. Not everything that governments do involves 'the distinctive functions of a sovereign' (Selznick 1969, p. 246), not everything private organizations are involved in should be understood as private. To the extent that non-state institutions both themselves 'become to some degree political communities' and affect participation in the larger polity, issues of governance are potentially engaged within them; 'This raises the question whether we have a theory of public law adjudication adequate to deal with the group structure of modern society' (Selznick 1969, p. 246).

Concepts of public law, he argues, should be applied 'wherever the social function of governing is performed, wherever some men rule and others are ruled' (Selznick 1969, p. 259). That relationship is not confined to state–citizen relations but nor does it extend to every relationship, not even every relationship where there are asymmetries of power. It occurs where there is '*a special form of human association*', different from kin relations, yet equally not the same as pure contractual association. It shares features of both: with contract it involves 'objective and impersonal standards, determined by the requirements of that system' (Selznick 1969, p. 270); with kinship (and citizenship) membership as a source of social identity: here the logic of institutionalization returns and generates a demand for recognition of *status*:

> Participation thickens, it takes on a new dimension, as people in organizations strive for personal satisfactions and for protection against threats to their personal security. . . . minimal affiliation ripens into membership. As this occurs, we see a movement from contract to status. What matters is who you are, what position you occupy, what role you play, rather than what voluntary agreements you may have entered. Nor is this only a product of personal psychology. Other forces, at least equally important, are also at work. Wherever there is an effort to create and sustain a going concern – based on continuing relationships rather than discrete transactions – a drift to status may be expected. (Selznick 1969, p. 271)

With this development of status in organizations where governance occurs, it will be both appropriate *and demanded* that rights of employees be put on a secure and adequate basis, adequate to the status of members of these organizations; 'With the emergence of status we may expect a claim of right' (Selznick 1969, p. 272). This bears analogies to the rights of *citizenship*, which is 'a special kind of group membership. It is known by the public rights accruing to the individual who occupies that status . . . minimally, the right to a civic identity and to civic participation' (Selznick 1969, p. 249). Contexts where it makes sense to speak of citizenship occur in both state and non-state settings, then, where membership of the association is a source of social identity and a basis for social demands.

In response to such developments, it becomes appropriate to seek contribution from the side of state law, at the same time to legality and to governance. Such a contribution can be made by the public law of due process, the principles of which Selznick explores and explicates, and takes to represent 'a *common law of governance*' (Selznick 1969, p. 256) whereby 'the rule of law [may be extended] to areas hitherto controlled only by concepts of private law' (Selznick 1969, p. 250).

Of course, as critics have observed, Selznick commends and recommends these developments. But it is too swift to dismiss this whole enterprise as a wish list with sociological trimmings. True, Selznick does not try to hide what he hopes for, and that goes way beyond due process minimally understood. Thus, he suggests, the key is personal adherence, status, the shift from 'minimal affiliation' to 'membership'. As that sense of connection deepens and broadens, so too will grow demands of a political character, demands for recognition of members as persons, demands for protection from arbitrary power; 'the transition from an administered machine – in which human beings are deployed as fully manipulable resources – to a system of governance will have begun' (Selznick 1969, p. 273). And there is more in store. For not only might we expect (or at least have reason to hope for) a richer legality within organizations, but it is possible that further evolution might bring in train something more than legality:

> Legality has a strong affinity with the ideal of political democracy, and . . . a legal order should be seen as transitional to polity. It follows that there is latent in the law of governance a norm of participation. Due process strains to take account of all legal interests, provide opportunities for the offering of proofs and arguments, and deepen the legitimacy of authority. These premises invite new forms of legal and political participation. Without yielding the position that democratic forms are not to be imposed mechanically on uncongenial settings, the perspective of governance sounds a note of caution and of hope: In the end, the quest for justice may be indistinguishable from the quest for civic competence and personal autonomy. (Selznick 1969, pp. 275–276)

On the other hand, you can't always get what you want. In the particular case, Selznick is sceptical that all that he would wish to come to pass is likely to; 'we can speak with far greater assurance about the social foundations for limiting arbitrary power than for sustaining democratic decision-making. By the same token, it is easier to see a basis for managerial self-restraint than for affirmative social responsibility' (Selznick 1969, p. 275). More generally, and crucially, none of this can simply be imposed by some enthusiastic Selznickian legislator. What is required, to repeat, is a '*receptive institutional setting*', without which legislators are just whistling in the wind. And if they wish to learn when and where their performances might be heard and heeded, they must be prepared to understand the specific settings in which they hope to intervene. And that must involve concrete institutional *assessment*, not merely an assumption or some abstract theorization:

> Where these conditions are approximated, *not as a result of external constraint but as the outcome of the group's own problem-solving*, we may speak of the evolution of government. Therefore we cannot argue from an abstract ideal to an institutional prescription. The whole point is that the conditions for governance must be found in the life of the institution itself. On that basis, the law of governance may be invoked. Without that basis the law is irrelevant, its application self-defeating. (Selznick 1969, p. 273)

This is, after all, merely to apply to the particular case the general point about state legislation and non-state law, which underlies this work of depth, complexity and broad implication:

> If social evolution has taken place, it does not follow that legal change is not needed or expected. On the contrary, the legal order is pressed to put into practice ideals that have always had an abstract validity but which may not, in the past, have reflected the institutional competence of the society. Law works best when appropriate social foundations exist, but those foundations do not obviate the need for legal support and direction, to confirm rights and to extend them. (Selznick 1969, p. 275)

9. CONCLUSIONS

There is room for debate about many things in this work. There is the very enterprise of mixing analysis and evaluation, which is at the heart of Selznick's 'humanist science' and anathema to positivist social scientists (Black 1972; Hertogh 2004). There is the theory of institutional evolution that Selznick has elaborated in several of his works, and that has aroused the ire of many empirically minded critics (Feeley 1979, p. 901; Blankenburg 1984, pp. 281–284). There is the book's particular assessment of the character and development of American industrial law (Bainbridge 2002). There are matters of methodology where some prefer Ehrlich's 'bottom-up' empirical methods to Selznick's allegedly 'top-down' normative theorizing (Hertogh 2004). There are evaluative matters too: is what Selznick clearly favours an example of, perhaps a contributor to, that 'creeping legalism' that Lon Fuller so opposed? Donald Black predicted that Fuller might think so (Black 1972, p. 714), and for once, perhaps just once, he was cleverer than he knew. In correspondence between Fuller and Selznick, that is exactly (though without that phrase) what Fuller complained of.[8] And one might develop, inspired by

Selznick's book, an analysis of the interaction of public and private that points to quite a different sort of outcome than the colonization of private by public that he hopes for and in part expects. Thus, Lauren Edelman sees organizations setting up internal grievance procedures to deal with allegations of discrimination, which they don't do very well, but then courts defer to these internal practices and take their existence without more, as satisfying the requirements of anti-discrimination legislation. As a result, Edelman argues, this practice of 'legal endogeneity' 'allows patterns of injustice that become institutionalized in the organizational realm to be incorporated into – and legitimated by – public legal rules and norms' (Edelman 2002, p. 201).

There are important issues here, both of principle and of empirical detail. Some of them have to do with American industrial and employment law, on which no enlightenment can be had from me; some I aim to explore in another place; some are legitimate differences that are the stuff of routine academic disputation. But some of the deepest matters that divide Selznick from many mainstream social scientists have to do with a sustained programme of thinking about actual and desirable social, legal and political developments, how to understand them, and what is involved in analysing them in depth. Moreover, in a world full of lawyers and policy advisers propagating state-centred institutional recipes for the rule of law, and then affecting disappointment that benighted beneficiaries still violate or deliberately ignore it, a reminder of the complexity of non-state conditions for the rule of law might be salutary. The rarity of such reminders suggests that we still await a 'social science that does not quite yet exist' (Soltan 2002, p. 357). It might, as Australian electoral posters used to have it, be time for a change.

NOTES

* This chapter is adapted from *Philip Selznick. Ideals in the World* by Martin Krygier, forthcoming with Stanford University Press, all rights reserved.

1. See, for example, Fuller (1969, pp. 123 ff). They did not always agree, however) in particular – as we shall see – on the normative theses of this book.
2. For two fertile and influential more recent elaborations of this theme, see Galanter (1981) and Moore (1981).
3. Chester Barnard's work on administration in the 1930s greatly influenced Selznick's earliest work in organizational theory, including *TVA and the Grass Roots*. Barnard had in turn expressed his debt to a 'chance reading of Eugene Ehrlich's *Fundamental Principles of the Sociology of Law*', a book which emphasized the social rather than doctrinal and formal roots of legal orders, and countered what Barnard took to be the prevailing 'legalism that prevents the acceptance of essential facts of social organizations' (Barnard 1938, pp. xxx, xxxi). Barnard clearly discerned a kinship and overlap between his understanding of organizations and Ehrlich's of law, and Selznick did so too. He refers to Ehrlich in his first article on sociology of law and later several times returns to him.

4. In correspondence with me, he has recently reflected: '[A]bout Ehrlich, I think the point is that he and I shared a sociological perspective. I don't think that his writings were a big influence on me but it was helpful to refer to him as someone who expressed the significance of a sociological perspective for jurisprudence. So I would not say that I depended in any way on Ehrlich's authority but I did see him as sharing the same point of view' (personal correspondence, 21 May 2007).
5. As he puts it in Selznick (1968): 'In context, this approach is more than an appeal to bring law into closer relation with social practice; it is an assertion that authoritative legal materials are to be found in the realities of group life. In other words, it questions the claim of the state to be the sole receptacle of legal authority' (p. 51).
6. A fact of which he was quite conscious, reflecting in interviews that he had never managed to tie it down conceptually. In his discussion of the principles of due process, near the end of *LSIJ* (Selznick 1969, p. 253), however, he suggests some examples: 'Rule-making that is based on evident caprice or prejudice, or that presumes the contrary of clearly established knowledge violates due process. Procedure cannot be "due" if it does not conform to the canons of rational discourse or if it is otherwise outside the pale of reasoned and dispassionate assessment. Thus legislative classification of persons or groups may be struck down as arbitrary and against reason if they have no defensible connection with, or inherently frustrate, the professed aims of the legislation. Similarly a host of administrative actions, though they may enjoy large grants of discretion, are subject to this ultimate appeal.'
7. 'My view of law and authority has certainly benefited from the stirrings of the sixties, especially on the campuses, where there has been a quest for enlarged student rights and for the reconstruction of authority' (Selznick 1969, Preface, p. v).
8. Lon L. Fuller, letter to Philip Selznick, 12 January 1972: 'If I have one fundamental criticism it is that in dealing with institutional procedures (such as adjudication) your thesis assumes a kind of continuum, and that one can be "adjudicative" in one's approach to a problem in varying degrees. Or again, it assumes that procedures of decision and authoritative direction can be "legalized" along a kind of continuum, with no clear stopping places en route.

   Coupled with this is a tendency to disregard the costs of judicialization and legalization. . . . There is, in the book, little sense of dilemma and none of tragic choice. . . .
   I have been suggesting that your book does not recognize sufficiently the costs and disadvantages of legalization and judicialization. . . .
   . . . processes have an internal integrity that cannot be violated without damage to their moral efficacy. Plainly this is true of contracts, elections and deciding issues by lot. I think it is also true of adjudication. . . .

   I am disturbed by what seems to be a too free-wheeling disposition toward the internal integrity of adjudicative forms.'

REFERENCES

Bainbridge, Stephen M. (2002), 'Employee Involvement Postcollective Bargaining', in Robert A. Kagan, Martin Krygier and Kenneth Winston (eds), *Legality and Community. On the Intellectual Legacy of Philip Selznick*, New York: Rowman & Littlefield Publishers, pp. 203–218.

Barnard, Chester (1938), *Functions of the Executive*, Cambridge, MA.: Harvard University Press.

Black, Donald J. (1972), 'Review of *Law, Society, and Industrial Justice*', *American Journal of Sociology*, **78**, 709–714.

Blankenburg, Erhard (1984), 'The Poverty of Evolutionism: A Critique of Teubner's Case for "Reflexive Law" ', *Law and Society Review*, **18**, 273–289.

Carothers, Tom (ed.) (2006), *Promoting the Rule of Law Abroad. In Search of Knowledge*, Washington, DC: Carnegie Endowment for International Peace.
Edelman, Lauren B. (2002), 'Legality and the Endogeneity of Law', in Robert A. Kagan, Martin Krygier and Kenneth Winston (eds), *Legality and Community. On the Intellectual Legacy of Philip Selznick*, New York: Rowman & Littlefield Publishers, pp. 187–202.
Ehrlich, Eugen (1936), *Fundamental Principles of the Sociology of Law*, Cambridge, MA: Harvard University Press (translation reissued, with a new introduction by Klaus A. Ziegert, New Brunswick: Transaction Press, 2002).
Feeley, Malcolm M. (1979), 'Law, Legitimacy, and Symbols: An Expanded View of Law and Society in Transition', *Michigan Law Review*, **77**, 899–907.
Fuller, Lon L. (1969), *The Morality of Law*, revised 2nd edition, New Haven: Yale University Press.
Galanter, Marc (1981), 'Justice in Many Rooms: Courts, Private Ordering, and Indigenous Law', *Journal of Legal Pluralism and Unofficial Law*, **19**, 1–47.
Hertogh, Marc (2004), 'The Living *Rechtsstaat:* A Bottom-Up Approach to Legal Ideals and Social Reality', in Wibren van der Burg and Sanne Taekema (eds), *The Importance of Ideals*, Brussels: Presses Interuniversitaires Européennes, pp. 75–95.
Jensen, Erik G. and Thomas C. Heller (eds) (2003), *Beyond Common Knowledge. Empirical Approaches to the Rule of Law*, Stanford, CA: Stanford University Press.
Krygier, Martin (2004), 'False Dichotomies, Real Perplexities, and the Rule of Law', in András Sajó (ed.), *Human Rights with Modesty. The Problem of Universalism*, Leiden and Boston: Martinus Nijhoff, pp. 251–277.
Krygier, Martin (2006), 'The Rule of Law. An Abuser's Guide', in András Sajó (ed.), *The Dark Side of Fundamental Rights*, Utrecht: Eleven International Publishing, pp. 129–161.
Krygier, Martin (2007), 'Law and the State', *Encyclopedia of Law and Society: American and Global Perspectives*, New York: Sage.
Krygier, Martin (2008), 'The Rule of Law: Legality, Teleology and Sociology', forthcoming in Gianluigi Palombella and Neil Walker (eds), *Relocating the Rule of Law*, Oxford: Hart Publishers.
Moore, Sally Falk (1981), 'Law and Social Change: The Semi-autonomous Social Field as an Appropriate Subject of Study, *Law as Process*, London: Routledge and Kegan Paul, pp. 54–81.
Nelken, David (1984), 'Law in Action or Living Law? Back to the Beginning in Sociology of Law', *Legal Studies*, **4**, 157–74.
Nonet, Philippe and Philip Selznick [1978] (2001), *Law and Society in Transition. Toward Responsive Law*, new edn, New Brunswick: Transaction Publishers.
Selznick, Philip (1949), *TVA and the Grass Roots: A Study in the Sociology of Formal Organization*, Berkeley: University of California Press.
Selznick, Philip (1961), 'Sociology and Natural Law', *Natural Law Forum*, **6**, 84–108.
Selznick, Philip (1965), 'Review of Lon L. Fuller, *The Morality of Law*', *American Sociological Review*, **30** (6), 947–948.
Selznick, Philip (1968), 'The Sociology of Law', *International Encyclopedia of the Social Sciences*, **9**, pp. 50–59.
Selznick, Philip (1969), *Law, Society, and Industrial Justice*, New York: Russell Sage.
Selznick, Philip (1976), 'The Ethos of the Common Law', in Irving Kristol and Paul Weaver (eds), *The Americans: 1976*, Lexington: D.C. Heath and Co.

Selznick, Philip (1984), *Leadership in Administration*, Berkeley, CA: University of California Press (first published 1957, New York: Harper & Row).
Selznick, Philip (1992), *The Moral Commonwealth*, Berkeley, CA: University of California Press.
Selznick, Philip (1996), 'Institutionalism "Old" and "New"', *Administrative Science Quarterly*, **41**, 271.
Soltan, Karol (2002), 'Selznick and Civics', in Robert A. Kagan, Martin Krygier and Kenneth Winston (eds), *Legality and Community. On the Intellectual Legacy of Philip Selznick*, New York: Rowman & Littlefield, p. 357.

4. The point of law: the interdependent functionality of state and non-state regulation

Sanne Taekema

1. INTRODUCTION

The relation between non-state law and state legislatures can be fruitfully understood in the context of alternatives to legislation. The search for alternatives to legislation is not a merely academic exercise; it is pursued because of the perceived defects of traditional legislation. Other governmental regulatory instruments, privatization and deregulation are among the options considered in order to make law work better. In this chapter, I will focus on the basic claim that underlies such discussions, namely that law should be assessed according to its success in performing key functions in society. More specifically, I will take a comparative perspective on the functionality of state and non-state regulation.

Following general results of socio-legal research that show the limited influence of official law on people's behaviour, the questions I wish to pursue here are the following. To what extent, and in which respects, is state law needed to fulfil important functions, claimed to be legal, in society? And to what extent, and in virtue of which characteristics, can non-state regulation fulfil these functions? In what way do state and non-state regulation interact in the performance of these functions? With regard to this interaction, I will investigate what the remaining function of state legislation is when compared with forms of non-state regulation.

Underlying this project is an interest in the question of the scope of the concept of law; more specifically, the extent to which regulation by non-state actors deserves to be included in it. I will address this issue at the end of this chapter. For now, I will confine myself to a working definition of *state* law, leaving open the question whether the concept of law extends beyond the state. In the following I will use Roger Cotterrell's definition of state law as 'the hierarchically organized, centrally coordinated, and systematized official law of the state, promulgated and enforced only by its legislative, judicial, and administrative agencies' (2006, p. 33). I will speak of state regulation, or official state rules, versus non-state regulation, or informal non-state rules, meaning by the latter regulation by actors that are not agencies instituted by the state.

As the theoretical background for this chapter I have chosen a classic functionalist theory: the legal realist work of Karl Llewellyn. My approach consists of a discussion of studies by other authors in the light of his law-jobs framework, in order to draw out problems and promises of non-state regulation. The limited space available makes my analysis slightly impressionistic: I have selected studies about non-state regulation that are interesting regarded from a functionalist perspective but that are not necessarily representative. In the following I will combine discussion of these studies with theoretical discussion of the implications for a functional approach.

2. THEORETICAL BACKGROUND: LLEWELLYN'S LAW-JOBS

As I said, my theoretical starting point is the law-jobs theory developed by Karl Llewellyn (1940). The theory identifies a limited number of five jobs that need to be done in any social group for that group to survive. According to Llewellyn, these broad functions could be performed by official legal institutions and by other normative institutions in society. He distinguished two aspects to the performance of these functions: in its 'bare-bones aspect' each job must be done minimally in order for society to survive; in its 'questing aspect' each job points to the directions in which a society may flourish (1940, p. 1375).

At first sight, Llewellyn's ideas seem vulnerable to the common criticism raised against functionalism: that it connects legal functions so tightly to the survival of society that the theory is self-fulfilling, meaning that wherever a working society is found, these essential functions are performed by law (e.g. Tamanaha 2001, p. 36). This seems true of Llewellyn also, because he claims that performance of the law-jobs is essential for the existence of a group (Llewellyn 1940, p. 1381), entailing that wherever a functioning group is found the law-jobs must be performed.

However, on consideration the criticism does not hold, for three reasons. First of all, the law-jobs theory is best interpreted as a heuristic device, a tool to look for legal, or law-like, phenomena (De Been 2005, p. 110).[1] The theory provides a specific focus for research more than an argument that law must perform these functions. Secondly, because of the focus on two distinct aspects of the law-jobs, basic and aspirational, Llewellyn makes room for judgments of variable achievement of the law-jobs, of more or less successful performance. Finally, in his broad approach he explicitly acknowledges that the law-jobs need not be performed by what is usually regarded as (official) law (Llewellyn 1940, p. 1389). Other forms of social ordering may be involved, such as religion, education or the economy.

Using Llewellyn as a starting point for me implies a 'thin' type of functionalism: my focus is on the tasks state law aims, and claims, to perform with the explicit recognition that law need not effectively perform them.[2] In other words, my aim is to assess the success of state law in fulfilling its point or purposes in comparison to non-state regulation. I will focus on finding out which characteristics of state or non-state rules support or hinder their success. Moreover, it is important to study the interactions between state and non-state regulation in order to see in what ways they presuppose and depend on each other.

In essence, my approach consists of a comparison of regulatory schemes on two dimensions: the extent to which the scheme in question is successful in performing a function and the extent to which the scheme in question involves state or non-state regulation. That allows for a scale with four extremes: A. a regulatory scheme that is functional because it involves state regulation; B. a scheme that is non-functional despite being state regulation; C. a scheme that is non-functional because lacking the characteristics of state regulation; D. a scheme that is functional precisely because its characteristics are different from state regulation. These four possibilities are extremes because both the functionality and the state-dependence of a regulatory scheme are matters of degree. The advantage of such an approach is that it is non-tautological: it does not take for granted that if a function is fulfilled, this means that the scheme that fulfils it is therefore legal.[3]

The five law-jobs distinguished by Llewellyn are the following (1940, p. 1373). The first of the jobs is what he calls 'the disposition of trouble-cases'. By this he means the resolution of disputes, conflicts and grievances. Conflicts threaten the order of the group and therefore the order needs to be 'repaired' by the resolution of the dispute. The second law-job is that of 'the preventive channelling and the reorientation of conduct and expectations so as to avoid trouble'. This includes the idea that the legal rules make clear what people can expect of each other and create ways to reorganize their relations. The third law-job concerns 'the allocation of authority and the arrangement of procedures that legitimatize action as being authoritative'. This job involves determining who has the power to make decisions and in what way such decisions need to be made. The fourth law-job is 'the net organization of the group or society *as a whole* so as to provide direction and incentive'. This concerns coordinating diverging perspectives into one focused vision, of which Llewellyn rightly says that it is often achieved to an important extent by other cultural symbols, which then still need to be made effective by legal mechanisms. The fifth law-job is that of juristic method. This job is of a different character, it is more an aspect of the other four than a separate activity: 'The law-jobs of trouble-handling, of channelling, of say-allocation, of the Net Drive, all need doing, and they all drive toward the emergence of some type of institutional machinery' (1940, p. 1392). Juristic method includes typical legal mechanisms, e.g. the use of precedent. In the following, I will not use it as a separate function of law; to my mind, juristic method is more fruitfully seen as part of what defines the legal than as something the legal should do. I will take each of the other four jobs as my unit of analysis in the following four sections.

For assessing the successful performance of law-jobs or legal functions, I will focus on the aspirational, 'questing', aspects of the jobs. The basic aspect of the law-jobs cannot really distinguish better from worse performance, but the aspirational aspect can. As Llewellyn points out, the aspirational side consists of two dimensions: the dimension of efficient, smooth performance of the law-job and the dimension of value-realization (1940, p. 1375). The criteria of the first dimension are fairly clear, but what counts as ideal is less so, and Llewellyn limits himself to a vague reference to justice to explain it. In order to make it slightly more concrete, I will formulate the value dimensions that I believe to be implicit in the different law-jobs.[4]

The resolution of trouble-cases is primarily concerned with the value of peace, by which I mean restoring relations to the satisfaction of all those concerned. Secondly, it involves redressing the balance that was disturbed by the trouble: restorative justice. Channelling conduct also has two main values connected to it: security of expectations and distributive justice, how to organize relations and expectations in such a way that there is a fair distribution of burdens. The ideal side of allocating authority is to achieve legitimate, accountable and competently exercised power of decision. This includes procedural fairness and well-considered judgments. The questing aspect of organizing net-drive is the hardest to formulate. It involves providing clear and legitimate direction and a vision of the common good. What the latter should be, however, is not really explicable in the abstract: there are side-constraints on normatively acceptable visions of the good, to exclude evil regimes, but there is a wide range of possibility within those boundaries. Overall, I should note that the ideal dimension of the law-jobs brings in criteria that transcend the stated purposes of the actors who make the rules: evaluation need not be limited to assessing whether the explicit goals of the actor are reached.

A final thing to note about Llewellyn's discussion of the law-jobs is that he recognized that they imply each other, in the sense that performance of one job has consequences for the others. For instance, resolving trouble-cases also helps channel future conduct because it makes clear what is expected in the situation that was at issue in the case. It is also imaginable that all law-jobs are performed by one institution at the same time.[5] A King Rex who does not rule proactively by formulating rules, but solely by way of pronouncements in trouble-cases that arise, is possible.

3. RESOLVING CONFLICTS

The first law-job on Llewellyn's list is that of adjusting trouble-cases. Settling disputes has been one of the central tasks of state officials, in this case judges, for a long time. However, it is also an area in which the limitations of legal solutions are clearly felt. This is evident, for instance, in the rise of mediation and alternative dispute resolution. Although it sometimes seems as if the alternatives to state courts are only a fashionable reaction to failures in the court system, such alternatives have existed informally alongside state courts for a long time. Therefore, the question whether state law is needed to resolve conflicts cannot be answered as a matter of either state or non-state dispute resolution performing the function. People always solve at least some of their conflicts outside of the official legal institutions. The question is rather, given that there are non-state, informal resolution mechanisms, whether the state system always influences the informal solutions for conflicts and is necessary as a back-up to those solutions.

The preferred way of referring to this issue is derived from a phrase by Mnookin (Mnookin and Kornhauser 1979): do the informal alternatives operate 'in the shadow of the law'? Whether this is true generally is contested, most interestingly by Ellickson (1991). Ellickson claims that there are situations in which conflicts are solved 'beyond the shadow of the law', where the state legal system no longer plays a significant role. Although his empirical research yields interesting results that alter the role of state law, I believe that his conclusion that conflicts in such a context are solved without influence of state law is unwarranted.

Ellickson studied how Shasta County cattle ranchers resolved issues involving liability for damage caused by trespassing cattle. In Shasta County there are complicated liability rules distinguishing between open and closed range rules applying to unfenced land (Ellickson 1991, p. 3). When an area is declared open range, the cattle owner is generally not liable for an animal trespassing on another's land. In a closed range area, owners are strictly liable for damage caused by their cattle. Ellickson shows that people do not solve their conflicts on the basis of these rules. Appeal to a legal official, even an attorney, is extremely rare. In most cases, no damages are paid but neighbours keep what Ellickson calls 'mental accounts' of transgressions, not only of cattle damage but of other offences as well (1991, pp. 55–56). As long as the accounts are roughly balanced, nobody presses for payment. Ellickson explains this by reference to informal norms of neighbourly cooperation (p. 53), which include the norms that everyone is responsible for his animals and that minor transgressions need not be compensated. As long as these norms are respected, state legal rules seem to exert no influence at all. However, things are different when someone does not behave as a good neighbour should. Then, informal sanctions, such as gossip or self-help, are applied and eventually complaints to public officials and legal claims for compensation are made (p. 57).

The question is whether this is so different from bargaining in the shadow of the law. Mnookin and Kornhauser studied attorney-assisted bargaining between divorced couples. In such a situation, it does not seem surprising that the official law plays a role, because legal experts are already involved. Ellickson has a good point when he argues that the actual formal rules do not exert influence: in Shasta, they were simplified because neither lay people nor attorneys completely understood them. To the extent that official divorce rules form a complicated system, I would also expect them to be interpreted differently in bargaining. In both these situations, however, official law definitely exerts an influence, only not the exact influence that it was meant to have.[6] The situation of cooperating neighbours, using informal norms, is not addressed by Mnookin and Kornhauser. They explicitly exclude divorcees with altruistic motives, and do not explicitly distinguish between attorney-assisted and completely informal conflict resolution (1979, p. 969). If that is taken into account, the difference between the two approaches of the shadow of the law is reduced. But what does the shadow of the law really imply?

For Ellickson, the shadow of the law is influence on the substantive norms as informally applied; because of this focus on the substantive issues, state law is said to have no influence. However, when we look at the broader picture, state law does influence the procedural options people have and employ: against non-cooperative neighbours, formal legal alternatives are indeed invoked. Official law is needed to deal with individuals who refuse to cooperate; the shadow that law extends is thus more of a threat in the background than an influence on the rules applied in normal situations.

In terms of Llewellyn's law-job, this actually makes perfect sense if the 'trouble' of the trouble-case is analysed more carefully. If we see trouble not so much as a dispute between a few individuals, but as a disruption of the order of a larger community, then state law is indeed needed for trouble-cases. Llewellyn's own discussion seems to allow for both interpretations of trouble. He describes the resolution of trouble-cases as: 'garage-repair work on the general order of the group when that general order misses fire, or grinds gears, or even threatens total break-down' (1940, p. 1375). This connects trouble to the well-being of the group, but he goes on to say that this is usually minor trouble, which does not threaten the group as a whole. Although Llewellyn includes all dispute resolution in the scope of this law-job, it seems that on the basis of the distinction between minor and major trouble, it is possible to see state law as needed only for major trouble. On the basis of Ellickson's research, we may add that minor trouble is that which members of a group manage to resolve among themselves, and that major trouble involves individuals who rebel against the group's solutions. Only in the second type of trouble is there a need for the threat of official legal intervention.

4. CHANNELLING CONDUCT

For a Dutch person, the law-job of channelling conduct conjures up images of engineers trying to control the course of a river. Such an image transferred to law implies the existence of an external authority who does the channelling, for instance by making rules. I will focus on the making of rules, not as the activity of external rule-makers but as self-regulatory activity. Under what circumstances does self-regulation appear to help rechannel conduct?

One area in which self-regulation has become popular is that of transnational industry, where businesses draw up codes of conduct. Such codes are really a mix of self-regulation in a strict sense – meaning a company or group of companies making rules to control their own behaviour – and other-regarding regulation – companies making rules to control the behaviour of others down the value chain. Codes of conduct play an important role in the regulation of issues with an ethical component: for instance, environmental protection or labour rights. In Llewellyn's terms, addressing these issues in regulation is a matter of rechannelling conduct so as to realize the questing aspect of this law-job, aimed at achieving a fair reorganization of burdens and benefits.

Although codes of conduct play a role in a national context as well, such as the codes of national professional organizations, their role in international trade relations is potentially more significant. Many national governments, especially of poorer countries, have only limited power to control the behaviour of companies that can choose where and at which costs to produce. Because states have to compete for production, in order to ensure economic growth and employment, state regulation is less concerned with demanding ethical conduct than with creating an attractive business environment. Other states with a stronger economic position might be willing to make regulation demanding green or ethical production, but are inhibited by other factors. They have committed to free trade through treaties with other states; or the problems do not concern their territory or citizens directly; or they think problems are best dealt with by concerted action, together with other states; and perhaps most importantly, these are not issues that are considered the most pressing in the national political forum. It thus appears that codes of conduct may have genuine added value.

In order to see what advantages and disadvantages codes may have compared with state legislation, I will use a study focusing on the specific issue of fair labour conditions: *Corporate Responsibility and Labour Rights* (Jenkins et al. 2002). With regard to labour-related issues, at least four types of codes are operative: codes adopted by individual companies, industry or branch codes agreed by business associations, codes drawn up by a diverse group of stakeholders, and government-initiated codes (Jenkins 2002, p. 18). Jenkins points out that there are significant differences in the content and stringency of the norms in these types of codes. Using the International Labour Organization (ILO) labour standards as the point of reference,[7] he shows that less than half of the company codes and a third of the business association codes contain clauses against forced labour and child labour. Codes made by multiple stakeholders fare better; around two-thirds contain these clauses. The most striking difference between business association codes and multi-stakeholder codes is the reference to freedom of association and collective bargaining: only 13 per cent of the former and 95 per cent of the latter include them (Jenkins 2002, p. 19). The most popular norms across the codes of conduct are vague commitments to a 'reasonable working environment' (Jenkins 2002, p. 20). These figures seem to yield the cynical conclusion that companies themselves, whether individually or collectively, are not really interested in serious improvement and merely use a code of conduct as window-dressing. In the case of business association codes, there is the familiar problem of getting a consensus on particular norms, which enlarges the influence of the least committed companies. It is therefore not so surprising that the branch codes are the least demanding. The good score of multi-stakeholder codes suggests the importance of a democratic aspect of procedure: involving non-governmental organizations (NGOs) and trade unions is effective in ensuring that core standards are included. In this respect, codes of conduct clearly resemble state legislation: it is important to include different perspectives in the decision-making process and the most straightforward way of doing this is by having representatives of these perspectives as participants. This is not a matter of procedural fairness alone, it also supports the robustness of substantive norms.

After adopting norms, the next step of implementation, and especially monitoring implementation, is a commonly acknowledged difficulty. A functional perspective highlights this problem: rules can only work to rechannel conduct if they are effective in practice and are not only laid down on paper. Codes therefore include monitoring regimes in order to have an independent check whether the code's norms are adopted in practice. Here, it is instructive to look at the specific problem of codes that are imposed on all the agents in a production chain. Clothing, for instance, is a product made mostly for Western consumers in low-wage countries; it is typically not produced in a brand's own factories but by subcontractors.[8] A particular brand that has adopted a code of conduct with norms against forced labour or child labour does not control the production process in the subcontracting factories. Theoretically, a brand can demand that its subcontractors respect a minimum working age and a maximum of working hours. In practice, such demands are difficult to enforce. The first problem is that a good inspecting regime needs to be carried out: knowledgeable inspectors who do not allow management to organize who they talk to and what they see. This is not easy to do: many commercial monitoring agencies do not have specialized agents and work fairly bureaucratically, relying on paper reports (O'Rourke 2002). Furthermore, the main sanction available to a brand is terminating the contract. Unfortunately, that sanction does nothing to improve conditions of workers, or it may even worsen it, because the amount of work decreases. The economic realities of such industries are that consumers make conflicting demands: ethical production, on the one hand, and low prices, on the other. The financial demand usually prevails. In this respect the clothing industry differs from situations where the financial demand is subordinate to another interest: for instance, the food safety issue studied by Havinga (2006). Food safety, unlike fair labour conditions, is a priority for consumers as well, as it involves their own health, which makes it much easier to implement industry-wide safety norms.

In comparison to non-state implementation of codes, state regulation seems to have the advantage of independent inspection and enforcement of norms. Being outside the mutually dependent relations of production makes it easier to enforce norms: the state has a separate interest in upholding the norms and the ability to set norms for the industry nationwide. However, as I noted above, in the case of these transnational industries, the power of the state is limited. Except by way of intergovernmental legal cooperation, the national state is not really able to set or enforce norms for actors that are not clearly based within its borders. In such cases, it seems that state and non-state regulation are equally weak: neither is able to channel conduct effectively.

Thus, the limits and challenges of this legal function become clear: both states and non-state actors face difficulties and pressures when trying to influence the behaviour of others. For setting fair rules, it appears difficult to transcend immediate self-interest in a business setting. Actors that have a clear interest in strong norms, either ideologically or practically, need to be involved in the process of making the rules. Procedurally, state legislatures have the advantage here, although here too there is the pressure of narrow self-interest dominating. Implementing rules is difficult when the people who actually need to adjust their behaviour do not genuinely support the rules, for instance because there are other more pressing influences on their behaviour. I have pointed to examples of this in a transnational context, but the same problem has been noted in regard to state legislation. There is ample evidence that a change of behaviour by way of legislation is difficult to realize if the desired change does not build on tendencies that are already present.[9]

5. ALLOCATING AUTHORITY

Since Hart's *The Concept of Law* (1994), secondary rules have been seen as the most distinctive trait of law and as the province of the state's power. It is not so much the making of rules of conduct themselves, but the determining by whom and how such rules are made and applied, that is the main task of the state. A clear example of this line of thinking is the well-known argument that private law is really public law, in the sense that the law of contract which allows parties to determine their own contractual rules is a framework of power-conferring rules set by state legislation. When we look at this issue in terms of the law-job of allocating authority, the job to be done seems the state's job: determining who makes or enforces the rules of conduct is what the state does, choosing between public or private bodies. The move towards deregulation, co-regulation and self-regulation can then all be understood as public decisions about who should have the decision power on particular issues.

However, not in all situations is it the state that makes the decision about allocation of powers. In some cases, companies in a particular sector, such as the food industry (Havinga 2006), agree on a set of standards, devise their own monitoring procedures and choose monitoring agencies without any obligation deriving from state law. One of the more popular mechanisms for private monitoring is certification: subjecting to quality standards and the accompanying inspections, usually in order to obtain a quality label such as various ISO labels.[10] In terms of allocating authority, the interesting questions are: Who decides on the inspecting agencies and the procedures to be followed? And what strengths and weaknesses of private authority allocation become apparent?

These questions cannot be separated from the more substantive issues involving the exercise of authority: whether allocation of powers by non-state actors works well, is dependent on the functioning of the agencies who actually exercise these powers. With the use of certification, it is often the company that is being certified that has the choice of inspecting agency (usually with the constraint that the agency must be accredited by the certification body). This free choice influences the quality of the monitoring procedure and decisions as does the character of these inspecting agencies themselves: do they have the knowledge of the field that is needed to hold serious inspections, for instance?

Looking at examples of certification schemes with the allocation of authority as the focus, two actors are of interest: the certification institution, such as the ISO or the Forest Stewardship Council (FSC), which sets the standards and procedures, and the certifier, the inspecting agency which makes the actual judgment on whether the company under scrutiny fulfils the standard. In a number of respects, the certification institution resembles the state as allocator of authority: it determines the procedures to be followed and which agencies are qualified to certify. The main difference, of course, is in the certification institution's authority itself: the voluntary commitment of a company to take part in the certification programme and thereby recognize the authority of the ISO or FSC is unlike the automatic authority the state has over its subjects. One interesting corollary of this voluntary submission to authority is pointed out by Meidinger: in many contexts, competing certification programmes have appeared (2006, pp. 4–5).[11] Meidinger argues that such competition often serves to improve the way these programmes work: they copy the best aspects of each others' schemes. This beneficial effect of competition, to my mind, depends on the public scrutiny of certification. Programmes and labels need to be taken seriously by the public in order to be a selling point for companies.

A second issue with the certification institutions runs parallel with the problems noted in relation to codes of conduct in the previous section: it matters highly who is involved in the setting of the certification standards and procedures. The FSC is a multi-stakeholder system that is highly developed, while other certification systems are dominated by industry interests (Meidinger 2006, pp. 4–5). Here, similar differences as in the labour codes of conduct between strict standards in multi-stakeholder programmes and lax standards in industry-based programmes are to be expected.

As to the role of the certifier, the most interesting issue is the triangular relationship between certification institution, certifying agency and the company to be certified. Under most programmes, the certifying agencies operate commercially, meaning that they are chosen and paid for by the company to be certified. This seems to invite the certifier to make his inspection as (un)demanding as the company wants; a tendency that may be reinforced by the incentive to work as cost-effectively as possible. Much then depends on the role of the certification institution and its subordinate organizations to make sure that certifiers apply standards correctly and in the same way. The certification institution also has to ascertain that certifiers have all the qualifications needed to judge the particular standards and situations involved. O'Rourke (2002) as I mentioned earlier, points out that this can be a serious problem. A promising way out seems to be the involvement of local NGOs and experts either as monitors or informants;[12] again, it is the task of the certification institution to design procedures in such a way that the dangers of 'customer-friendly' inspection are minimized.

As Meidinger argues, state regulation can support the regulation by certification programmes in the background. Some of the mechanisms available to the state are familiar, such as requiring certification or making it a condition for preferential treatment (Meidinger 2006, p. 20). Others are at the moment no more than interesting possibilities, such as using certification standards to fill in duties of reasonable care in tort law (Meidinger 2006, p. 24). Although the direct involvement with this exercise of private authority is limited, state regulation can be a significant back-up.

I should note here that the examples Meidinger gives of state support for certification are mostly not traditional legislation, but other regulatory instruments. They involve administrative policy, such as making certification a reason for preferential treatment, or judiciary rule-making, such as filling in duties of reasonable care in tort cases. Legislation turns out not to be a necessary back-up for certification schemes, although it is a significant part of the mix of regulatory instruments available to the state.[13]

The law-job of allocating authority is certainly not by definition the state's prerogative or task. Private institutions are quite capable of making such decisions under the right conditions: the institutions should represent multiple interests, be open to public scrutiny, and prevent self-interested and lax monitoring. With regard to this law-job I see similar patterns as with channelling conduct: non-state regulation suffers from problems that are often similar to those of state legislation. Private institutions that allocate authority can be seen as quasi-legislators that need similar conditions to function well and that cannot automatically be seen as better or worse than state legislation.

6. PROVIDING DIRECTION AND INCENTIVE

Of all the law-jobs, the task of organizing 'net-drive' as Llewellyn calls it, is most closely connected to the central notion of the group. From his description, we can gather that this function of law is to transcend plurality in society by providing it with a sense of direction and the incentive to do things for society as a whole (1940, p. 1387).[14] This is the law-job that is most clearly the traditional province of state legislation: ideally, after public and parliamentary deliberation on the basis of a plurality of perspectives, the legislature chooses to enact general rules that incorporate its vision of where society should be headed. At the start of this chapter, I noted that state legislation is now seen as not necessarily the most effective instrument to perform legal functions. The question here is: what possibilities are there for non-state alternatives to provide direction and incentive? That question in turn raises some difficult points for the law-jobs theory.

Llewellyn himself saw other aspects of culture and their symbols as important contributors to this law-job, such as religion, education, economic organization and patriotism. He emphasizes the role of emblems (such as the flag) and slogans as symbols that are 'heavily charged with a philosophy of felt rightness and heavily charged with emotional incentive' (1940, p. 1390). Although these cultural symbols nicely fit the description of non-state alternatives to legislation, there are at least two major ways in which they challenge the functionalist framework. First of all, they are quite elusive phenomena to pin down as the performers of this law-job: the functions of the symbolic are more akin to those of language, i.e. to express and communicate (van Klink 1998, pp. 35–39), than to the jobs identified by Llewellyn.[15] Expressing values can, of course, have the effect of providing direction, but this involves an additional causal link that is tenuous. Although the US flag is an important patriotic symbol, it no longer serves to steer people in the direction of supporting the war in Iraq, for instance. The changeable effects of cultural symbols challenge the idea of function as the fulfilment of a purpose consciously set by an identifiable actor, which makes the cultural difficult to evaluate in terms of being (non-)functional.

The second issue raised by cultural symbols is actually a broader point, which is also implicit in the discussion of the job of channelling conduct: the concept of a group. In the context of contemporary society, the pertinent question about cultural symbols is: whose symbols and whose culture? This is not only a question of acknowledging the multicultural character of modern societies; it is the question whether the main presupposition underlying the law-jobs theory is tenable. For Llewellyn, the notion of the group, or entirety, is central. The group needs to deal with tendencies that (threaten to) disturb the group's order (1940, p. 1373). It is significant that he uses the concept of the entirety as a synonym for the group: the unit of observation is the whole and its constituting subgroups and individuals. This, however, makes the theory neglect the difficulty of pinning down the relevant group or totality and, as a consequence, also the interaction between groups that cannot be situated within one larger whole. To take religion as an example, the Roman Catholic Church and Islam are important, symbolically charged, institutions that are capable of uniting their followers to some extent. However, it is not really sensible to look at all Catholics, or all Muslims, as one group. Such communities, if they can be called that, partly overlap with others: they cannot really be visualized as a subgroup completely within another entirety, or an overarching supragroup that unites other groups. Because groups overlap and interconnect, we should study pluralities of groups and not the order of one society, but the stability and success of the interactions between different groups. Coming back to the labour codes of conduct can clarify the point that it is difficult to identify one entirety. There is not one state or a particular industry that forms the relevant whole, but there is a set of different groups or stakeholders that interact in relation to a particular problematic, here: fair labour conditions.[16] In terms of the distinctions made by Marc Hertogh, Llewellyn can be said not to have enough eye for non-state law *beyond* the state.

With this contextualized adaptation of the law-jobs framework, a few of my earlier observations are reinforced. It is important to ensure that all groups involved in a problem field are active participants, or at the very least heard, in processes of regulation. With regard to the law-job of providing direction and incentive, there is a genuine but limited role for state legislation. Problems with a national scope that involve diverse groups within the confines of one state still call for deliberation on, and the formulation of, general rules. Where problems concern groups that cannot be identified as part of a state, non-state alternatives are necessary. For both state and non-state regulation, the expectations of what they can achieve are modest: providing direction to multiple groups is always difficult. The prospects look better, however, if involvement of all the groups affected by a piece of regulation can be ensured.

7. THE PLACE OF JURISTIC METHOD: DEFINING LAW?

Finally, I want to devote some space to the fifth 'law-job' of juristic method. As I said at the beginning, I see it not as a function to be fulfilled but I want to explore the possibility of using juristic method for the concept of law. So far, by speaking of state and non-state regulation I have avoided the need to address the question whether the non-state phenomena I discuss deserve to be called legal. This is a big question that I will not attempt to answer in full. Rather, what I will do is consider one particular option: using juristic method as the defining characteristic of law.

As I said in section 2, the law-job of juristic method sits uneasily within the functional framework. Do the style and reasoning of jurists in themselves perform a role in the preservation of order and the promotion of justice? Llewellyn himself seems to recognize the rather different character of juristic method:

> This problem, seen as reaching over all the law-job foci, or seen if you will as one phase of the play of the fourth upon the first three, I take in any event to be worth isolation for study. I shall call it the problem of *juristic method*, that of the *ways* of handling 'legal' tools to law-job ends, and of the on-going upkeep and improvement of both ways and tools. (1940, p. 1392)

Juristic method is secondary; it supervenes upon the other jobs. What it has in common with the other law-jobs is a basic and an ideal aspect; perfecting the methods and institutions of law can be a genuine quest. As a specific way in which to perform the (other) law-jobs, juristic method is a recognizable feature of regulation. It encompasses particular forms of persuasive reasoning,[17] making use of formal rules and institutions, developing a specialized language,[18] and a special focus on correct procedure.

As a particular way of handling jobs to be done, juristic method is best seen as more or less present. If the legal is equated with the use of juristic method, the legal also becomes a gradual concept: the more specialized, formal, rule- and procedure-oriented a practice becomes, the more legal it is.[19] The idea that legal character is a matter of degree may seem counterintuitive; we are used to regarding law as a binary concept: something either is or is not legal. There are many important phenomena, however, that are not fully law in the traditional sense, modelled on state law, but that share many of its characteristics, for which we use terms such as 'soft law', 'emergent law' and 'implicit law'. For my purposes here, it is important to be able to say that some non-state regulation resembles state law more closely than others. If something has all the characteristics of juristic method except being made and enforced by state agencies, is there good reason to withhold the label 'law'? I think not.

8. CONCLUDING REMARKS

Looking back at the different areas discussed in the previous paragraphs, it seems to me that the most significant difference can be found in the operation of non-state regulation in Shasta County conflict resolution versus international labour codes of conduct. The conflict resolution between neighbours in a small rural area works as a non-legal solution, informally without special procedures or language.[20] International regulation by codes of conduct, on the other hand, is highly legalized: it uses the specialized language developed in law and depends on formal procedures. Following Ellickson, I would suggest that the less homogeneous groups are, and the more distant the interactions, the more a legal solution is necessary. In terms of the scale I described in section 2, only when there is a sufficiently strong social bond between people can non-state rules function well without resembling state law. In settings where different groups are involved and there are few mechanisms of social control, legal instruments are necessary, which may be more or less connected to the state.

To what extent a legal solution can and should involve state legislation depends largely on the scope of the problem and the kinds of groups involved. For many problems in the world today, the state is only one of the actors involved and there non-state law without the state, as indicated in Chapter 2, may be the only form of regulation with some chance of success. State legislation remains the preferred form in those situations where different groups need to be brought together *and* a relevant whole can be identified within a national context. Moreover, the principles that have evolved to ensure good legislation, such as representativeness, clear procedure, fairness etc., turn out to be as important for non-state regulation as for state legislation. To focus attention on these legal safeguards, it is wise to include regulation that displays the features of juristic method in the domain of law, regardless whether it is made by state or non-state actors.

NOTES

1. This is most clear in his application of the law-jobs theory in his study together with the anthropologist Hoebel among the Cheyenne Indians (Llewellyn and Hoebel 1941).
2. I borrow the term 'thin functionalism' from William Twining (2003, p. 238).
3. This is common criticism of legal pluralism, that the concept of law is inflated to include everything that provides social order.
4. This is based on my earlier work on the ideals of law (see Taekema 2003, pp. 171–196).
5. Here it is helpful to recall Robert Cover's distinction between a functional and an institutional approach: either the function or the institution can be the unit of analysis. In the institutional approach, one institution can be found to perform several functions; in the functional approach, one function can be performed by a number of institutions (Cover 1979, pp. 910–911). Taking a functional approach tends to underplay the interrelations of different functions.
6. Compare socio-legal literature, e.g. Moore (1973), Griffiths (2003).
7. The so-called core labour standards were laid down in the ILO's Declaration on Fundamental Principles and Rights at Work in 1998. They were first adopted in different ILO conventions and include principles such as a ban on forced labour and child labour, freedom of association and the right to collective bargaining, and elimination of workplace discrimination (Jenkins 2002, p. 19).
8. For a view on the situation of workers in such factories, the documentary *China Blue* (2005, directed by Micha X. Peled) is instructive.

9. Griffiths (2003, p. 12) points to a good example of a successful law that changed behaviour: US smoking bans in public, referring to research done by Kagan and Skolnick (1993). Public opinion in this case was already against smoking, and the laws reinforced that opinion.
10. The International Organization for Standardization (ISO) is the main standard-setting body, which supervises a number of certification programmes, such as ISO 9000 (for good management) and ISO 14000 (for environmental management). Many other certification programmes use approaches similar to the ISO model (see Meidinger 2006, pp. 8–9).
11. Meidinger focuses on forestry certification, but Havinga points to a similar phenomenon in food safety (2006, pp. 523–524).
12. E.g. the way the CITES treaty on endangered species is monitored. Thanks to Saja Erens (Tilburg University PhD student) for this information.
13. For an in-depth discussion of mixed regulatory regimes, see the chapter by Neil Gunningham.
14. William Twining has pointed out that in his later work Llewellyn talks more about law-government than about law as a separate practice, which seems to suggest that this law-job is not so much a job of the legal system as of the government (Twining 1973, pp. 175–180). In his 1940 article, however, Llewellyn explicitly rejects the idea that direction is more a matter of leadership than of law. Although he acknowledges that an individual leader may be the one to start giving direction, that needs to be incorporated not only in the work of his subordinates but also in the legal institutions (p. 1388).
15. From a communicative perspective, law itself can fruitfully be regarded as symbolic as well (as van Klink 1998 shows).
16. Such a contextual, problem-oriented approach fits a pragmatist theory of law (see Taekema 2006). This is by no means contradictory to legal realism: De Been shows that pragmatist philosophy unites the different currents in the legal realist approach (2005, pp. 209–251).
17. Typical of legal reasoning is a reliance on precedent and authority: what has been decided in the past counts as does the importance of the person who decided.
18. I.e., the technical–legal terminology which jurists are trained to use.
19. I should stress that I move away further from Llewellyn's theory by this move: he defined the rudiments of law in terms of supremacy, enforcement and officialdom (1940, p. 1367). However, he did see the legal as a gradual concept (1940, p. 1366).
20. Although, as I argued earlier, the legal (in the form of state law) is never far away: when the informal solution no longer works, people turn to state law eventually.

REFERENCES

Cotterrell, Roger (2006), 'Living Law Revisited: Communitarianism and Sociology of Law', in Paul van Seters (ed.), *Communitarianism in Law and Society*, Lanham [etc.]: Rowman & Littlefield, pp. 33–48.

Cover, Robert M. (1979), 'Dispute Resolution: A Foreword', *Yale Law Journal*, **88**, 910–915.

De Been, Wouter (2005), *Realism Revisited*, dissertation, Tilburg University, the Netherlands.

Ellickson, Robert C. (1991), *Order without Law: How Neighbors Settle Disputes*, Cambridge, MA: Harvard University Press.

Griffiths, John (2003), 'The Social Working of Legal Rules', *Journal of Legal Pluralism and Unofficial Law*, **48**, 1–84.

Hart, H.L.A. (1994), *The Concept of Law* (2nd edn), Oxford: Clarendon Press.

Havinga, Tetty (2006), 'Private Regulation of Food Safety by Supermarkets', *Law & Policy*, **28**, 515–533.

Jenkins, Rhys (2002), 'The Political Economy of Codes of Conduct', in Rhys Jenkins, Ruth Pearson and Gill Sefang (eds), *Corporate Responsibility and Labour Rights: Codes of Conduct in the Global Economy*, London: Earthscan, pp. 13–30.

Jenkins, Rhys, Ruth Pearson and Gill Sefang (eds) (2002), *Corporate Responsibility and Labour Rights: Codes of Conduct in the Global Economy*, London: Earthscan.

Kagan, Robert and Jerome Skolnick (1993), 'Banning Smoking: Compliance without Enforcement', in R. Rubin and S.D. Sugarman (eds), *Smoking Policy: Law, Politics and Culture*, Oxford: Oxford University Press, pp. 69–94.

Llewellyn, Karl N. (1940), 'The Normative, the Legal, and the Law-Jobs: The Problem of Juristic Method', *Yale Law Journal*, **49**, 1355–1400.

Llewellyn, Karl N. and E. Adamson Hoebel (1941), *The Cheyenne Way: Conflict and Case Law in Primitive Jurisprudence*, Norman: University of Oklahoma Press.

Meidinger, Errol (2006), 'Multi-interest Self-governance through Global Product Certification' (Buffalo Legal Studies Research Paper Series No. 2006–016), http://ssrn.com/abstract=917956, accessed July 2006.

Mnookin, Robert H. and Lewis Kornhauser (1979), 'Bargaining in the Shadow of the Law: The Case of Divorce', *Yale Law Review*, **88**, 950–997.

Moore, Sally Falk (1973), 'Law and Social Change: The Semi-autonomous Social Field as an Appropriate Subject of Study', *Law and Society Review*, **7**, 719–746.

O'Rourke, Dara (2002), 'Monitoring the Monitors: A Critique of Third-Party Labour Monitoring', in Rhys Jenkins, Ruth Pearson and Gill Sefang (eds), *Corporate Responsibility and Labour Rights: Codes of Conduct in the Global Economy*, London: Earthscan, pp. 196–208.

Taekema, Sanne (2003), *The Concept of Ideals in Legal Theory*, The Hague: Kluwer Law International.

Taekema, Sanne (2006), 'Beyond Common Sense: Philosophical Pragmatism's Relevance to Law', *Retfaerd: Nordisk Juridisk Tidsskrift*, **29** (4), 22–36.

Tamanaha, Brian (2001), *A General Jurisprudence of Law and Society*, Oxford: Oxford University Press.

Twining, William (1973), *Karl Llewellyn and the Realist Movement*, London: Weidenfeld & Nicolson.

Twining, William (2003), 'A Post-Westphalian Conception of Law', *Law and Society Review*, **37**, 199–257.

Van Klink, Bart (1998), *De wet als symbool: over wettelijke communicatie en de Wet gelijke behandeling van mannen en vrouwen bij de arbeid*, Deventer: Tjeenk Willink.

5. Can there be law without the state? The Ehrlich–Kelsen debate revisited in a globalizing setting

Bart van Klink

1. GLOBAL BUKOWINA *VS* BRAVE NEW WORLD

In his provocative essay 'Global Bukowina: Legal Pluralism in the World Society', Gunther Teubner (1996) returns to what he considers to be one of the first heralds of legal pluralism: Eugen Ehrlich (1862–1922). According to Teubner (1996, p. 3), Ehrlich's vision of 'Global Bukowina' consisted of a civil society globalizing its legal orders and thereby distancing itself from 'the political power complex in the Brave New World's Vienna'. In prophetic terms Teubner (1996, p. 3) announces: 'Although Eugen Ehrlich's theory turned out to be wrong for the national law of Austria, I believe that it will turn out to be right, both empirically and normatively, for the newly emerging global law.' Empirically, Ehrlich is deemed to be right because 'the political–military–moral complex' – formerly known as the state, I suppose – will increasingly lose 'the power to control the multiple centrifugal tendencies of a civil world society'. Normatively, Ehrlich is claimed to be right because his theory, by relocating rule-making activities to local contexts, complies with the ideal of democracy. However, Teubner (1996, p. 7) distances himself from (what he sees as) Ehrlich's 'romanticizing' of 'the law-creating role of customs, habits and practices in small-scale rural communities'. The concept of 'living law' will in the current globalization process still have significance, albeit a 'different and quite dramatic' one which is based on 'cold technical processes' instead of 'warm communal bonds'.

Although I am not sure whether Ehrlich's theory 'turned out to be wrong for the national law of Austria' and I seriously doubt whether 'it will turn out to be right, both empirically and normatively, for the newly emerging global law' (for one thing, because I do not believe that this can be established in such a quick and easy way), I do not mean to deny the relevance of his thinking for the current debate on the role of the state and the meaning of law in a globalizing world. In this chapter I would also like to return to Ehrlich, and in particular to his main work: *Fundamental Principles of the Sociology of Law*, and confront it again[1] with the critical review thereof two years later by Hans Kelsen (1881–1973). It is worthwhile to juxtapose these positions since they seem to represent two extremes on a sliding scale in a still continuing debate about the meaning and significance of non-state law: at one end, Ehrlich's allegedly pluralist and decentred position in which society takes precedence over the state in the process of law creation and, at the other, Kelsen's allegedly monolithic and state-centred view in which law always has to originate from the state. I have written 'allegedly' twice intentionally, because both these characterizations are based on a superficial and traditional reading of the views involved, which have to be corrected in due course. However, as a first appropriation of the battlefield, they suffice.

It is my purpose to clarify the underlying conceptions of law and to show what is at stake, politically speaking, to endorse one conception or the other. What do these two conceptions of law imply for the distribution, maintenance and limitation of power on a national and transnational scale? And which conception of law is conceptually the strongest and normatively the most attractive? I intend to show how a Kelsenian conception of law can be defended that is both sensitive to the political and sociological concerns that underlie Ehrlich's work and is tenable in a globalizing setting. What these concerns on Ehrlich's part are, I will try to explain in more detail below but, roughly speaking, they have to do with the effectiveness of law and its democratic quality. By 'globalizing setting' I refer to the changing context in which the nation state has to operate nowadays in competition, cooperation and/or co-existence with other regulatory actors outside or beyond the state. On the one hand, nation states have to cooperate more and more closely with other states by designing transnational legal frameworks in order to cope with worldwide problems such as environmental protection, immigration and safety. On the other hand, to a growing extent norms seem to be produced in 'relative isolation'[2] from the state. Many examples of non-state norms, produced within or without the state, can be found in Chapter 2; Teubner's favourite example is the new *lex mercatoria*, consisting of the transnational norms of economic transactions (Teubner 1996, pp. 8–11).

Firstly, I will try to clarify Ehrlich's conception of law, including the relationship between state and society it presupposes (section 2). Secondly, I will discuss the critique Kelsen formulated against it (section 3). In addition, I will sketch his own conception of law and, in close connection, of the state that he later developed in his pure theory of law. It will be shown under which conditions non-state law may be recognized in Kelsen's conception of law. Thirdly, the conceptual merits of both conceptions will be assessed and their political implications will be uncovered and evaluated (section 4). Finally, I will address the question whether Kelsen's conception of law and, by implication, of the state is still relevant in a globalizing setting (section 5). Or are we leaving the old Brave New World and heading to a new, Global Bukowina, in which the nation state is no longer the privileged site of power, as Teubner claims?

2. LAW AND SOCIETY

However, let us first turn to the local Bukowina that Ehrlich inhabited – with a small 'l' and supposedly many warm communal bonds. Throughout his entire work, Eugen Ehrlich contested what he called the 'vulgar, state-centred conception of law' (Ehrlich [1925] 1996, p. 82; my translation). According to him, this conception of law can only recognize law produced or sanctioned by the state, 'state law' (*Staatsrecht*) for short, or simply statute law (*Gesetze*). Ehrlich ([1936] 1975, Chapters V–VIII) identifies three types, or sources, of law.[3] The first two types of law are still related closely to the state and are, therefore, generally recognized, also by adherents of the 'vulgar' conception of law: firstly, the state or public law, set down in statutes; and, secondly, the 'juristic' law developed by judges and jurists. Public law in the broad sense consists, on the one hand, of legal norms that constitute the state and its institutions (public law in the narrow sense, including administrative law); and, on the other hand, also of legal propositions (*Rechtssätze*) that contain general provisions (including penal law and procedural law) aimed at protecting public law in the narrow sense and 'private' law, that is, norms developed in society. On the basis of these general provisions (if available), judges and jurists devise, on a more concrete level, legal norms for decision-making (*Entscheidungsnormen*) upon which judges rely to resolve conflicts in society.

More important to Ehrlich, and also far more controversial, is the third source of law that he claimed to exist independently of the two aforementioned types of public, state-centred, law: the so-called facts of the law (*Tatsachen des Rechts*). In his view, the main function of law is to create order in and between associations within society. It does so by providing norms by which people can regulate and coordinate their actions. In most cases, these order-creating norms are not produced by the state, but flow from the institutions and structures of which the people are a part. Ehrlich refers to these norms as the 'facts of the law'. These facts of the law can be classified in four categories: custom or usage (*Übung*), relations of domination and subjection (*Herrschaft*), relations of possession (*Besitz*), and declarations of will (*Willenserklärungen*), such as contracts and testaments.

According to Ehrlich, the norms contained in these facts of the law have a far greater impact on people's lives, quantitatively as well as qualitatively speaking, than the norms laid down in the state and the judicial law. Here is where the living law resides, the law made and maintained by the people themselves: by contrast, the 'official' law would always run the risk of becoming a mere dead letter by losing touch with the society in which it operates.

Ehrlich considers the demarcation between legal norms and non-legal or, more accurately, *extra*-legal (*außerrechtliche*) norms in general to be very difficult. What is needed, in his view, is 'a thorough examination of the psychic and social facts, which at the present time have not even been gathered' (Ehrlich [1936] 1975, p. 164). The psychic and social facts Ehrlich is referring to in particular are the different kinds, or 'overtones', of feelings (*Gefühlstöne*) that the transgression of the different kinds of norms is supposed to bring about. According to Ehrlich (ibid, p. 165), a violation of law evokes 'the feeling of revolt' (*Empörung*), a violation of a moral prescript induces 'indignation' (*Entrüstung*) and indecency is accompanied by 'the feeling of disgust' (*Ärgernis*), and so on. In the end, law is, in Ehrlich's view, a matter of social perception. Yet, in daily practice the conceptual issue almost never occurs: 'Difficult though it may be to draw the line with scientific exactitude between the legal norm and other kinds of norms, *practically* this difficulty exists but rarely' (Ehrlich [1936] 1975, p. 164).

3. LAW AND STATE

3.1 Kelsen's Critique

This blatant attack on the positivist thought presumably prevalent at that time (vulgar or not) could and would not remain unanswered. In 1915, two years after its first edition, Kelsen (2003) published a highly critical review of Ehrlich's *Fundamental Principles of the Sociology of Law*. Basically, Kelsen argues that Ehrlich had confused facts and norms in his conception of law – a distinction that would later become the cornerstone of his pure theory of law. According to Kelsen, the phenomenon of law can be approached from two different perspectives. On the one hand, the law can be conceived of as a norm, that is, a rule that articulates a specific kind of 'ought' (*Sollen*): something *has* to be done or not be done. On the other hand, the law may be taken as a part of social reality, as a fact or an occurrence that takes place regularly. Here, the law takes the form of an 'is' (*Sein*) proposition with respect to human behaviour: some action *is* done or not done on a regular basis. These two perspectives correspond with two different disciplines from which law can be studied: respectively, a *normative* science of law that determines deductively which rules are valid (*gelten*), and an *explanatory* sociology of law that establishes inductively a certain regularity for which it tries to find a causal explanation. Thus, the science of law is a normative and deductive science of value, like ethics and logics, whereas the sociology of law, like other branches of sociology, is a science of reality, and conforms more generally to the methodological practices of the natural sciences. It is equally possible and legitimate to study law from both perspectives, but not at the same time. An object cannot be construed as something that is done or happens regularly and that ought to be done or happen simultaneously. Biology, as an explanatory science, may establish a causal link between two factual occurrences (e.g., between firing a gun and somebody's death), but is not capable of evaluating this link in terms of good/bad or legal/illegal. Conversely, ethics and the science of law, as normative sciences, may dismiss a certain action (e.g., killing someone by firing a gun) as bad, if it violates an ethical norm, or illegal, if it violates a legal norm; however, they are not able to explain this action. In Kelsen's view, a combination of perspectives is 'inadmissible' and would lead to a 'methodological syncretism' (Kelsen 2003, p. 5; my translation).

Kelsen criticizes Ehrlich for trying to combine what he considers are incompatible perspectives. In describing the internal order within associations in society, from past to present, Ehrlich constantly and inconsistently mixes factual observations about law with normative statements about what the law should be. For example, Ehrlich claims that in ancient times the legal institution of marriage existed, although legal propositions (*Rechtssätze*) formalizing marriages were lacking. There were no general legal prescripts, promulgated by the state, only contract law applied. In other words, valid marriages could be 'contracted' in the absence of 'official' law. According to Kelsen, this is a normative claim that presupposes a legal point of view. A vow between two persons can only constitute a contract with legal consequences if at least the legal proposition is presupposed to be valid that declarations of will of this kind – not only in one particular case, but in general – ought to be legally binding. 'Otherwise,' Kelsen (2003, p. 14; my translation) asks rhetorically, 'how can one speak of right and duty?'

Ehrlich's concept of 'facts of the law' suffers from the same methodological confusion. A fact – be it a usage, a relation of domination or possession, or a declaration of will – can never constitute law or a legal relation, because this fact, postulated as something that *is*, is in itself value indifferent. Only by confronting it with a norm, a fact requires an objective value: it is judged to be good or bad, legal or illegal, beautiful or ugly, and so on. Kelsen, however, argued that usage (*Übung*) actually is the only fact of the law. 'Usage' means that a fact is repeated on a regular basis; it is an 'is' rule. Facts, such as a declaration of will or a relation of domination, can only become a fact of the law by repetition, that is, by means of a usage. This is only possible under the pre-condition of an 'ought' rule that prescribes that something that used to be done, has to be done. Following this rule, certain facts become legally relevant, that is, facts of the law. In itself, usage is not a fact of the law. Ehrlich's 'facts of the law' were, according to Kelsen, nothing but the possible content or object of legal (or other kinds of social) regulation.

According to Kelsen, Ehrlich's concept of law threatens to become boundless and indistinguishable from that of a social norm or a rule in general, because he deliberately refrains from referring to the state in defining law. As a result, from a sociological perspective, Ehrlich's project 'loses itself' – as Kelsen (2003, p. 46) puts it – in an identification of law and society. Consequently, the sociology of law has great problems to establish itself as a separate discipline, independent from a general sociology.

3.2 Kelsen's Conception

Kelsen, by contrast, advocates a clear separation between legal norms and other norms, leading to an identification of law and state. In his words, the state is 'the personification of a legal order' (Kelsen 1973, p. 197). In his pure theory of law he aims at describing the set of valid legal norms in a certain territory at a certain time, irrespective of their ethical value and empirical working. According to Kelsen, a norm is a legal norm, if and only if it can be traced back to a higher legal norm that authorizes the creation of the legal norm on a lower level. Ultimately, the validity of all legal norms depends on the implicit acceptance of the basic norm, or *Grundnorm*, of a legal system (e.g., Kelsen 1970, p. 193ff. and Kelsen 1973, p. 113ff.). The basic norm states that the norms of a state's first Constitution constitute law and, by implication, the norms following from the first Constitution also constitute law. Whereas Ehrlich is not able to differentiate between law and power (section 4), Kelsen can do so, but only under the assumption that a person is willing to adopt the legal perspective. Someone who does not recognize the basic norm perceives the enforcement of norms as nothing but the exercise of naked power. Thus, for Kelsen, law is a matter of perception too; however, not as a social fact, but as a transcendental datum: in order to identify norms as legal, it has to be presupposed that a prior higher legal norm was accepted that validates all other legal norms that follow. According to Kelsen (1973, p. 26), coercion is an essential element of law. He conceives of a legal norm as a conditional statement that authorizes an individual to apply the sanction prescribed in the norm in case the specified behaviour occurs (e.g., 'If a person steals, a judge is authorized to send this person to jail'). Fear of sanctions does not need to be the primary motivational force to obey the law, but the legal order simply has to provide for sanctions if the law is not obeyed. If one ignores this specific element of law, as Ehrlich did, one is unable to distinguish it from other social phenomena.

Taken together, the legal norms of a given legal order build a hierarchical structure (or *Stufenbau*), consisting of different levels of norms and norm applications, starting from the basic norm, moving down to statutes, governmental regulations, court decisions, contracts, and so on, and ending in the factual execution of a legal command (e.g., the imprisonment of a criminal by a police officer; cf. Kelsen 1970, p. 221ff.). Because the norms belonging to a given legal order owe their validity ultimately to the basic norm, the basic norm brings unity in the diversity of existing norms. This unity makes it possible to describe the legal order at hand as a coherent set of legal sentences that do not contradict each other (Kelsen 1970, pp. 205–208). Consequently, legal pluralism *within* one legal order is impossible: 'If there is to exist *one* community, there can only be *one* order' (Kelsen [1928] 1962, p. 190; my translation).

Irrespective of how they are created and by whom they are created, legal norms owe their validity to the state, not to society. Whereas in Ehrlich's view the state is nothing more than 'an essentially military association' even in the present day (Ehrlich [1936] 1975, p. 138), Kelsen (2003, pp. 42–46; my translation) considers it to be a 'special form of society', 'social unity' or a 'legal organization' (*Rechtsorganisation*) to which all legal norms can be traced back, whether they are produced by state officials or by members of an association. Every individual whose actions are imputed or ascribed to the state can be designated as an 'organ' of the state, including a voter or a contract party. By implication, in the creation of law, no principal distinction can be made between 'ordinary' people and state officials: everyone who is authorized to issue legal norms is, by definition, part of the state (Kelsen 1973, pp. 181–206). Neither can the rights of private law, or 'private rights', and the rights of public law, or 'political rights', be distinguished fundamentally: 'all law [is] state law' (*Staatsrecht*; Kelsen [1928] 1962, p. 216; my translation). At the same time, Kelsen did not consider every legal order to be a state. A state presupposes at least an administration and courts, and possibly but not necessarily a legislature in a later stage of development; that means that there has to be a certain degree of centralization. Both the legal order of primitive society and the international legal order are fully decentralized coercive orders and therefore not states (Kelsen 1970, pp. 286–287). However, Kelsen (1971, p. 256) did not rule out the possibility of 'world state' in the future (section 5). Because he acknowledged that there can be law without the state in primitive society as well as in the international legal order, it is more accurate to say that, in Kelsen's view, all law has to be *public* law (*öffentliches Recht*). But as soon as an administration and courts have been installed within a certain legal community, which are responsible for the application of legal norms created either on a centralized or on a decentralized level, all law is by definition state law. In other words, non-state law is only thinkable in contexts where there is no state or no state yet.

4. THE POLITICS OF LAW

4.1 Conceptual Merits

After having described two competing conceptions of law, I will now compare and assess them, firstly on a conceptual level. To what extent are the conceptions at hand helpful in understanding and defining law and in distinguishing it from other social phenomena? According to Ehrlich ([1936] 1975, p. 9), 'juristic science has no scientific concept of law'. If jurists refer to law, they mean, in his view, 'exclusively that which is of importance in the judicial administration of justice' instead of 'that which lives and is operative in human society as law' (Ehrlich [1936] 1975, p. 10). As shown above, Ehrlich prioritizes the latter meaning in developing his allegedly scientific conception of law, that is, law as it is perceived in society. He acknowledges that it is not possible, at least not yet, given the 'present state of the science of law', to provide a well-defined conception of law. In his view, more research is called for in the field of social psychology.

However, the few clues that Ehrlich offered himself for a social psychological understanding of law are not very promising. Obviously, emotive reactions aroused by the violation of a legal norm – that is, the 'feeling of revolt' (*Empörung*) – can never be a serious and solid foundation for law: feelings are in a constant flux and do not, by themselves, involve legal entitlement. People may experience revolt when confronted with their tax assessment; unfortunately for them, it still constitutes law. Conversely, the absence of feelings is also not a very reliable indicator for the existence or non-existence of law: although many people cycle frequently and carelessly through the red light, their behaviour remains punishable by law. Feelings of whatever kind – anger, bitterness, resignation, relief, joy, and so on – are possible by-products of law, never its defining characteristic. As Kelsen (2003, p. 34; my, somewhat free, translation) notices, '[I]t is an all too cheap pleasure to test Ehrlich's criteria for categorizing social norms.' So let's not push this point too far.

Principally, the question is: What if the perceptions of law within or between the different associations of society conflict with each other? In other words, how does one proceed when the beacon of practice is not as reliable as Ehrlich hoped it would be? If practice is divided on the issue of law – which is more the rule than the exception in our post-conventional era – it loses its function as a guiding light. In the absence of a normative, authoritative standard for the assessment of competing perceptions of law, in actual practice power will inevitably trump law: certain norms prevail not so much because a legal authority has issued them, but because some people or groups in society are capable – due to their superiority in terms of physical or intellectual strength, wealth, charisma, and so on – of imposing these norms on others. The 'living law' is the 'law' that survives in the social struggle for recognition. In the end, what lives on is not law but naked power. Or, as boils down to the same thing, both concepts get blurred to the point of indistinction.

Consequently, for lack of any clear criteria of identification, it is no longer possible to maintain Ehrlich's division into three sources or types of law. In particular, it remains completely unclear on which grounds the third source or type, the so-called facts of the law, or the order-creating norms which are not promulgated by the state but are supposed to flow from the institutions and structures of society, can lay a claim to legal validity. Why and when are observed regularities in, for instance, custom-based behaviour legally binding? Morally, people may feel obliged, for example, to execute a testament or to comply with the agreements of a contract they have entered into. However, why does it have to be assumed that *legal* entitlements also follow from these social institutions? The answer to this pertinent question can never be given from the perspective of social psychology as Ehrlich thought and contemporary researchers into legal consciousness still seem to believe. At the most, psychology can show what people experience, think or feel to be law on a factual level; it can never settle objectively why and when these subjective assessments have to count as law on a normative plane. As Kelsen (1971, p. 214) rightfully claims: 'The "existence" of a legal norm is no psychological phenomenon. The "existence" of a legal norm is its validity.'

In sum, Ehrlich's conception of law fails because it cannot describe and explain in which respects legal norms differ from other norms (moral, ethical and religious norms, norms of decency, customary rules, and so on) and from power. Clearly, Kelsen's conception of law is preferable, because it provides an adequate account of what is distinguishingly legal about law and, thereby, how it can be differentiated both from other social norms and power. In this conception, a norm is a legal norm if, and only if, it can be traced back to a higher legal norm that authorizes the creation of the legal norm on a lower level. Ultimately, the validity of all legal norms depends on an implicit and presupposed acceptance of the basic norm of a legal system. Beside legal norms, there are many other possibly more important or more influential norms, but they are created in other ways, or they are not created at all but have grown out of existing practices, and, therefore, they are based on different basic norms. No one can be forced to take a legal perspective. What might appear, from an empirical point of view, to be the sheer execution of power, may normatively be considered a rightful application of a legal norm. That is essentially an *ideological* choice – which brings us to the next topic.

4.2 Political Implications

Every conception of law, however 'pure' it claims to be, has political implications. It not only describes what law is, but it also prescribes either on conceptual or on normative grounds, implicitly or explicitly, what ought to be considered as law; in other words, which norms may acquire a legal status and, thereby, a *legitimate* title to enforcement by state officials. As a result, every conception of law has – at least on a discursive level – consequences for the distribution, maintenance and exertion of power in society. The next question I will address is: What are the political implications of the two conceptions of law described above and how are they to be evaluated? By way of forewarning: implications do not, by necessity, equal intentions. It might well be that a certain conception of law has political consequences that its originator has neither foreseen nor intended. Moreover, the evaluation of these political consequences is not possible without subjective value judgments. Giving preference on political grounds to one conception of law over the other is, in the end, a matter of personal choice. The same applies to the following evaluation.

According to Michaels (2005, p. 1227), there often is a 'political project' behind legal pluralism. Early expressions of legal pluralism were frequently directed against the dominance, or even 'dictatorship', of Western state law, to begin with in the colonies and subsequently in Western countries themselves. As I have argued elsewhere,[4] Ehrlich's concept of living law is basically a slogan or buzz-word without any scientific content; it is synonymous either with valid law (from a legal perspective) or with effective law (from a sociological point of view). Its main function lies in the rhetorical–political sphere, where it may call out powerful pleas for the recognition of norms that have originated in society, independently of the state. This actually happened in Japan and Indonesia, as Stefan Vogl and Franz and Keebet von Benda-Beckmann respectively demonstrate.[5]

In his biographical account, Vogl (2003, pp. 73–107) shows that Ehrlich was motivated by different political ideals in different periods of his intellectual life. In his early years in Vienna, Ehrlich was an 'undogmatic socialist', who sought to solve the 'social question' caused by capitalism by means of economic growth and social reforms induced by the state (Vogl 2003, p. 213). Later in Czernowitz, he became sceptical of the possibilities of state-induced social reforms. In his view, the state's main functions had to be limited to taking care that the goods produced were distributed fairly, to 'channelling' and stimulating in a non-coercive way the economic forces active in society and to protecting individual rights within communities (Vogl 2003, pp. 229–239). Self-regulation had to be promoted by establishing, among other things, people's educational centres (*Volkshochschulen*) and agricultural cooperatives (*Genossenschaften*). Ehrlich's initial social and socialist position was replaced by a social–liberal and egalitarian democratic attitude.

Whether these are Ehrlich's 'real' intentions or not, one cannot fail to notice that they do not sit comfortably with his conception of law. By stressing the importance of non-state norms and fighting for their 'official' recognition both by jurisprudence and state law, Ehrlich seems to promote essentially one political value above others, and that is the value of freedom: the freedom to live according to self-made rules, to enter into contracts of one's own design, to make one's own will, and so on. As Vogl (2003, p. 308) acknowledges, on a dogmatic level Ehrlich strived for a strengthening of private autonomy, in particular freedom of contract and freedom of property. It is entirely possible to ground this call for freedom in some populist bottom-up notion of democracy, although Ehrlich did not do so himself explicitly. But it will be very hard, if not downright impossible, to set limits to this private autonomy on social grounds (as Ehrlich, according to Vogl, intended), if one does not have any clear conception of the state, its main functions and its necessary relation to law. Lacking legitimacy as well as capability, the state is bound to preserve and reproduce the power relations existing in society, with all the inequalities and other injustices they may entail.

Thus what remains, politically speaking, from Ehrlich's concept of living law – despite his intentions possibly otherwise – is a defence of the value of freedom, grounded in some vague idea of democracy. It is the freedom to create and apply (supposedly legal) norms outside the official arena of the state. Special credit is given to the freedom of contract and property, exactly the kinds of freedom capitalism needs to flourish. It is, therefore, not without ground that Teubner links Ehrlich's conception of law to the upcoming *lex mercatoria* (section 1). It is equally justifiable to invoke his conception in defence of social norms endorsed by suppressed peoples and communities and against the suppressing norms of state law. Ironically, although non-state law finds itself in permanent competition with state law, it can never fully liberate itself from, by breaking with, the state and state law. Legal pluralism condemns the two types of law forever to unpeaceful co-existence without granting the one or the other the right to overrule.

On a superficial level, Kelsen seems to share many political ideals with his opponent Ehrlich. It may seem odd to look for values in a work that aims so desperately at 'purifying' the science of law from moral and political elements. Kelsen does not deny that in the creation and application of law inevitably moral and political elements creep in, but he considers these elements not to be its defining characteristics; morally and politically despicable norms could still be conceived as law. Although he believes that an objective, scientific assessment of values is impossible, in his later thinking Kelsen engaged on a personal basis more and more with moral and political questions. As it turned out, he defended many of the values that Ehrlich also deemed important, notably freedom, equality, democracy and the peaceful ordering of society. Yet, their conception of these values differs fundamentally, just as did their view on the role that law, state and society may play in protecting or promoting these values.

Kelsen's effort to depoliticize the science of law has a huge political impact. In his critical variant of legal positivism, he opposes the natural-law doctrine that, in his view, wrongly identifies law (or state) and justice and misconstrued law as an absolute value, which can be deduced objectively from the unchanging laws of nature (see, e.g., Kelsen [1945] 1973, pp. 5–13; Kelsen 1970, pp. 217–221; Kelsen 1971, pp. 137–173). Instead, he stresses the dynamic character of law creation: law is constantly created and re-created through decisions of individual people authorized to do so. Law is never simply given, waiting to be discovered, but it is a construction, a product of conscious and subjective choices. As a result, law can only have a relative value. According to Kelsen (1971, p. 150), the natural-law doctrine has, 'on the whole, a strictly conservative character'. Despite its appeal to norms superior to law, its function is 'not . . . to weaken, but to strengthen the authority of positive law'. If legal norms are presented as absolute commands, deduced from the laws of nature, they are immunized against criticism and change. If, on the other hand, legal norms are taken for what they are, that is, man-made constructions in which some interests are protected at the expense of others, their fallible and changeable character becomes apparent.

According to Kelsen ([1928] 1962, p. 46), modern sociology had, in general, replaced the natural-law doctrine. Both disciplines tried to ground their normative conception of law in factual statements in the 'nature of things', either in a supposedly ideal or in a supposedly real world. That may explain why Kelsen reviewed Ehrlich's *Fundamental Principles of the Sociology of Law* so critically (section 3.1). By promoting the 'living law', the law that lives and breathes in 'real life' in contrast to the (potential) 'dead' law in the books, Ehrlich transgressed the boundaries of an empirical sociology and entered the realm of politics. That is not problematic *per se*, if he had been honest about it and had not pretended to sell his personal preferences as an objective account of the origins of law in his pseudo-history of the emerging 'facts of the law'. Instead of trying to prove that law can be found in the daily practices of people, Ehrlich could have better rephrased his claim – in Kelsen's opinion – as his own political wish to elevate certain privileged social norms to the rank of legal norms.

So Kelsen's pure science of law is not – as is sometimes argued (see, e.g., Dreier 1990, pp. 19–20) – meant to disguise the political nature of law but, on the contrary, to expose it in order to enable a critical discussion about it, albeit outside the forum of science. Consequently, as a scientist, Kelsen does not give preference to one kind of legal order over another; every state he considers to be a *Rechtsstaat* dedicated to the rule of law, since it, by definition, exerts its power by means of law.

That does not keep him, however, from embracing democracy on a personal level (see, in particular, Kelsen 1963). He rejects the raw and direct form of democracy, in which the 'people's voice' is transmitted without any apparent interference, as in the instances of self-regulation proposed by Ehrlich, but opts for the mediating form of parliamentary democracy instead. He considers parliamentary democracy to be both a valuable and inevitable compromise between the democratic requirement of freedom, on the one hand, and the need for a division of labour caused by social–technical progress, on the other. Parliamentary democracy can only be, Kelsen (1963, pp. 72–76) argues, a 'democracy of legislation', that is, a democracy where it comes to the creation of law on the highest level of the state. A so-called 'democracy of administration', in which the application of law in the lower ranks of the state would be democratized, would unavoidably undermine democracy on the legislative level. At first glance, legality leads to a limitation of democracy, but it appears to be a necessary element of its maintenance. Through its voting system democracy attests to a worldview of relativism: in the absence of absolute truths, every opinion and every vote should count equally. Autocracy, on the contrary, is based on political absolutism which grants no freedom to the ruled and does not treat them as equals (cf. Kelsen 1971, pp. 201–202).

Kelsen's defence of democracy, building on the principles of freedom and equality, does not, of course, follow logically from his conception of law but is very well compatible with it. In his view, democracy presupposes a hierarchical structure of norms, the so-called *Stufenbau*. In order to protect the unity of the legal system, higher norms (created by the legislature) are entitled to overrule norms on a lower level (created by, for example, the government or the court) in case of conflict. Within the confines of his scientific theory, he cannot and does not choose one system of norm creation (e.g., democracy) over the other (e.g., autocracy). However, politically speaking, one great advantage of Kelsen's conception of law is that it, *irrespectively of the system of norm creation in use*, provides clear rules to solve conflict between legal norms – something which is entirely lacking in Ehrlich's conception.

In at least three other respects I consider, from a political point of view, Kelsen's conception of law to be superior to Ehrlich's. To begin with, in case of conflict between two normative systems, Ehrlich's appeal to the 'living law' can only be perceived, from the viewpoint of the dominant system, as a noncommittal request to incorporate the norms of the subordinate system in the dominant system of law, the 'official' law of the state. Thereby, the 'living law' makes itself vulnerable to appropriation by and assimilation into the state's law. Because the 'living law' is presented not so much as an alternative, concurring legal order but as a *supplement* to the existing legal order, it is doomed to be transformed and devoured by it. Consequently, as Michaels (2005, p. 1232) observes acutely, 'Ehrlich's insight that the production of law mainly happens in the periphery, within society . . . loses its revolutionary potential.' By means of Kelsen's conception of law one is able to reconceptualize the relationship between two competing normative systems in far more radical terms: not as a relationship of dependency in which the subordinate one is begging for recognition by the dominant one, but as a relation of competition, or possibly even war, in which ultimately only one normative system can establish itself as 'the law'. What is at stake in a revolution is exactly this question (cf. Kelsen [1945] 1973, pp. 117–118): Whose basic norm will triumph? In my view, this account is not only a more accurate description of what is going on in a clash of normative systems; it also offers, on a political level, a far more attractive point of departure for any liberation movement that seeks to establish its norms as law, independently and/or instead of the existing regime of oppression, than Ehrlich's shallow notion of the 'living law'.

Subsequently, Kelsen's conception of law provides a far more dynamic picture of law creation than Ehrlich's. Whereas in Kelsen's account the legal order finds itself in a permanent process of creation and re-creation on the different levels of the *Stufenbau*, it is not at all clear from what source, according to Ehrlich, the legal order can be renewed. In Ehrlich's conception, law is basically what people in different associations of law perceive to be law. The state is summoned, generally speaking, to respect and reproduce the norms created in society. It is allowed to act only if the norms produced in the legal 'free zones', granted by the freedom of contract and property, lead to an unfair distribution of goods or if internal conflicts cannot be solved within society itself. In these cases, the 'official' law (juristic or state law) is an indispensable supplement, complementary to the living law and capable of overruling it. This supplement should, however, be used very sparingly: 'The legislature . . . ought to attempt to mould life according to his own ideas only where this is absolutely necessary; and where he can let life take care of itself, let him refrain from unnecessary interference' (Ehrlich [1936] 1975, p. 184). So law has, following Ehrlich, predominantly a conservative, status quo-confirming character: law codifies or should codify what already is perceived in society to be law. As a result, it becomes very difficult to see how change can enter into this way of thinking. What can we do if the existing social norms are oppressive? In Kelsen's conception, law may derive its norms, not only from custom or established practices, but from any source (morals, politics, religion, decency, and so on) – as he claimed, 'any kind of content might be law' (Kelsen 1970, p. 198) – so the potential for modifying the existing law is far greater. What follows from the 'nature of things' on a factual level is not necessarily what ought to be done on a normative–legal level.

The final advantage of Kelsen's conception of law I want to highlight here, is that it places an important restraint on the creation and modification of legal norms. Although in principle 'any kind of content might be law', the norm to be created has to fit in the existing legal order; otherwise it can be annulled on the basis of the higher norm that authorizes the creation of the norm on a lower level. That means a significant limitation of arbitrariness in the exertion of power and gives some prospect that values such as equality of citizens before the law, legality and legal security are being protected. A similar mechanism, or another functional equivalent, is totally absent in Ehrlich's conception of law. In the legal 'free zones' granted by the freedom of contract and property, members of society are allowed to produce whatever norms they like, without having to concern themselves too much about equality, legality, legal security and the consistency of the legal order in general. As a result, individuals can never be sure at the mercy of which norms they find themselves. Moreover, if we connect Kelsen's conception of law with his view on democracy, we discover another mechanism that sets limits to the execution of power: the norms created on the highest level of the state, that of the legislature, are created by individuals who are elected by the people. According to Kelsen, both the members of the legislature and the people in their capacity as voters are part of the state. Because in a democracy both sides, the rulers and the ruled, can easily switch roles and the competency to rule has been granted only temporarily, man's inclination to maximize his power might be tempered. According to Kelsen (1963, p. 57; my, somewhat free, translation), 'the parliamentary procedure with its technique of argumentation and counter-argumentation . . . aims at forging a compromise'. As goes without saying, guarantees can never be given; the challenge is to design an institutional framework that reduces the chances of arbitrariness and abuse of power. A third limitation can be found in Kelsen's rejection of a 'democracy of administration' in favour of a 'democracy of legislation'; thereby, a certain separation of powers is implemented (which, by definition, can never be absolute, since creation and application of law cannot be distinguished fundamentally; cf. Kelsen 1970, pp. 348–351). Building on an overly simplistic dichotomy between state and society, Ehrlich was never able to appreciate the importance of such an institutional framework.

In sum, Kelsen's conception of law is, in my view, preferable by far to Ehrlich's on political grounds, since it makes it at least conceivable that, in a revolutionary context, arbitrary power is overthrown and a new legal order establishes itself that is not merely a supplement to the old legal order begging for recognition. Furthermore, it makes it possible, within the context of an existing and functioning legal order, to reduce arbitrariness in the exertion of power.

5. THE FUTURE OF LAW AND STATE

The time has come to return to the contemporary state of Global Bukowina, with a capital 'G' and less warm communal bonds apparently. Kelsen's conception of law may well be superior to Ehrlich's both in conceptual and political respects, but has it not become obsolete in the face of the current proliferation of norm producers outside or beyond the state? Teubner (1996, p. 11) seems to think so, when he asks mockingly: 'Where is the global *Grundnorm* . . .?' On the contrary, I believe that Kelsen's conception of law is still relevant in our age of globalization and will increasingly be so, for two major reasons.

Firstly, although it is undoubtedly true that, in a globalizing setting, the role of the nation state in the production and enforcement of legal norms has changed significantly and will continue to change in the future (in Chapter 7, many interesting examples thereof are given), that does not mean that the nation state does not, cannot or should not play *any* role at all. For example, in protecting security on a global scale, Loader and Walker (2007, in particular Chapter 7) still assign a pivotal role to the state. In their view, the state (or a functional equivalent of the state) has to fulfil several tasks, which they label as follows (Loader and Walker 2007, p. 176):

1. Identification, or the 'imaginative construction of identity';
2. Resource mobilization and allocation of collective resources;

3. Deliberation, or decision-making on the basis of evidence and reasoning;
4. Regulation, or designing an appropriate legal framework;
5. Commitment, or ensuring that people have confidence in the state's actions.

If there were no entity like the state that takes responsibility for these five tasks, 'there is simply no guarantee that each and all will be effectively performed, or even performed at all' (Loader and Walker 2007, p. 172). Moreover, there are problems of coordination and capacity that only a state or a state-like entity can solve. That does not imply that the state operates in splendid isolation. On the contrary, for security's sake, it is of vital importance that state actors cooperate closely with non-state actors, both on a national and transnational level. However, ultimately these combined efforts have to be coordinated and regulated by some central instance. As Loader and Walker (2007, p. 175) put it: 'What remains distinctive to the state's role in the tasks of identification, mobilization and allocation, deliberation, regulation and commitment is that *its* exercise of each must *in the last analysis* take precedence over the exercise of a similar role at any other public or private site.' When it comes to regulation, the state should be seen as a 'meta-regulator' (Loader and Walker 2007, p. 193). The state's regulatory primacy fits perfectly in Kelsen's conception of law: in the end, all legal norms are imputable to the state (section 3.2).

Secondly, his conception does allow for the creation of legal norms outside or beyond the state. In his view, international law has to be understood 'either as a legal order delegated by, and therefore included in, the national order; or as a total legal order comprising all national legal orders as partial orders, and superior to all of them' (Kelsen 1970, p. 333). The choice for one of these monistic conceptions is an ideological one. The conception in which international law has primacy is part of a pacifistic ideology, whereas the conception that departs from the primacy of national law, and thereby the state's sovereignty, reflects an imperialistic ideology. In both cases, international law, though not originating from one particular nation state, constitutes law. However, if the international legal order would centralize further, it could become one day a state in its own right (Kelsen 1971, p. 256):

> One may assume that the technical development of international law is progressing on the same path as that already taken by the development of the legal orders of the state. To the extent that the direct obligating and authorizing of individuals and centralization increases in international law, the boundary between national and international law tends to disappear, and the legal organization of mankind approaches the idea of a world state.

In the absence of such a world state in the present time, international law constitutes, beside primitive law (section 3.2), the only type of non-state law that Kelsen would recognize.

Moreover, in Kelsen's conception of law, legal norms do not need to be produced by the 'higher' or central organs of the state only, that is, by the court or the legislature. By signing a marriage contract, writing a will, selling a company, buying a house, and so on, individuals may add legal norms to the existing legal order, under the condition that the norms created ensue from and are in accordance with higher legal norms and, ultimately, the basic norm. As Michaels (2005, pp. 1228–1235) shows, there are various ways in which the state may react to non-state norms. To begin with, the state may simply reject any claim by non-state normative orders as law; for instance, non-Islamic states are in general not very willing to apply the Shari's. Subsequently, if it does recognize these claims, there are three possibilities: *incorporation*, that is, the norms originated in society are adopted by or integrated into the 'official' law (as happened with the *lex mercatoria* old and new style); *delegation*, that is, the norms are treated as a semi-autonomous body of norms which, from the state's perspective, constitute subordinated or delegated law (all contracts could be perceived as such, as well as different types of so-called self-regulation); and *deference*, that is, the norms are considered to be autonomous law strictly in the private space of a non-state normative order (e.g., in case of customs or social expectations); outside this space these norms only have the status of 'facts for the purpose of legal analysis' (Michaels 2005, p. 1233). Only in the case of incorporation and delegation is there – from the state's perspective – law, but this law is always subjected to and part of the state or public law and, therefore, it is never fully autonomous. Building on Kelsen, no principal distinction can be made between incorporation and delegation: delegation is, by definition, a kind of incorporation by which means the delegated law is annexed by and assimilated into the public law. In the third case of deference, there are even, again from the state's perspective, no legal norms at all but only facts that a legal authority (e.g., a judge) might or might not ignore. This is generally considered to be the answer of legal doctrine to Ehrlich's challenge of the 'living law' (Michaels 2005, p. 1233).

In conclusion, Kelsen's pure theory of law is not at all outdated by current phenomena. However, it gives access to these phenomena from a specific and specifically legal perspective. In this perspective, law has a necessary connection to the state, at least as soon as there is one. Therefore, within a state, non-state law cannot exist. That does not exclude the possibility that many legal norms – or even the most important ones, judged from some normative point of view – might be created by members of what Ehrlich calls associations in society. However, as soon as an individual in one way or the other is involved in the process of law creation, he has to be considered an organ of the state. This has important consequences for two of Ehrlich's major concerns: the effectiveness of the law and its democratic quality. As soon as a norm is recognized as belonging to the state or public law, the state is authorized to enforce it with all of its power. That will never be a sufficient condition for its effectiveness, but in many cases it might just be a necessary one. Furthermore, because the norm belongs to the hierarchical structure of the *Stufenbau*, it may be annulled if its content is not compatible with the higher legal norm that authorized its creation (on the basis of the principle of non-contradiction, cf. Kelsen [1945] 1973, p. 406). Since any norm has to comply with higher legal norms and, in the end, with the highest or basic norm, the value of democracy of legislation is being served.

By implication, neither Ehrlich's 'facts of the law' nor Teubner's *lex mercatoria* are law simply because some people might perceive it as such (in Ehrlich's view) or in some discourse the binary legal/illegal code is being used (according to Teubner 1996, pp. 12–14). Social norms have to be adopted by the existing legal order and filtered through it first before they become legal norms. That might, however, not be such a bad idea if we want to put some normative (democratic or other) as well as factual restraints on the execution of power in society, especially now the communal bonds which seemed to keep people together in earlier and happier times are weakening.

NOTES

1. Previously I have written a paper on the Ehrlich–Kelsen debate, entitled 'Facts and Norms. The Unfinished Debate between Eugen Ehrlich and Hans Kelsen', which I presented at the Ehrlich workshop in Oñati, 4–5 May 2006. This paper will be published soon and is currently available at: http://papers.ssrn.com/sol3/papers.cfm?abstract_id=980957, accessed 1 July 2007.
2. This expression from Anthony Giddens is quoted by Teubner (1996, p. 3).
3. Whenever I think it more useful, I will quote from the German edition (Ehrlich [1913] 1967).
4. See my paper, mentioned in note 1, p. 33.
5. See their contributions to the Ehrlich workshop (soon to be published; cf. note 1).

REFERENCES

Dreier, Horst (1990), *Rechtslehre, Staatssoziologie und Demokratietheorie bei Hans Kelsen*, Baden-Baden: Nomos Verlagsgesellschaft.

Ehrlich, Eugen [1913] (1967), *Grundlegung der Soziologie des Rechts*, Berlin: Duncker & Humblot.

Ehrlich, Eugen [1925] (1996), *Die juristische Logik*, Aalen: Scientia Verlag.
Ehrlich, Eugen [1936] (1975), *Fundamental Principles of the Sociology of Law*, New York: Arno Press.
Ehrlich, Eugen (1986), *Gesetz und lebendes Recht. Vermischte kleinere Schriften*, ed. Manfred Rehbinder, Berlin: Duncker & Humblot.
Kelsen, Hans [1928] (1962), *Der soziologische und der juristische Staatsbegriff. Kritische Untersuchung des Verhältnisses vom Staat und Recht*, Aalen: Scientia Verlag.
Kelsen, Hans (1963), *Vom Wesen und Wert der Demokratie*, Aalen: Scientia Verlag.
Kelsen, Hans (1970), *The Pure Theory of Law* (translation from the second [revised and enlarged] German edition by Max Knight), Berkeley: University of California Press.
Kelsen, Hans (1971), *What is Justice? Justice, Law, and Politics in the Mirror of Science*, Berkeley: University of California Press.
Kelsen, Hans [1945] (1973), *General Theory of Law and State* (translated by Anders Wedberg), New York: Russell & Russell.
Kelsen, Hans [1934] (1992), *Introduction to the Problems of Legal Theory. A Translation of the First Edition of the* Reine Rechtslehre *or Pure Theory of Law* (translated by Bonnie Litschewski Paulson and Stanley L. Paulson), Oxford: Clarendon Press.
Kelsen, Hans (2003), 'Eine Grundlegung der Rechtssoziologie', in Hans Kelsen and Eugen Ehrlich, *Rechtssoziologie und Rechtswissenschaft. Eine Kontroverse (1915/1917)*, Baden-Baden: Nomos Verlagsgesellschaft, pp. 3–54.
Kelsen, Hans and Eugen Ehrlich (2003), *Rechtssoziologie und Rechtswissenschaft. Eine Kontroverse (1915/1917)*, Baden-Baden: Nomos Verlagsgesellschaft.
Loader, Ian and Neil Walker (2007), *Civilizing Security*, Cambridge: Cambridge University Press.
Michaels, Ralf (2005), 'The Re-*state*-ment of Non-State Law. The State, Choice of Law, and the Challenge from Global Legal Pluralism', *Wayne Law Review*, **51**, 1209–1259.
Teubner, Gunther (1996), 'Global Bukowina: Legal Pluralism in the World Society', in Gunther Teubner (ed.), *Global Law without a State*, Aldershot: Dartmouth, pp. 3–28.
Vogl, Stefan (2003), *Soziale Gesetzgebungspolitik, freie Rechtsfindung und soziologische Rechtswissenschaft bei Eugen Ehrlich*, Baden-Baden: Nomos Verlagsgesellschaft.

6. Ehrlich's non-state law and the Roman jurists

Olga Tellegen-Couperus

1. INTRODUCTION

At first sight, it may seem strange to find Roman law and Roman jurists featuring in a volume on twentieth century non-state law. However, it is no longer so strange when it is realized that the first person to introduce the concept of non-state law was a professor of Roman law. It is only natural that this person, Eugen Ehrlich (1862–1922), used his expertise in legal history when developing his new theory on the sociology of law. It is not his fault that he did so in a way that was generally accepted in his day but which is now regarded as questionable. Therefore, it is interesting to return to his fundamental work on the sociology of law and see whether the arguments that he put forward then still hold today.

In his *Grundlegung der Soziologie des Rechts* (1913), Ehrlich argued that, in all times, the development of law is not centred in legislation, nor in jurisprudence or jurisdiction, but in society itself.[1] Law, and particularly private law, is and must be free from state influence. He seems to base his theory on a historical argument, for, throughout the book, he refers to Roman law, *ius commune*, and common law. In this contribution, I will concentrate on Ehrlich's use of Roman law as an example of law developed in society by independent jurists who were free from state influence.

According to Ehrlich, in the time of the Republic, i.e., in the first 500 years of Roman history, Roman law was not created by the state but by jurists. He therefore qualified it as '*ausserstaatliches Recht*', non-state law, and as '*lebendes Recht*', living law. In the following centuries, when Rome was ruled by emperors, the law was dictated by the state and judges were allowed to judge according to state law only. Ehrlich therefore qualified the law of this period as '*staatliches Recht*', state law.

It was not the first time that Ehrlich had used these concepts. Ten years before he published his *Grundlegung*, Ehrlich wrote a book on the sources of law: *Beiträge zur Theorie der Rechtsquellen*.[2] In that book, he discussed the sources of Roman law, particularly the notions of *ius civile* and *ius publicum*. He interpreted them in a way that, in his day, was and even now is still rather unusual. The common view was and still is that *ius civile* was the law made by and for Roman citizens, and that *ius publicum* was the law referring to matters in which the Roman government was directly involved.[3] In Ehrlich's view, *ius civile* was that part of private law that had been developed by the Roman jurists; it was non-state law. *Ius publicum* was '*Staatsrecht und staatliches recht*', state law.[4] *Beiträge zur Theorie der Rechtsquellen* was announced as a first part, but Ehrlich never wrote a following part. Instead, he laid the foundations of sociology of law.

In Chapter 2 of this volume, Ehrlich is mentioned as belonging to that part of the international socio-legal literature which focuses on multiculturalism.[5] Ehrlich had found his inspiration in the Austro-Hungarian Empire where many different ethno-cultural groups lived side by side. In 1811, the new Austrian Civil Law Code had been introduced but, at least in the Bukowina of around 1900, it was not fully complied with by all citizens. They rather lived according to their own norms. Ehrlich began to study this form of legal pluralism and argued that legal scholars should no longer confine their attention to the state and to state law.

The first part of this contribution is about Ehrlich's interpretation of *ius civile* as law developed by the Roman jurists. In the second part, I will argue that the Roman jurists were not independent persons creating a non-state law and that, in fact, it is an anachronism to distinguish between state law and non-state law. However, the concept of legal pluralism was a well-known phenomenon. I will finish this chapter by giving some other examples of legal pluralism that Ehrlich could have used.

2. *IUS CIVILE* AS LAW DEVELOPED BY THE ROMAN JURISTS

In his *Beiträge*, Ehrlich quoted many texts from Roman law to support his interpretation of *ius civile* as law developed by the Roman jurists. In the *Grundlegung*, however, he refers to only two of them, namely to a text by the second century jurist Pomponius and to a text by the sixth century philosopher Boethius. I will confine myself to these two texts.

The two texts may both connect *ius civile* to the Roman jurists but, in all other respects, they have nothing in common. They differ as to author, kind of work and time. Of Pomponius we hardly know anything, whereas Boethius' life is well documented. Pomponius' text forms part of a monograph on the history of Roman law; that by Boethius belongs to his comment on Cicero's *Topica*. Pomponius lived in the second century, in the heyday of the Roman Empire; Boethius was born just after the (western)

Roman Empire had ceased to exist. If Ehrlich's interpretation of *ius civile* in these two texts holds, the differences will make it even more convincing.

2.1 Pomponius on the *Proprium Ius Civile*

The text that – according to Ehrlich – clearly describes the proper meaning of the words *ius civile* is to be found in Justinian's *Digest*, and particularly in the title D. 1.2. This title mainly consists of (part of) a monograph by Sextus Pomponius on the origin of law and of all magistracies and on the succession of the jurists. Pomponius lived in the second century AD. He has left an extensive amount of legal literature, but nothing is known about his personal background or career.[6] For Ehrlich, the most relevant passage is D. 1.2.2.12. I will quote the text with my own translation:

> *Pomponius libro singulari enchiridii. Ita in civitate nostra aut iure, id est lege constituitur, aut est proprium ius civile, quod sine scripto in sola prudentium interpretatione consistit, aut sunt legis actiones, quae formam agendi continent, aut plebiscitum, quod sine auctoritate patrum est constitutum, aut est magistratuum edictum, unde ius honorarium nascitur, aut senatus consultum, quod solum senatu constituente inducitur sine lege, aut est principalis constitutio, id est, ut quod ipse princeps constituit pro lege servetur.*
>
> Pomponius in his monograph *Enchiridium*. Thus, in our community, everything is established either by law, that is by statute law; or there is our own *ius civile*, which exists without writing solely in the interpretation of the jurists; or there are statutory actions which contain the form of procedure; or a plebiscite which is passed without the authority of the senate; or there is the edict of the magistrates whence derives honorary law; or there is a *senatus consultum* which is based upon the action of the senate alone, without any statute; or there is an imperial constitution, that is whatever the emperor himself decrees shall be observed as the law.

This text contains a list of all sources of law that existed from the time of the beginning of the Republic to Pomponius' own time, i.e., the second century AD. One of these sources is 'our own *ius civile*', '*proprium ius civile*' in the second line of the text; according to Pomponius, it exists only in the interpretation of the jurists but not in writing. This explanation has puzzled many legal historians. Since the nineteenth century, various interpretations have been given. Many authors assume that Pomponius' *Enchiridium* is rather unreliable and that, therefore, this text cannot be taken to prove anything.

Ehrlich admits that Pomponius' writings are often not in accordance with other texts that may have been better preserved, but he states that Pomponius must have had a proper knowledge of the basic terminology.[7] Moreover, Ehrlich argues, it can be deduced from this text that Pomponius must have used a very old manuscript, probably dating from the time of the Republic. Therefore, Pomponius' definition of *ius civile* must be taken literally: originally, the notion must have been used exclusively for the unwritten opinions of the jurists, and it must have been used in this sense until the end of the classical period (235 AD).

In my view, this interpretation is not convincing. Ehrlich is right to assume that Pomponius' text is basically trustworthy, but he does not clarify why his definition of the words *ius civile* is so special that it should be taken literally. It consists of two elements. First, *ius civile* is used for the interpretation given by the jurists. This explanation of the notion *ius civile* seems to refer to another remark that Pomponius made earlier, in D. 1.2.2.5. There, he explained that, after the Law of the Twelve Tables had been enacted, there arose the necessity of forensic debate, and that this debate and the resulting interpretations were not given a name of their own, but were called by the common name of *ius civile*.[8] So, in both texts, the notion *ius civile* is used to indicate the interpretation given by the jurists. However, as Pomponius declares, this was a general term that was used only because there was not one particular word to indicate the jurists' interpretation. The Law of the Twelve Tables, dating from about 450 BC, and later statutes belonged to *ius civile* as well.

The second element is the fact that the interpretation was given 'without writing'. However, it seems that, by adding the words '*sine scripto*', Pomponius only stressed the fact that he was writing about the very beginning of Roman law, in the time of the early Republic. At that time, the ability to read and write was not yet widespread. Later on, opinions were written down, and it was precisely because they were, that they could be collected and, later still, be included in Justinian's famous *Digest*.

In other words, Pomponius' remark on 'our own *ius civile* that without writing exists solely in the interpretation of the jurists' does not indicate that *ius civile* has always had only this one meaning, it only indicates that, in the early days of the Republic, jurists' law belonged to the *ius civile* and that the jurists did not keep records of their interpretations.

2.2 Boethius on the Authority of the Jurists

Anicius Manlius Severinus Boethius was born into a patrician family in Rome in 480.[9] At the time, Rome had only just been conquered by the Ostrogoths. Boethius gained fame as a philosopher, poet and politician. For many years, he occupied a position of trust under King Theodoric but, eventually, he fell from favour and was accused of treason. In 524 (or 526), after a term of imprisonment at Pavia, Boethius was put to death. It is now widely accepted that he was unjustly accused.

Boethius' works include *The Consolation of Philosophy*, one of the masterpieces of Western literature. He also wrote a series of commentaries on Aristotle's logical works and other books on logic. To this part of Boethius' work belongs the book from which Ehrlich has taken a quotation. It is a commentary on Cicero's *Topica*. I will quote the text as provided by Ehrlich[10] and give my own translation:

> *Iuris peritorum auctoritas est eorum, qui ex XII tabulis vel ex edictis magistratum ius civile interpretati sunt, probatae civium iudiciis creditaeque sententiae.*
>
> The authority of the jurists belongs to those who have explained *ius civile* on the basis of the Twelve Tables or the edicts of the magistrates, and whose opinions have been approved and accepted by the judgments of the citizens. (Boethius, *In Top*. 321 Or.)

This text forms part of a commentary by Boethius on Cicero's explanation of the *topos* definition in *Topica* 28.[11] By writing this book, Cicero wanted to provide a method for topical argumentation. In section 28, Cicero states that some definitions consist of partitions, others of divisions. As an example of the first, he gives a definition of *ius civile* as consisting of statutes, decrees of the senate, judicial decisions, the authority of the jurists, the edicts of the magistrates, custom and equity.[12] Cicero then moves on to the other category of definitions, consisting of divisions. Boethius, however, in his commentary, first deals with the parts of *ius civile* mentioned by Cicero. In that context, he also explains the authority of the jurists.

According to Ehrlich, this text shows that *ius civile* cannot have the meaning that it is usually given, namely that of law for and by the Roman citizens.[13] The fact that the jurists are said to interpret not only the Law of the Twelve Tables but also the edicts of the magistrates makes it necessary to see *ius civile* not as the object of interpretation, but as its result. It should be interpreted in the same vein as Pomponius did: as opinions that were approved and accepted by the citizen-judges. The reference to these judgments also shows, according to Ehrlich, that Boethius must have had a source from the time of the Republic. Since the time of Emperor Augustus, only the opinions of jurists who had the *ius respondendi* were relevant. Moreover, an author from the time of the early Empire would have mentioned the senatorial decrees and the imperial constitutions together with the Twelve Tables and the edicts of the magistrates.

A hundred years ago, such an interpretation may have been acceptable, but standards are different now. The first duty of someone interpreting a text from Roman law is to put it into context. If Ehrlich had done so he would have had to recognize that, according to Cicero and Boethius, the authority of the jurists is only one of the parts of *ius civile*. The other parts (statutes, decrees of the senate, judicial decisions, edicts of the magistrates, custom and equity) are considered as belonging to *ius civile* as well. Therefore, Ehrlich is not justified in saying that, at the time of the Republic, *ius civile* was only jurists' law. Moreover, this context also excludes his ingenious suggestion that *ius civile* should be taken to mean the result of interpretation: when all the other parts of *ius civile* form its objects, then it does not make sense to qualify the interpretation of the jurists as its result.

Finally, there is a grammatical argument for my view. The words '*ius civile*' in Boethius' explanation (that the authority of the jurists belongs to those who interpret the *ius civile* on the basis of the Law of the Twelve Tables and the edicts of the magistrates) form the object of the verb '*interpretati sunt*'. Therefore, they must be taken to refer to the Law of the Twelve Tables and the edict of the magistrates as the actual texts to be interpreted by the jurists. In no way do the words '*ius civile*' in this text mean exclusively 'jurists' law'.

3. THE ROMAN EMPIRE AND ITS JURISTS

In his *Grundlegung*, Ehrlich suggested that there was a contrast between the jurists of the Republic and the jurists of the time of the emperors: the first were independent, they created non-state law; the latter were not independent, they were bound by the emperor by means of the *ius respondendi*. This suggestion is based on the remark by Boethius that only those jurists had *auctoritas* whose opinions were approved and accepted by the judgments of the citizens. According to Ehrlich, this remark only held for the jurists of the time of the Republic, because only then were the citizens free to decide which opinions they accepted and approved. The introduction of the *ius respondendi* by Emperor Augustus limited the *auctoritas* of the jurists: the opinion of the jurist who had this privilege was binding for the judges, the opinions of all other jurists became irrelevant. However, I do not think that the *auctoritas* of the Republican jurists forms a contrast with that of the later jurists who had the *ius respondendi*.

In my view, Boethius' remark must be explained in a different way. In Rome, until the second century, there were no officials acting as judges but only private persons doing so.[14] Every year, the praetor drew up a list of citizens who could be chosen to give judgment in a particular lawsuit. These persons belonged to the upper class, to the senatorial elite. They were well acquainted with Roman law, but they were not necessarily experts. In some cases, a jurist is known to have acted as judge.[15] The litigant parties used to turn to one or more jurists to ask an opinion that was in their favour. The judge then decided which interpretation/opinion was to win. By doing so, he accepted and approved the opinion of (one of) the jurists and acknowledged that jurist's *auctoritas*.

When Augustus became the first Roman emperor, he reorganized the administration of justice.[16] One of the changes was the introduction of the so-called *ius respondendi*: the emperor was to authorize the top jurist to give opinions that would be binding for the judges.[17] His purpose was to streamline the loose ways in which, until then, the opinions had been given. He did not intend to introduce state influence and limit the jurists' freedom to develop law. In other words, his purpose was not to undermine the authority of the jurists, but to add his own authority to theirs. For a number of reasons, Augustus did not grant this privilege himself. In fact, only his successors were to do so. However, the judgments were still given by citizens, and because the *ius respondendi* was granted to more than one top jurist at a time, these citizens still had to make up their own minds as to which opinion from which jurist they would prefer. Therefore, Ehrlich was not justified in suggesting that the *ius respondendi* created a form of state law that contrasted with the jurists' law of the Republic as a form of non-state law.

Ehrlich's view of the Roman jurists was largely formed by the German Historical School. This School was founded by Friedrich Carl von Savigny in the early nineteenth century but was still dominant by the turn of that century. For the Historical School, law was the result of the historical development of a people; it is not made arbitrarily by a legislator like the natural law-based *Code civil* in France, but it emanates from the historical development of national societies, from the *Volksgeist*. When, in the course of time, society becomes more complicated, jurists become the interpreters of the people and independently 'find' the law. In this way, law grows until it has reached maturity. At the beginning of the nineteenth century, German law had not yet reached this stage of development. In Rome, however, law was fully developed in the second century AD, at the time of the jurists Papinian, Ulpian and Paul. Their work contained a perfectly logical system of legal science. Savigny and the other followers of the Historical School assumed that, in legal science, time was not a relevant factor; legal concepts were historical because they had developed historically. However, once they were fully grown, they could be used any time, any place. Therefore, they could also be applied in the German territories in the nineteenth century. In the same way, the classical jurists were timeless persons, '*fungibele Personen*', who strictly separated legal science from daily life.

Ehrlich followed the Historical School in its theory of the jurists as autonomous interpreters of the *Volksgeist*.[18] It is striking that Savigny and Ehrlich were not at all interested in the social background of the Roman jurists. They seem to have identified the Roman jurists with the jurists of their own day; in other words, they seem to have thought that the Roman jurists formed a group of persons who practised a particular profession, were entitled to practise that profession and earned their living by doing so. Consequently, they regarded them as a separate group in society, free from state influence. They suggested that the Roman concepts of *iurisprudens*, *iurisperitus* and *iurisconsultus* were synonymous with *Fachjurist*. We do not know much about the Roman jurists, but what we do know does not support these views.

In Justinian's *Digest*, about forty persons are mentioned as authors of books on private law. These persons, who are usually called the Roman jurists, belonged to a period beginning in 100 BC and ending in 235 AD. With a few exceptions, they are all known to have had a splendid political career. They all belonged to the senatorial elite that governed Rome. As from the middle of the second century BC, the jurists had started to write down their opinions on legal problems that had been put to them. The next generations did the same, but they also referred to opinions of other and/or older jurists. These opinions were particularly important when they had been confirmed by a judge in a lawsuit. No official records of judgments were kept. Instead, the jurists made their own records and these are the books, or rather scrolls, from which, in the sixth century, Justinian's *Digest* was compiled.

It follows that the Roman jurists had very little in common with the jurists of modern times: they did not form a separate group in society, the legal profession was not regulated by law, and the words *iurisprudens*, *iurisperitus* and *iurisconsultus* were only used as adjectives, not as nouns denoting a profession.[19] As senators, they took part in politics. They influenced political decision making, but they themselves were also influenced by political trends. Therefore, the Roman jurists cannot be regarded as completely independent persons whose only aim was to create a pure, autonomous legal science. Their work of interpretation of written and unwritten law cannot be regarded as non-state law.

4. 'THE ROMAN STATE' AND 'STATE LAW'

Is there any other part of Roman law that can be regarded as non-state law, or was Ehrlich wrong from the very start in dividing Roman law into state law and non-state law? Was there a Roman state in the sense used by Ehrlich?

In his *Grundlegung der Soziologie des Rechts*, Ehrlich describes the origin and essence of a state and state law in the following manner.[20] Originally, every state comes into being as a military union that, for an unlimited time, has chosen a leader, a king. This union or state must provide the king and his retinue with the necessary means and must keep the peace. In a later stage, it organizes a state administration of justice and, later still, legislation. Finally, constitutional law is created.

In this reconstruction, state law enters history relatively late, namely when the state orders the judges or other officials how to decide. Of course, the state can only do so when it has a strong military and policing power. In Antiquity, this situation first arose in Egypt, and then also in city-states such as Athens and Rome. According to Ehrlich, society uses the state to provide powerful support for its own law and to impose that law on those elements that are its subjects.[21]

This reconstruction may be true for some states, but the history of Rome does not really fit in. Rome began as a city-state. During a period of 500 years, it conquered a large territory and built an enormous empire, but all the time it was governed as a city-state. It was not a state in the sense of one territorial entity with a ruler as 'landlord'.[22] The root idea of *imperium* was the giving of commands by a general, and that of imperial expansion was the compelling of other peoples to obey orders. It was not one ruler but the Roman senate that was in command. Moreover, the conquered communities were left a considerable amount of freedom or self-regulation. It was only under the Empire that strings were pulled. By that time, the law had already been fully developed. Terms such as *civitas* and *res publica* may have been used by Roman authors to denote the community of Roman citizens, but there never was a Roman state as described by Ehrlich. In fact, it was only in the sixteenth century that national states emerged.[23] It is, therefore, an anachronism to speak of 'the Roman state'.

According to Ehrlich, state law is constitutional law and law that emanates from the state. In Rome, there was little or no constitutional law, but there were many laws that emanated from the state. They could be made in various ways. The oldest form is the *lex*, i.e., the decision of a popular assembly on a bill proposed by a magistrate and approved by the senate. Usually, these statute laws dealt with political issues, but sometimes they introduced changes in private law as well. Then, there are the senatorial decrees dealing with political and religious matters and the edict of the magistrates providing a basis for legal procedures. All these forms of law can be called state law because they emanate from the senate or a state official. However, this qualification does not hold because Roman authors also sum them up under the name *ius civile*. The notion of state law as used by Ehrlich does not coincide with a particular part of Roman law. Therefore, it is also an anachronism to speak of 'Roman state law' and to distinguish between state law and non-state law in the Roman Empire.

5. SOME EXAMPLES OF LEGAL PLURALISM IN ROMAN LAW

Ehrlich may have been wrong in distinguishing between state law and non-state law in the Roman Republic, but he could have used the history of the Roman Empire to illustrate his theory of multiculturalism. Eleven years before Ehrlich published his *Beiträge zu den Quellen des römischen Rechts*, Ludwig Mitteis had demonstrated that, from the beginning, the eastern provinces of the Roman Empire had resisted the application of Roman law.[24] They continued to follow their own norms and traditions, although the sources show traces of Roman law as well. Even after the grant of citizenship to all inhabitants, Greek and demotic Egyptian law persisted in these parts, sometimes in its pure form and sometimes mixed with Roman elements. The title of his book, *Reichsrecht und Volksrecht in den östlichen Provinzen des römischen Kaiserreichs*, makes it clear that Mitteis was writing about more or less the same phenomenon of legal pluralism as Ehrlich later did.

Mitteis' theory still holds, albeit that new evidence has now put his views in perspective. A useful survey is to be found in Andrew Lintott's book on the politics and administration of the Roman Empire.[25] Following older authors, he argues that, from the very start, the senate recognized the importance of local jurisdiction in the provinces. However, he shows that the interaction between Roman law and local law led to different results in different parts of the Empire. In a special chapter on Roman law and indigenous law, he elaborates on the similarities and the differences.

Generally speaking, the Roman law of procedure and substantive law had a much larger impact in the western provinces than in Greece, Asia Minor, Syria and Egypt. However, things were not always as simple as that. The *Tabula Contrebiensis*, an inscription of 87 BC containing a decree of the Roman governor of the Spanish provinces, shows that the Spaniards were expected to understand the Roman ways of civil procedure, but also that the governor was operating within the context of local tradition. On the other hand, more or less recently published documents testify that forms of Roman law were applied from Britain to Dacia and Syria. Egypt had a special position. Rome allowed the Egyptians to apply their native law, even if it meant a fundamental breach with its own laws and traditions.

When, in the early third century, Roman citizenship was granted to all inhabitants of the Empire, the non-Roman communities may have been more willing to give up their own traditions and accept Roman law, but it is more likely that they did not do so. Mitteis demonstrated that, in Egypt and Syria, even legal principles that were against Roman law continued to be applied. In the sixth century, Emperor Justinian subsumed local laws under customary law, which formed part of *ius civile*. For him, custom was no longer the tradition of the Romans, whether unwritten or having no identifiable origin, but reasonable local deviations from the 'Roman' law that was the *ius commune* of the whole Empire.[26]

Two millennia ago, Romania, including Ehrlich's Bukowina, formed part of the Roman Empire. Particularly after they had acquired Roman citizenship, the people may have applied Roman law, but it is more likely that they went on living according to their own customs. It seems that their situation did not differ much from that of Ehrlich's fellow-countrymen: around 1900, the Austrian Civil Law Code was formally in force, but in that region it was not fully applied. It would have made sense for Ehrlich to compare local law in the Roman provinces with that in the outer parts of the Austrian Empire. That he did not do so, but referred to the Roman jurists instead, can only be explained by the overwhelming influence of the Historical School which, in continental Europe, is still being felt even now.

6. CONCLUSION

The question that I posed at the beginning of this chapter was whether Ehrlich could underpin his theory on the sociology of law by referring to the Roman jurists. It will be clear that the answer must be negative. The distinction between state law and non-state law did not exist in the Roman Empire.

Still, Ehrlich deserves to be complimented on his effort to – at least partly – break away from the Historical School. He was right to question the focus on legal science and to turn his attention to the development of law. Looking for historical arguments to support his theory on the sociology of law was only natural. He was well versed in Roman law, which, in his time, still 'ruled the waves'. However, he was wrong to identify the concepts of *ius publicum* and *ius civile* with state law and non-state law, respectively. It seems that he could not resist the temptation of interpreting unclear texts on Roman law in a way that suited his theory.

There is no reason to assume that, at the time of the Republic, the Roman jurists were developing law independently and that, in the Early Empire, they were restricted by state influence. All the time, the jurists were closely connected to or even part of the powers-that-were. Therefore, Ehrlich's reference to the Roman Republic as a time when law was developed by independent jurists lacks foundation and cannot support his theory on the sociology of law. In the provinces of the Roman Empire, however, local law may have functioned as non-state law.

NOTES

1. Ehrlich (1913), Vorrede.
2. Ehrlich (1902).
3. Tellegen-Couperus (1993, p. 18).
4. He also dealt with a third element, namely *ius privatum*, which he regarded as a combination of *ius civile, ius gentium* and *ius naturale*. For the purpose of this chapter, only the first two concepts are relevant.
5. Hertogh (this volume, Chapter 2).
6. Kunkel (1967, p. 171).
7. Ehrlich (1902, pp. 1–3).
8. D. 1.2.2.5. *Pomponius libro singulari enchiridii. His legibus latis coepit (ut naturaliter evenire solet, ut interpretatio desideraret prudentium auctoritatem) necessariam esse disputatione fori. Haec disputatio et hoc ius quod sine scripto venit compositum a prudentibus, propria parte aliqua non appellatur, ut ceterae partes iuris suis nominibus designantur, datis propriis nominibus ceteris partibus, sed communi nomine appellatur ius civile.* (After the enactment of these laws, there arose a necessity for forensic debate, as it is the normal and natural outcome that problems of interpretation should make it desirable to have guidance from learned persons. This forensic debate and the law which without formal writing emerges as expounded by learned men has no special name of its own like the other subdivisions of law designated by that name (there being proper names given to these other subdivisions); it is called by the common name '*ius civile*'.)
9. For details of Boethius' life, work and influence in later times, see Gruber (1997 II, pp. 719–723). See also Marenbon (2003, pp. 7–16).
10. Ehrlich (1902, p. 16). According to Stump (1988, p. 14), two modern editions of Boethius' commentary exist, that in the *Patrologia Latina* and that in the *opera omnia* of Cicero's works by Orelli and Baiterus (1833). It seems that both Ehrlich and Stump used the Orelli edition. I have not been able to consult either edition. For the translation, see Stump (1988, p. 89).
11. For more information, see Stump (1988, pp. 89 and 210).
12. Cicero, *Topica* 28: '*Atque enim definitiones aliae sunt partitionum aliae divisionum; partitionum, cum res ea quae proposita est quasi in membra discerpitur, ut si quis dicat ius civile id esse quod in legibus, senatus consultis, rebus iudicatis, iuris peritorum auctoritate, edictis magistratuum, more, aequitate consistat.*'
13. Ehrlich (1902, p. 16).
14. On the regular procedure in private lawsuits, see Tellegen-Couperus (1993, pp. 54–59).
15. For instance, Publius Mucius Scaevola in the lawsuit brought by Gaius Gracchus' widow Licinia against her late husband's heirs (D. 24.3.66 pr.). On this lawsuit, see Tellegen-Couperus (2001, pp. 5–10).
16. In 17 BC, in the *leges Iuliae iudiciorum publicorum et privatorum*.
17. The nature of the *ius respondendi* is not clear. For a survey of the older literature and a new, convincing theory, see Tellegen (1988, pp. 279–287); also in Tellegen-Couperus (1993, pp. 96–98). However, Robinson (1997, pp. 10–13), for instance, still adheres to the traditional, more limited interpretation: 'Any grant must have been more of the nature of an honour (rather like appointing silks – King's or Queen's Counsel – in the English tradition) than of authority, even for a particular case' (p. 13).
18. In the same vein, still, Frier (1985, pp. 184–196).
19. These terms were used for all sorts of people, and not always in a positive and complimentary sense. Cicero, for instance, referred to Aebutius, the opponent of his client Caecina, as *inter mulieres iuris peritus et callidus*, 'a shrewd and clever lawyer among women'. See Cicero, *Pro Caecina*, 14.
20. Ehrlich (1913, p. 111).
21. Ehrlich (1913, p. 123).
22. See Lintott (1993, p. 22).
23. See Opello and Rosow (2004, pp. 77–97).

24. Mitteis (1891, pp. 30–32).
25. Lintott (1993, pp. 154–160).
26. According to Robinson (1997, p. 29).

REFERENCES

Ehrlich, Eugen (1902), *Beiträge zur Theorie der Rechtsquellen. 1. (einziger) Teil. Das ius civile, ius publicum, ius privatum*. Berlin, reprinted Aalen: Scientia Verlag 1970.

Ehrlich, Eugen (1913), *Grundlegung zur Soziologie des Rechts*, Paris, reprinted Berlin: Duncker & Humblot 1967.

Frier, Bruce (1985), *The Rise of the Roman Jurists*, Princeton: Princeton University Press.

Gruber, Joachim (1997), s.v. Boethius' in *Der neue Pauly. Enzyklopädie der Antike*, Stuttgart-Weimar: J.B. Metzler.

Kaser, Max (1971), *Das römische Privatrecht*, Volume I (2nd edn), Munich: C.H. Beck.

Kunkel, Wolfgang (1967), *Herkunft und soziale Stellung der römischen Juristen*, Graz, Vienna and Cologne: Böhlau.

Lintott, Andrew (1993), *Imperium Romanum. Politics and Administration*, London: Routledge.

Marenbon, John (2003), *Boethius*, Oxford: Oxford University Press.

Mitteis, Ludwig (1891), *Reichsrecht und Volksrecht in den östlichen Provinzen des römischen Kaiserreichs*, Leipzig, reprinted Hildesheim, Zürich and New York: Georg Olms Verlag 1984.

Opello, Jr. Walter C. and Stephen J. Rosow (2004), *The Nation-State and Global Order. A Historical Introduction to Contemporary Politics*, Boulder and London: Lynne Rienner Publishers.

Robinson, Olivia (1997), *The Sources of Roman Law. Problems and Methods for Ancient Historians*, London and New York: Routledge.

Stump, Eleonor (1988), *Boethius's In Ciceronis Topica*, translated, with notes and an introduction, Ithaca and London: Cornell University Press.

Tellegen, Jan Willem (1988), 'Gaius Cassius and the Schola Cassiana in Pliny's Letter VII 24,8', *Zeitschrift der Savigny Stiftung, romanistische Abteilung*, **105**, 263–311.

Tellegen-Couperus, Olga (1993), *A Short History of Roman Law*, London and New York: Routledge.

Tellegen-Couperus, Olga (2001), 'The Role of the Judge in the Formulary Procedure', *Journal of Legal History*, **22**, 1–13.

PART 2

Non-state law in practice

7. Environmental regulation and non-state law: the future public policy agenda

Neil Gunningham

1. INTRODUCTION

Over the last decade, considerable thinking has gone into the issue of how to design more efficient and effective regulation. Much of this thinking has been in the field of social regulation and that of environmental regulation in particular. While not all the innovations and insights that have emerged from a radical re-conception of the roles of environmental regulation have broad application to other fields of regulation, nevertheless, many of them do. This chapter draws from the writer's previous work on this area and seeks to identify some broad themes and insights based around the themes of 'smart regulation' and regulatory reconfiguration (see in particular Gunningham and Sinclair 2002, Ch. 9) and their broader connection with non-state law.

The chapter reviews the changing role of the regulatory state, and the evolution of a number of next generation policy instruments, intended to overcome, or at least to mitigate, the considerable problems associated with previous policy initiatives, and traditional forms of regulation in particular. The goal is, in the words of the US Environmental Protection Agency (EPA) 'to adapt, improve and expand the diversity of our environmental strategies' (ibid) and to address the circumstances not only of laggards but also of leaders.

However, policy reform has taken place in what is, in many respects, a hostile political and economic environment. The 1980s and 1990s saw a resurgence of free-market ideology which, assisted by the economic and political collapse of the former Soviet Union, enabled neo-liberalism to triumph almost unchallenged, for most of that period and beyond. And while public opposition precluded the sort of wholesale deregulation which occurred in some other areas of social regulation, environmental regulatory budgets were substantially cut in almost all jurisdictions. This trend shows little sign of changing under the lower taxation regimes that now characterize the large majority of economically advanced states, irrespective of the party in power.

During the same period, governments have also experienced considerable pressure from industry to reduce the economic burden of complying with environmental regulation. Although on most calculations, the costs of compliance are relatively modest, nevertheless industrial lobby groups have argued strongly, and often successfully, that the imposition of such regulation would put industry at a competitive disadvantage. In an era of globalization, in which capital flight to low tax, low regulation regimes is increasingly plausible (though far less often demonstrated), governments have listened particularly closely to industry concerns and have frequently responded sympathetically. Thus the confluence of economic and political pressures has often precluded the application of direct regulation.

But while government regulators have been losing both their power and resources, others have begun to fill the regulatory space they previously occupied. For example, environmental non-governmental organizations (NGOs), aided by advanced techniques for information gathering (from digital cameras to satellite imaging) have become increasingly sophisticated at communicating their message (via global television, international newspapers and the Internet) and in using the media (and sometimes the courts) to amplify the impact of their direct action campaigns. They have not only sought to shape public opinion to lobby governments and to pressure industry directly, but also to influence consumers and markets through strategies such as orchestrating consumer boycotts or preferences for green products. Indeed, they have commonly bypassed governments altogether where they perceived them to be overly sympathetic to industry or incapable of effective action.

At the same time, a variety of commercial third parties have also begun to take a considerable interest in environmental issues. Banks and insurance companies seek to minimize their financial risk by scrutinizing more closely the environmental credentials of their clients. And financial markets themselves have become responsive to good or bad environmental news, rewarding environmental leaders with a share price increase and discounting the share price of laggards. So too is supply chain pressure increasingly important, with a substantial number of companies seeking accreditation under ISO 14001 – not because regulators require it or because they believe it necessary but rather because their trading partners insist upon it.

As part of this reshaping of the regulatory landscape, a number of environmental stakeholders have to some extent departed from their traditional roles. Some business groups, such as the World Business Council for

Sustainable Development, have become proactive, arguing that business is part of the solution rather than merely the problem, and have sought to develop a variety of voluntary initiatives through which business seeks to shape its own environmental destiny. Environmental NGOs, frustrated with their limited impact on governments, or at the ineffectiveness of government in protecting the environment, have redirected their attention towards corporations through strategies ranging from confrontation to partnership. And government policy makers, constrained by diminishing resources and noting the increasing power of NGOs and financial markets, and the potential for industry self-management, have become increasingly enamoured with the possibilities of 'steering not rowing' in policy design.

What has evolved is not a retreat of the regulatory state and a return to free markets but rather a regulatory reconfiguration. The US EPA's Reinventing Environmental Regulation programme, negotiated agreements in Western Europe, a plethora of informational regulation initiatives, various forms of industry self-management and a variety of enterprises (commonly using supply chain and financial market pressure) built around harnessing third parties as surrogate regulators, nevertheless involve a continuing government role. Even in relation to problems which the state is ill equipped to address directly, it almost invariably retains a supporting role, underpinning alternative solutions and providing a backdrop without which other, more flexible options, would lack credibility, and stepping in where they fail. That is, in almost all circumstances the state is still involved in engineering solutions to environmental problems rather than trusting the market, unaided, to provide them.

This reconfiguration is still in process, and the next generation instruments that have emerged are very diverse. Some seek out and nurture win–win solutions, some seek to replace conflict with cooperation between major stakeholders, and others seek to mitigate power imbalances, and to increase transparency and accountability, as is the case with informational regulation. Many, in stark contrast to the first generation of command and control, seek to encourage and reward enterprises for going beyond compliance with existing regulation. And the large majority exemplify the changing role of the state, which in the domestic environmental arena at least, retains a substantial role, albeit one that involves less direct intervention in the affairs of business than previously. Nevertheless there is much evidence of what, in the terminology of Chapter 2, can be termed 'legal pluralism at home'.

But neither the precise direction of this reconfiguration nor its results are yet known. Much work remains to be done in mapping progress, identifying what works and what doesn't, and why, and in providing a better understanding of how to match types of instruments, and institutions, with particular environmental problems. The following sections provide a broader perspective on this regulatory reconfiguration. First, they examine it through a variety of different lenses and in terms of a number of different conceptual frameworks. Second, they reflect on some broader lessons for the future of regulatory reform.

2. CONCEPTUALIZING REGULATORY RECONFIGURATION

Below, five different frameworks, or lenses, are examined through which one might better understand regulatory reconfiguration. None of these lenses offers (or necessarily purports to offer) a complete prescription for what the next generation of policy instruments should involve. However, as will be demonstrated, individually and collectively, they enrich our understanding of individual policy instruments and what they might achieve. They also provide insights into the challenges facing regulatory reconfiguration and how they might be resolved.

3. REFLEXIVE REGULATION

The literature on reflexive law recognizes that the capacity of the regulatory state to deal with increasingly complex social issues has declined dramatically. As Teubner (1983) and others (Teubner et al. 1994) have argued, there is a limit to the extent to which it is possible to add more and more specific prescriptions without this resulting in counterproductive regulatory overload. Traditional command and control regulation (a form of 'material law') is seen as unresponsive to the demands of the enterprise and unable to generate sufficient knowledge to function efficiently. In sum: 'the complexity of society outgrows the possibilities of the legal system to shape the complexity into a form fitting to the goal-seeking direct use of law' (Koch and Nielsen 1996). To give a concrete example, one cause of the Three Mile Island nuclear accident and near melt-down was that operators simply followed rules, without any capacity for strategic thinking, and as events unfolded which were not covered by a rule, they had no capacity to read the situation and respond appropriately.

In contrast, reflexive regulation, which uses *indirect* means to achieve broad social goals, has, according to its proponents, a much greater capacity to come to terms with increasingly complex social arrangements. This is because it:

> focuses on enhancing the self-referential capacities of social systems and institutions outside the legal system, rather than direct intervention of the legal system itself through its agencies, highly detailed statutes, or delegation of great powers to the courts . . . [it] aims to establish self-reflective processes within businesses to encourage creative, critical, and continual thinking about how to minimize . . . harms and maximize . . . benefits. (Orts 1995, p. 1232)

Put differently, reflexive regulation is procedure-oriented rather than directly focused on a prescribed goal, and seeks to design self-regulating social systems by establishing norms of organization and procedure.

Such a strategy can also be viewed as a form of 'meta risk-management' whereby government, rather than regulating directly, risk manages the risk management of individual enterprises. This is what happens under the 'safety case' regime, instituted on North Sea oil rigs following the Cullen enquiry into the Piper Alpha disaster where 167 lives were lost (Cullen 1990). This involves what is in effect a safety management system being developed by the rig operator and submitted to the regulator for scrutiny and approval. Similarly, the safety regime established for the nuclear power industry, post Three Mile Island, ceased to be primarily about government inspectors checking compliance with rules, and more about encouraging the industry to put in place safety management systems which were then scrutinized by regulators and, in this case, by the industry association in the form of the Institute of Nuclear Power.

A number of the second generation instruments could be readily interpreted as examples of reflexive law, whose goal, rather than regulating prescriptively, is to encourage organizations to establish processes of internal self-regulation to monitor, control and replace economic activities injurious to the environment. Take the use of environmental management systems, which form the principal component of regulatory flexibility initiatives and some forms of negotiated agreement. Such systems seek by law to stimulate modes of self-organization within the firm in such a way as to encourage internal self-critical reflection about its environmental performance. They establish processes and procedures that encourage self-reflexive learning and thinking about reducing environmental impact rather than seeking to influence behaviour directly by proscribing certain activities. Similar mechanisms are being devised to suit the circumstances of SMEs (small and medium-sized enterprises). These include not only 'slimmed down' EMSs (environmental management systems) but also self-inspection, self-audits and checklists.

In part, informational regulation can also be viewed in these terms (although it is much else besides). For example, requiring facilities to track and report their emissions (as under the TRI (toxic release inventory)), not only empowers community groups, and enables markets to make more informed judgments, but it also leads to a degree of self-reflection on how things might be done differently. Dow Chemicals is among those firms which freely acknowledge that they had not previously measured their wastes and as a result had no idea how much they were discharging. Once they did so, they realized that there was a business opportunity to make pollution prevention pay, through reuse, recycling, the substitution of different substances and the use of less chemicals. Thus a strategy which involved no requirement to do anything other than estimate discharges and disclose them, had a variety of broader consequences, including generating internal organizational change (and corporate shaming) which in turn resulted in substantially improved environmental performance for many companies.

On close inspection, a number of other strategies also contain elements of reflexive regulation. Industry self-management initiatives certainly fall within this category, to the extent that they deliberately build in a variety of mechanisms to generate internal compliance and self-organization. Even economic incentives, on one view, have reflexive elements, though whether their designers would have viewed them in these terms is debatable. Nevertheless, Fiorino (1999, p. 450) argues that marketable permits, such as emissions trading and acid rain allowance trading programmes in the US, 'induce reflection by specifying a goal and allowing firms to decide how to achieve it, given their circumstances'. However, he also notes that because they are implemented in the context of technology requirements such permits involve a combination of substantive and reflexive law.

4. REGULATORY PLURALISM

For present purposes, the term 'smart regulation' is used to refer to an emerging form of regulatory pluralism that embraces flexible, imaginative and innovative forms of social control which seek to harness not just governments but also business and third parties. For example, it is concerned with self-regulation and co-regulation, with using both commercial interests and NGOs, and with finding surrogates for direct government regulation, as well as with improving the effectiveness and efficiency of more conventional forms of direct government regulation. All this, in the terminology of Chapter 2, involves harnessing non-state actors *within* the context of the nation state.

The central argument is that, in the majority of circumstances, the use of multiple rather than single policy instruments, and a broader range of regulatory actors, will produce better regulation. Further, that this will allow the implementation of complementary combinations of instruments and participants tailored to meet the imperatives of specific environmental issues. By implication, this means a far more imaginative, flexible and pluralistic approach to environmental regulation than has so far been adopted in most jurisdictions.

To put this concept in context, it is important to remember that traditionally, regulation was thought of as a bi-partite process involving government and business, with the former acting in the role of regulator and the latter as regulatee. However, a substantial body of empirical research reveals that there are a plurality of regulatory forms, that numerous actors influence the behaviour of regulated groups in a variety of complex and subtle ways (Rees 1988, p. 7), and that mechanisms of informal social control often prove more important than formal ones. In the case of the environment, the regulatory pluralism perspective suggests that we should focus our attention on the influence of: international standards organizations; trading partners and the supply chain; commercial institutions and financial markets; peer pressure and self-regulation through industry associations; internal environmental management systems and culture; and civil society in a myriad of different forms.

These insights have led some policy makers to investigate how public agencies may harness institutions and resources residing *outside* the public sector to further policy objectives in specific concrete situations. This approach can be seen as part of the broader transition in the role of governments internationally: from 'rowing the boat to steering it' (Osborne and Gaebler 1992, p. 32) or choosing to 'regulate at a distance' by acting as facilitators of self- and co-regulation rather than regulating directly. Thus for regulatory pluralists, environmental policy making involves government harnessing the capacities of markets, civil society and other institutions to accomplish its policy goals more effectively, with greater social acceptance and at less cost to the state (Gunningham et al. 1999). And since parties and instruments interact with each other and with state regulation in a variety of ways, careful regulatory design will be necessary to ensure that pluralistic policy instruments are mutually reinforcing, rather than being duplicative, or worse, conflicting (Gunningham and Grabosky 1998, Chapter 6).

A substantial number of next generation instruments are pluralistic in conception. Some, such as the regulatory flexibility initiatives established under the Clinton–Gore 'Reinventing Environmental Regulation' initiative, were directly inspired by one version of regulatory pluralism (and by Osborne and Gaebler's (1992) concept of 'steering not rowing' in particular). Seeking to embed environmental values and processes within the corporate culture in such a way that it becomes self-regulating, and relying upon oversight from local communities and perhaps third party auditors, to supplement or even replace direct regulation, is a quintessential pluralist strategy.

Many informational regulation initiatives can also be understood in pluralist terms. Providing communities and financial markets with greater information about corporate environmental performance effectively empowers both of these groups. Communities and environmental NGOs respond by using this information to shame bad corporate performers, while the same information apparently influences share prices, thereby indirectly punishing bad performers and rewarding environmental leaders. In particular, the powerful impact of the TRI as a surrogate regulatory tool is well documented (Fung and O'Rourke 2000).

5. ENVIRONMENTAL PARTNERSHIPS

Environmental partnerships came of age in the 1990s when parts of industry, government and NGOs recognized that conflict and confrontation were not necessarily the best means of achieving either the best economic or environmental results. Governments sought alternatives to direct regulation, and business enterprises, dissatisfied with the cost and inflexibility of command and control regulation, and sometimes seeking win–win outcomes, sought more flexible and less confrontational alternatives. NGOs, too, began to see virtue in 'green alliances' with environmentally proactive enterprises. Sometimes these partnerships involve agreements between business and NGOs, or between governments and business, or even between business and business along the supply chain. On other occasions, they may embrace governments, NGOs, business *and* a range of other third parties, which held out the promise of acting as surrogate regulators and performing many of the functions that government regulation was no longer ready, willing and able to fulfil.

According to their proponents, environmental partnerships provide an additional policy option which steers a middle course between the two extremes of traditional regulation on the one hand and self-regulation and voluntarism on the other, and in so doing take advantage of their respective attributes while compensating for their particular weaknesses (Long and Arnold 1994). Environmental partnerships also provide opportunities to replace adversarialism with cooperation, and in doing so may provide benefits for all sides. For example, through 'green alliances' business may obtain the political goodwill and credibility which NGOs bring to the partnership while, in return, environmental groups gain commitments to improved environmental practices on the part of their business partner. In industry–government partnerships, governments can offer resources, expertise, regulatory relief and external legitimacy in return for improved industry environmental performance. Government can also play a broader role in encouraging, facilitating, rewarding and shaping a variety of partnership forms.

In Europe, negotiated agreements between government and individual companies or industry sectors have rapidly become one of the principal environmental management and policy instruments at a national level. The goal here is often to fill in the gaps not covered by regulations, to encourage companies to go beyond compliance or even to find a more politically acceptable alternative to regulation. Public voluntary programmes also fit the partnership model, with government offering technical support and public relations benefits in return for industry commitments to improved environmental performance. In the US they have also become an important component of 'Reinventing Environmental Regulation' (Clinton and Gore 1995) under which government seeks to replace the typically adversarial relationship which has existed between business and government in that country with a more cooperative approach based on trust and reciprocity.

6. CIVIL REGULATION AND PARTICIPATORY GOVERNANCE

As defined by Murphy and Bendell (1998, p. 8): 'civil regulation is where organizations of civil society, such as NGOs, set the standards for business behaviour. Enterprises then choose to adopt or not to adopt those standards.' Those who advocate a greater role for civil regulation argue that the regulatory state is starved of resources, lacking in political will, and incapable of reaching the many businesses which can now operate outside national territorial boundaries. The goal of civil regulation is to fill the vacuum left by the contracting state, and to compensate for 'the deficit of democratic governance that we face as a result of economic globalization' (Bendell 2000, p. 201). As such, there is considerable overlap between this perspective and some aspects of regulatory pluralism, discussed above.

Under civil regulation, the various manifestations of civil society act in a variety of ways to influence corporations, consumers and markets, often bypassing the state and rejecting political lobbying in favour of what they believe to be far more effective strategies. Sometimes NGOs take direct action, usually targeted at large reputation-sensitive companies. Greenpeace's campaign against Shell's attempted deep sea disposal of the Brent Spar oil rig is one example. Sometimes, they boycott products or producers deemed to be environmentally harmful, as with the effective boycott of Norwegian fish products organized by Greenpeace in protest against that nation's resumption of whaling. Market campaigning, focusing on highly visible branded retailers, is a particularly favoured strategy. Less so are campaigns which seek to provide a market premium for 'environmentally preferred' produce, due largely to the unwillingness of consumers to support such a strategy. More recently certification programmes such as the Forest Stewardship Council have been 'transforming traditional power relationships in the global arena. Linking together diverse and often antagonistic actors from the local, national and international levels . . . to govern firm behavior in a global space that has eluded the control of states and international organizations' (Gereffi et al. 2001, pp. 64–65).

However, the evolving role of civil regulation has not taken place entirely divorced from state intervention. On the contrary, either in response to pressure from the institutions of civil society or in recognition of the limits of state regulation, governments are gradually providing greater roles for communities, environmental NGOs and the public more generally. Thus a number of next generation policy instruments are geared to empower various institutions of civil society to play a more effective role in shaping business behaviour. In effect, they facilitate civil regulation (and regulatory pluralism). These include public participation provisions under the various US 'Reinventing Environmental Regulation' initiatives, CRTK (Community Right to Know) legislation, some second generation voluntary agreements which contemplate a significant role for third parties, and some forms of environmental partnership in which the public, or public interest groups, are major players.

Arguably the most powerful forms of civil regulation are those in which environmental NGOs or communities have the capacity to threaten the social licence and reputation capital of large corporations. Sometimes they do so independently of government, but more commonly government and next generation instruments play a crucial facilitative role.

7. ECOLOGICAL MODERNIZATION AND THE 'GREENGOLD THESIS'

Another emerging paradigm is what has become known as 'ecological modernization'. In contrast to many analyses which suggest that a radical reorientation of our current economic and social arrangements will be necessary to avert ecological disaster, ecological modernization suggests that ecologically sound capitalism is not only possible, but worth working towards. This good news message may indeed be a substantial part of the attraction of the ecological modernization approach. Beyond this, the main tenets of this perspective are difficult to encapsulate, since writings under the ecological modernization banner are diverse and draw from a number of different schools of thought.

For present purposes the focus is on its core, which emphasizes how strategies such as eco-efficiency can facilitate environmental improvements in the private sector (particularly in relation to manufacturing) by simultaneously increasing efficiency and minimizing pollution and waste. This will require switching to the use of cleaner, more efficient and less resource-intensive technologies, shifting away from energy- and resource-intense industries to those which are value- and knowledge-intensive, anticipatory planning processes, and the 'organizational internalization of ecological responsibility' (Cohen 1997, p. 109).

However, this is not to suggest that markets unaided, or past environmental policy, will provide the appropriate messages and incentives to enable industry to achieve these goals. On the contrary, such an outcome requires action on a number of fronts, and government regulation in particular will need to promote innovation in environmental technology. In terms of public policy prescriptions, Mol (one of the most influential proponents of this perspective) suggests two directions that should be pursued. First, state environmental policy must focus not on prescription but rather on prevention and participatory decentralized decision making, which 'creates favourable conditions and contexts for environmentally sound practices and behaviour on the part of producers and consumers' (Mol 1995, p. 46). The second option includes a transfer of responsibilities, incentives and tasks from the state to the market, which provides the flexibility and incentives to enable more efficient and effective outcomes. Under this approach, 'the state provides the conditions and stimulates social "self-regulation", either via economic mechanisms and dynamics or via the public sphere of citizen groups, environmental NGOs and consumer organizations' (Mol 1995, p. 47).

In these respects, the ecological modernization literature has resonance with a number of other perspectives described in this chapter, especially civil society, regulatory pluralism and, to some extent, reflexive regulation. However, on one fundamental issue, ecological modernization departs substantially from these other perspectives, namely in its assumption that by following the precepts of ecological modernization there will be a 'dissolution of the conflict between economic progress and responsible environmental management because it will be possible to achieve both objectives simultaneously' (Cohen 1997, p. 109).

In arguing that the business community could successfully combine the objectives of environmental protection and economic growth, ecological modernization resonates with the views of a variety of business strategists, environmental commentators and corporations who subscribe to what has become known as the 'greengold thesis'. This group argues that by preventing pollution and thereby cutting costs and avoiding waste directly, by more effective risk management, by gaining an increasing share of expanding 'green markets' or price premiums within them, and by developing the environmental technology to compete effectively in the global environmental market, businesses can achieve win–win outcomes, gaining economically from environmental improvements (Smart 1992; Schmidheiny 1992).

Of particular influence have been the views of Porter (1991), who has argued that in a highly regulated world, innovative companies can acquire competitive advantages or cut costs by developing novel methods of reducing environmental problems. Notwithstanding some differences of emphasis, a common refrain has been that going beyond compliance is both good for business and good for the environment. However, both Porter and the ecological modernization theorists acknowledge that there may be more scope for win–win outcomes in some sectors and circumstances than in others (Porter 1998; Baylis et al. 1998).

A number of next generation instruments might facilitate win–win outcomes. For example, instruments which harness market forces, so as to encourage rather than inhibit commercial drive and innovation (including many economic instruments and performance standards), meet with approval. Various other flexible and arguably cost-efficient mechanisms for curbing environmental degradation, such as self-regulation, information-based strategies, the use of liability rules and other financial instruments, are consistent with Mol's two directions summarized above. Government's role includes nudging firms towards cleaner production, heightening their awareness of environmental issues, providing them with financial incentives (which at the margin may be crucial), and encouraging the reordering of corporate priorities in order to reap the benefits of improved environmental performance.

The question of whether in a particular set of circumstances there are opportunities for win–win outcomes or not, is both highly contentious and important, because in the absence of such opportunities, it cannot be assumed that organizations will voluntarily become greener, or that they have any incentive to pursue beyond compliance environmental strategies in the absence of external pressure to do so. As regards the latter issue, Reinhardt (2000) has demonstrated that it makes sense to pursue beyond compliance policies if they increase the enterprise's expected value, or if they appropriately manage business risk, but in a substantial number of circumstances, they do neither.

8. IMPLICATIONS OF NON-STATE LAW FOR THE LEGISLATURE

While each of the perspectives described above provides insights concerning how best to approach the task of regulatory reconfiguration, there are considerable disparities between them, and none provides unproblematic or comprehensive answers as to what next-generation environmental regulation should involve, or to the normative question: what should be the implications of 'non-state law' (or in the language of this chapter, 'surrogate regulators') for the legislature?

Nevertheless, both the commonalities and the differences between these perspectives provide insights as to how best to approach the journey ahead. To begin, there is general agreement that returning to the policies of the past is not an option. A common theme is that traditional state regulation is not suited to meet many contemporary policy needs (although, as is emphasized below, it still has a role to play), and indeed it is partly in response to the perceived shortcomings of the regulatory *status quo* that each of these conceptual frameworks evolved. As Fiorino (1999, p. 464) puts it: 'underlying each strand in the literature is the belief that the increased complexity, dynamism, diversity, and interdependence of contemporary society makes old policy technologies and patterns of governance obsolete'.

There is also recognition that regulated enterprises have a diversity of motivations and that it cannot be assumed (as in some versions of command and control regulation) that deterrence (a traditional tool of the state) is the principal weapon available to regulators and policy makers. Notwithstanding differences of emphasis, there is a shared awareness of the complexity of motivational forces influencing environmental behaviour, and of the need to develop instruments and strategies to take account of this. In particular, they recognize that the state is only one source of law creation (broadly defined) and that its role may be, in Osborne and Gaebler's terms, more about steering than rowing.

For example, each of these perspectives to a greater or lesser extent recognizes the importance of such broader motivational drivers as the effects of negative publicity, informal sanctions and shaming, incentives provided by various third parties, the significance for private enterprise of maintaining legitimacy, and the necessity to maintain cooperation and trust. As a result, they all recognize that changing motivation is not something that can be achieved by the state alone.

Again, some instruments and approaches are common to almost all of these perspectives. For example, informational regulation (which empowers third parties) is important to reflexive regulation, civil regulation and regulatory pluralism, is supportive of environmental partnerships and at least consistent with the goals of ecological modernization. Similarly, process-based strategies such as EMS (which places greater emphasis on self-regulation with state oversight) are central to reflexive regulation, many environmental partnerships and ecological modernization, and, as a form of industry self-management, to some variants of regulatory pluralism. And none of these perspectives would deny that there is a role for public interest groups, although their role is conceived as more central in the case of environmental partnerships, regulatory pluralism and civil regulation, than it is for reflexive regulation or ecological modernization.

And in contrast to traditional forms of environmental regulation, each of the perspectives examined above sees virtue in engaging with environmental leaders and in encouraging or rewarding their further improvement rather than focusing only on bringing laggards up to compliance. This is perhaps most obvious in the case of environmental partnerships (which often only the best firms are willing to join) but regulatory pluralism and civil regulation also reward environmental leaders (for example in terms of reputation, or market advantage, or share price premium), as well as seeking to shame or otherwise provide negative incentives to laggards. Reflexive regulation, while less explicit, builds in processes which often lead to continuous improvement, while ecological modernization, with its emphasis on win–win outcomes and cleaner production, also seeks to encourage best practice rather than merely minimum standards and compliance.

However, when it comes to identifying where the focus of regulatory reconfiguration should be, there is much less agreement, and very different policy prescriptions flow from different perspectives. In terms of reflexive regulation, the perceived role of the state is to establish regulatory structures that strengthen the capability of individual institutions or enterprises for internal reflection and self-control. For regulatory pluralism, it is a plethora of instruments which enable the state to steer not row, and to harness the capacities of second and third parties to more effectively fill the space vacated by the contracting regulatory state. From a civil regulation perspective, the state's principal role is to provide mechanisms that will empower the institutions of civil society to make corporations more accountable. A partnership perspective would seek out opportunities to build reciprocal gains from cooperation with the state playing an additional role as facilitator. For ecological modernization, the aspiration is to create incentives which will facilitate industry moving towards sustainability using new technologies and techniques of production, with economic and environmental considerations being mutually reinforcing.

9. REGULATORY REFORM: THE NEVER ENDING JOURNEY

Each of the above frameworks has something valuable to offer and none of them is 'right' or 'wrong' in the abstract. Rather, they make differing contributions depending upon the nature and context of the environmental policy issue to be addressed. For example, ecological modernization has most to offer where industry can demonstrably benefit economically from environmental improvements (the so-called win–win scenario) but is far less persuasive in the variety of contexts where this is not the case. Civil regulation has considerable power when it comes to changing the behaviour of large reputation-sensitive companies, which are vulnerable not only to shaming but also to market forces and consumer pressure, but has far less to offer when dealing with the environmental excesses of many SMEs and firms which are not vulnerable to such pressures. Reflexive regulation is demonstrably effective in dealing with complex and sophisticated environmental issues such as regulating major hazardous facilities, but may be redundant when it comes to more traditional challenges. Environmental partnerships have attractions where both partners can see common ground and mutual benefits from constructive engagement, but not where there are irreconcilable philosophical differences between stakeholders (Poncelet 1999, 2001).

The limitations of each of the major policy innovations, and of the conceptual frameworks that drive next generation regulation, lead to a plea for pragmatism and regulatory pluralism. None of the policy instruments or perspectives examined above works well in relation to all sectors, contexts or enterprise types. Each has weaknesses as well as strengths, and none can be applied as an effective stand-alone approach across the environmental spectrum. In part, such a conclusion suggests the value of designing complementary combinations of instruments, compensating for the weaknesses of each with the strengths of others, while avoiding combinations of instruments deemed to be counterproductive or at least duplicative. This indeed was the central message of Gunningham and Sinclair's previous work, embedded within the pluralist perspective (Gunningham and Sinclair 1999a, b). From this perspective, no particular instrument or approach is privileged, whether it is reflexive regulation, civil regulation or the tenets of ecological modernization. Rather, the goal is to accomplish substantive compliance with regulatory goals by any viable means using whatever regulatory or quasi-regulatory tools might be available, including any or all of the next generation instruments. As Parker (2000) points out: 'the objective is to steer corporate conduct towards public policy objectives in the most effective and efficient way, without interfering too greatly with corporate autonomy and profit, rather than fruitless expenditure of government and business resources on traditional styles of regulation that ignore the effects of indigenous regulatory orderings'.

However, even in circumstances where one particular perspective (or combination of perspectives) and one set of policy tools seem well suited to apply to a particular problem, there may still be a substantial gap between theory and practice. Indeed, some of the policies at the very heart of next generation regulation are largely untested and their efficacy is uncertain. This is certainly the case with environmental management systems, which play an important role under a number of the frameworks reviewed above. There is only limited evidence available of how they work in practice and there remains a risk that they will produce the trappings of self-reflection and internal control without achieving more than business as usual (Coglianese and Nash 2006). Moreover, it has proved very difficult to develop incentives sufficient to persuade substantial numbers of organizations to participate in an EMS-based alternative regulatory track.

Some second generation agreements are much better designed but we still have incomplete evidence as to whether, or under what circumstances, they will be successful. Indeed, there remain considerable risks of wrong turnings and of re-enacting the mistakes of previous decades. Much the same can be said for many environmental partnerships (Gunningham 2007a). Even informational regulation, which has been generally hailed as a success story, has been challenged by its critics as not demonstrably achieving many of its objectives, at least in some jurisdictions (Brown et al. 2007) The limitations of our current experience are even greater in the case of SMEs, where the empirical picture remains extremely unclear.

Thus some of our knowledge about policy instruments and in particular about what works and when, is tentative, contingent and uncertain. We should not be too pessimistic about this, for we do know much more than we did a decade ago. For example, it will often be possible to identify which policy tool is best suited (at least in principle) to deal with a particular type of problem, or what mix of policy instruments is likely to be complementary (Gunningham and Grabosky 1998, Ch. 6), or what role state law should (still) play in NGO–business collaborations (Bastmeijer and Verschuuren 2005).

Nevertheless, recognizing that there is still much we do not know, there is virtue in adaptive learning, and in treating policies as experiments from which we can learn and which in turn can help shape the next generation of instruments. From this perspective, following Fiorino (1999, p. 468), it is important to ask: 'how may mechanisms that promote policy-learning . . . be strengthened? To what extent do policy-making institutions provide mechanisms for learning from experience and altering behavior based on that experience?' This might imply, for example, monitoring, ex post evaluation and revision mechanisms, and 'building reliable feedback mechanisms into policy-making, strengthening learning networks, creating conditions that would lead to more trust and more productive dialogue and building enough flexibility into the policy system so that it is possible to respond to lessons drawn from one's own experience or that of others' (Fiorino 1999, p. 468).

In particular, adaptive learning is heavily dependent on the depth and accuracy of an agency's statistical database and other information sources. Only with adequate data collection and interpretation can one know how effective or otherwise a particular regulatory strategy has been. There will be a need to establish databases which provide more accurate profiles of individual firms, hazards and industries. Environmental Information Systems have the potential to play a key role here. Work in this area is still in its embryonic stage, but some initiatives (Rapp et al. 2000) suggest it is developing quite rapidly. Of particular note is the Finnish compliance monitoring system (VAHTI), which comprises a database for the input and storage of information on the environmental permits of industry and their discharges into water, emission to air and solid wastes.

Finally, notwithstanding the growing importance of non-state law, it is helpful to return to the role of direct state regulation under a next generation approach. This is because it is important not to lose sight of the residual but nevertheless important role that command and control regulation can and should continue to play in environmental policy. It is only the state which can impose criminal sanctions and the full weight of the law, and only the state which, under statute, may have power of entry into private property to inspect, take samples and gather evidence of illegality more generally. While there may be some circumstances where, as advocates of civil regulation, reflexive regulation and regulatory pluralism would argue, far more can be achieved by various other forms of state and non-state action, this is certainly not the case across the board.

For example, there remain situations where SMEs in particular need the highly specific and concrete guidance that specification standards can provide. And in the case of large companies the most important 'step' changes in environmental performance in industries such as pulp and paper have been achieved through mandated technological change (Gunningham et al. 2003). Nor should it be forgotten that, according to various surveys, the single most important motivator of improved environmental performance is regulation. The more general conclusion, as the US EPA (2000, p. 4) has recognized, is that 'in some cases, nationwide laws and regulations will continue to be the best way to reduce risk. But in others, tailored strategies that involve market based approaches, partnerships, or performance incentives may offer better results at lower costs.'

The broader point is that many less interventionist strategies are far less likely to succeed if they are not underpinned by direct regulation. For example, under reflexive regulation some enterprises may be tempted to develop 'paper systems' and tokenistic responses which 'independent' third party auditors may fail to detect (O'Rourke 2000). However, the threat of sanctions if they fail to deliver on performance targets set by the state will substantially reduce the risk of free riding. Again, there is evidence that information based strategies cannot necessarily replace traditional regulation and enforcement practices but rather that the two instruments work best when they are used in a complementary combination (Foulon et al. 1999). So too in the case of small business, the fear of regulation or its enforcement can be used to good effect to complement other, more innovative approaches.

Once again, what we are witnessing is not the demise of the regulatory state but a regulatory reconfiguration, in which command and control retains a place, albeit no longer at centre stage but rather as a complement to a range of next generation policies and increasingly influential non-state law. But this reconfiguration remains a work in progress. Certainly, our knowledge of what works and why is much greater than it was a decade ago. Nevertheless, the journey to best practice environmental regulation is far from complete. Notwithstanding the considerable promise of the new generation of environmental policy tools, the road to regulatory reform is long and tortuous, and the journey is far from over.

REFERENCES

Antweiler, W. and K. Harrison (1999), 'Environmental Regulation vs Environmental Information: A View from Canada's National Pollutant Release Inventory' (Washington DC: paper presented to the Association for Public Policy Analysis and Management, November).

Bastmeijer, Kees and Jonathan Verschuuren (2005), 'NGO–Business Collaborations and the Law: Sustainability, Limitations of Law and the Changing Relationship between Companies and NGOs', in Istemi Demirag (ed.), *Corporate Social Responsibility, Accountability and Governance*, Sheffield: Greenleaf, pp. 314–329.

Baylis, R., L. Cornnell and A. Flynn (1998), 'Sector Variation and Ecological Modernization: Towards an Analysis at the Level of the Firm', *Business Strategy and the Environment*, **7**, 150–161.

Bendell, Jem (2000), 'Civil Regulation: A New Form of Democratic Governance for the Global Economy', in Jem Bendell (ed.), *Terms of Endearment: Business, NGOs and Sustainable Development*, London: Greenleaf, pp. 239–254.

Brown, H., M. De Jong and T. Lessidrenska (2007), 'Can Global Reporting Initiative Become a Global Institution' (Amsterdam, Holland: paper presented to Conference: Earth Systems Governance: Theories and Strategies for Sustainability, Amsterdam, May, http://www.2007amsterdamconference.org/, accessed 3 June 2007.

Clinton, W.J. and A. Gore Jr (1995), *Reinventing Environmental Regulation*, Washington DC: The White House.

Coglianese, Cary and Jennifer Nash (eds) (2006), *Leveraging the Private Sector*, Washington DC: RFF Press.

Cohen, M.J. (1997), 'Risk Society and Ecological Modernisation', *Futures*, **29** (2), 105–119.

Cullen, Lord (Chairman) (1990), *Piper Alpha Inquiry*, London: HMSO.

Fiorino, D. (1999), 'Rethinking Environmental Regulation: Perspectives from Law and Governance', *Harvard Environmental Law Review*, **23** (2), 441–469.

Foulon, J., P. Lanouie and B. Lapante (1999), *Incentives for Pollution Control: Regulation and Reinventing Environmental Regulation Information* (Washington DC, Policy Research Working Paper, World Bank).

Fung, A. and D. O'Rourke (2000), 'Reinventing Environmental Regulation from the Grassroots Up: Explaining and Expanding the Success of the Toxics Release Inventory', *Environmental Management* **25** (2) (February), 115–127.

Gereffi, Gary, Ronie Garcia-Johnson and Erica Sasser (2001), 'The NGO–Industry Complex', *Foreign Policy*, July/Aug., see http://info.worldbank.org/etools/docs/library/57460/Gereffi.pdf, accessed 20 August 2007.

Gunningham, Neil (2007a), 'Environmental Partnerships in Agriculture; Reflections on the Australian Experience', in Pieter Glasbergen, Frank Biermann and Arthur Mol (eds), *Partnerships, Governance and Sustainable Development*, Cheltenham: Edward Elgar, pp. 115–137.

Gunningham, Neil (2007b), 'Corporate Environmental Responsibility, Law and the Limits of Voluntarism', in Doreen McBarnett, Aurora Voicelescu and Tom Campbell (eds), *The New Corporate Accountability: Corporate Social Responsibility and the Law*, Cambridge: Cambridge University Press, pp. 476–500.

Gunningham, Neil and Peter Grabosky (1998), *Smart Regulation: Designing Environmental Policy*, Oxford: Oxford University Press.

Gunningham, N. and D. Sinclair (1999a), 'Regulatory Pluralism: Designing Environmental Policy Mixes', *Law & Policy*, **21** (1), 49–76.

Gunningham, N. and D. Sinclair (1999b), 'Integrative Regulation: A Principle-Based Approach to Environmental Policy', *Law & Social Inquiry*, **24** (4), 853–896.

Gunningham, Neil and Darren Sinclair (2002), *Leaders & Laggards: Next-Generation Environmental Regulation*, Sheffield: Greenleaf Publishing.

Gunningham, N., P. Grabosky and M. Phillipson (1999), 'Harnessing Third Parties as Surrogate Regulators: Achieving Environmental Outcomes by Alternative Means', *Business Strategy and the Environment*, **8** (4), 211–224.

Gunningham, Neil, Robert A. Kagan and Dorothy Thornton (2003), *Shades of Green: Business, Regulation and Environment*, Stanford, CA: Stanford University Press.

Koch, C. and K. Nielsen (1996), 'Working Environment Regulation: How Reflexive – How Political? A Scandinavian Case' (Lyngby, Denmark: Working Paper, Technical University of Denmark, June).

Long, Frederick and Matthew B. Arnold (1994), *The Power of Environmental Partnerships*, New York: Dryden Press.
Mol, Arthur (1995), *The Refinement of Production*, Utrecht: Van Arkel.
Murphy, D. and J. Bendell (1997), *In the Company of Partners: Business, Environmental Groups and Sustainable Development Post-Rio*, Bristol: Policy Press.
O'Rourke, D. (2000), *Monitoring the Monitors: A Critique of PricewaterhouseCoopers (PWC) Labor Monitoring*, Massachusetts: Department of Urban Studies and Planning, Massachusetts Institute of Technology.
Orts, W.E. (1995), 'Reflexive Environmental Law', *Northwestern University Law Review*, **89** (4), 1227–1340.
Osborne, David and Ted Gaebler (1992), *Reinventing Government: How the Entrepreneurial Spirit Is Transforming the Public Sector*, Boston: Addison-Wesley.
Parker, C. (2000), 'Summary of the Scholarly Literature on Regulatory Compliance', Annex to 'Reducing the Risk of Policy Failure: Challenges for Regulatory Compliance' (Paris, OECD, Working Paper 77).
Poncelet, E. (1999), 'In Search of the "Win–Win": Possibilities and Limitations of Multi-stakeholder Environmental Partnerships', Greening of Industry Conference, Best Paper Proceedings.
Poncelet, E. (2001), 'A Kiss Here and a Kiss There: Conflict and Collaboration in Environmental Partnerships', *Environmental Management*, **27** (1), 13–25.
Porter, M. (1991), 'America's green strategy', *Scientific American*, **264**, April, 8.
Porter, Michael (1998), 'How Competitive Forces Shape Strategy', in Henry Mintzberg, Joseph B. Quinn and Sumatra Goshal (eds), *The Strategy Process*, Bath: Prentice Hall, pp. 60–69.
Rapp, M., G. Wolschner and W. Hafner (eds) (2000), 'European Union Network on the Implementation and Enforcement of Environmental Law Conference on Environmental Compliance and Enforcement' (11–13 October, Villach, Austria: Klagenfurt, Flatschacherstrasse 70, November, Final Report).
Rees, Joseph (1988), *Reforming the Workplace: A Study of Self-Regulation in Occupational Safety*, Philadelphia, PA: University of Pennsylvania Press.
Reinhardt, Forest L. (2000), *Down to Earth: Applying Business Principles to Environmental Management*, Boston, MA: Harvard Business School Press.
Schmidheiny, Stephan (1992), *Changing Courses*, Cambridge, MA: MIT Press.
Smart, Bruce (ed.) (1992), *Beyond Compliance: A New Industry View of the Environment*, Washington DC: World Resources Institute.
Teubner, G. (1983), 'Substantive and Reflexive Elements in Modern Law', *Law & Society Review*, **17** (2), 239–286.
Teubner, Gunther, Lindsay Farmer and Declan Murphy (eds) (1994), *Environmental Law and Ecological Responsibility: The Concept and Practice of Ecological Self-organization*, Chichester, New York: Wiley.
US EPA (2000), *A Decade of Progress: Innovation at the Environmental Protection Agency*, Washington DC: EPA Innovation Annual Report.

8. The hardness of soft law in the United Kingdom: state and non-state regulatory activities related to nanotechnological development

Bärbel Dorbeck-Jung and Marloes van Amerom

1. INTRODUCTION

In the past three years regional and national regulators have become aware of the huge governance challenges of emerging nanotechnologies.[1] Nanotechnologies refer to technologies of the very small, with dimensions in the range of one to a hundred nanometers.[2] Although there is much concern about the risks of these new technologies, in most countries no specific legal action has been taken to anticipate potential damage to health, safety and the environment, and consumer protection. According to a recent OECD review of regulatory development on the safety of manufactured nanomaterials, the common regulatory approach includes standardization, research and development funding activities, the collection of evidence on nanotechnological risks, evaluations of existing legislative structures and the promotion of codes of conduct.[3] Presently, soft law is emerging at various levels of nanotechnological regulation. By soft law we understand rules of conduct which in principle have no legally binding force, but which nevertheless have effects in legal practice (Snyder 1995).

Soft law is playing an important role in non-state law, as well as in the state's legislature. At the European level, for example, the European Commission's Action Plan on Nanosciences and Nanotechnologies sets out certain rules for the regulation of nanotechnologies.[4] Other interesting examples of soft law are the voluntary reporting schemes on nanotechnological properties and risks that have been introduced in the United Kingdom and the United States. These two countries are also establishing best practices and codes of conduct. At the international level, the International Organization for Standardization (ISO) is developing a business plan including the standardization of nanotechnologies. Considering these regulatory activities we assume that soft law can be of great importance for legal regulation related to nanotechnologies. This is why we speak of the 'hardness' of this policy instrument.

In this chapter, the interplay between soft and hard law in emerging nanotechnological regulation will be explored. By focusing on the relations between soft and hard elements in public/private regulation we transcend the divide between the state's legislature and non-state law. In view of the central question of this volume we will examine the role that soft law plays in regulation related to nanotechnological development and the role that is 'left' for hard law. We also discuss the consequences that the use of soft law may have for the legislature's role. What are the 'weak' aspects of soft law and do they call for compensation by hard law facilities?

To answer these questions we first explore the challenges that nanotechnological development poses to public regulation, including specific risk problems, conflicting interests and undesirable lock-ins of technological development. By discussing these regulatory challenges we address the need for transcending the state law/non-state law divide. Secondly, an analytical frame will be set out. How can soft law be located in relation to the state's legislature and non-state law? What are the capacities and deficiencies of soft law and how can we analyse the interplay between soft and hard law? Thirdly, we describe how nanotechnological regulation has been evolved in the United Kingdom. The UK has been selected as a case study because it is one of the key players in this regulatory field. In our analysis we explore the interplay between soft and hard law and the roles that are attributed to them. We discuss 'weak' aspects of soft law in terms of problems related to effectiveness and legitimacy. This leads to conclusions regarding the compensation by hard law facilities.

2. REGULATORY CHALLENGES OF NANOTECHNOLOGICAL DEVELOPMENT

2.1 Nanotechnological Risk Problems

From the initial outset of technological governance, regulation has been confronted with particular problems, which refer to the uncertainty, complexity and ambiguity of technological risks (Lyall and Tait 2005; Sørensen and Williams 2002). When new technologies are emerging, potential hazards usually cannot be determined exactly. How can we regulate an emerging technology when the subjects of regulation cannot yet be identified? Complex technological development increases the uncertainty of risks. In the context of technological risk governance the notion of ambiguity denotes the variability of (reasonable) interpretations of risks, as well as the variability of normative evaluation with respect to the tolerability of observed effects on a given value or norm (International Risk Governance Council (IRGC) 2006, p. 34). In the context of pluralistic values and norms the importance of the values and norms involved is controversial. Stakeholders can diverge about whether assumed impacts of technology violate or meet predefined values. In this regard regulatory challenges concern the determination of risk interpretation and tolerability of risks.

At present there is much speculation, but hardly any certainty about nanotechnological risks (Maynard 2006). Due to the complexity and speed of nanotechnological development, there is hardly any certainty about the nature of the particular evolution paths (IRGC 2006, p. 34). More certainty is only expected after about two decades. The assessment of the social, ethical and legal consequences relies more on hypothetical assumptions than on rigorous scientific analysis.[5] It is expected that applications of nanotechnologies will penetrate and permeate nearly all sectors and spheres of life, and will be accompanied by immense changes in the social, economic, ethical and ecological spheres (IRGC 2006, p. 19). With regard to the impact of nanotechnologies, there is some evidence that downsized material structures will lead to surprising and unpredicted, or unpredictable, effects. Referring to similar cases (i.e. the asbestos case and drug disasters) many social scientists expect that nanotechnology will have far-reaching effects on our health, environment, safety and constitutional freedoms (Macnaghten et al. 2005). Several scientific studies have experimentally shown that there are human health risks, for example that large doses of nanoparticles can cause cells and organs to demonstrate a toxic response (European Environment Agency 2001; Oberdörster et al. 2004; Maynard 2006; IRGC 2006, pp. 15, 41). In addition, the higher surface reactivity and surface-area-to-volume ratio of nanopowders appears to increase the risk of dust explosion. It is expected that the impact of nanoparticles on the environment will be significant because of their potential for bioaccumulation and persistence (Colvin 2003).[6]

2.2 Conflicting Interests and Undesirable Lock-Ins of Technological Development

Nanotechnological regulation has to cope with potentially conflicting constitutionally recognized interests. In nanotechnological development the constitutionally recognized interests of health, environment, employment, occupational safety, privacy, equality, property, national security, scientific research and technological development are involved (EC 2004, p. 20; 2005, p. 10).[7] For example, in the manufacturing process of potentially highly beneficial nanoproducts, employees are exposed to nanoparticles, which may be harmful to their health. In this example, society's and industry's interests in technological innovation may be conflicting with an employee's interest in occupational safety.

To balance recognized interests may be rather difficult, when technological development becomes entrenched (Sørensen 2002, p. 23). When an area of technological development is getting locked in, other desirable development paths may be excluded (Rip 2006a). Entrenched or locked-in technologies pose a particular challenge to public regulation, because the space for regulation becomes quite limited and difficult to extend. Regarding the promise of huge profit-making that is ascribed to nanotechnological products it is likely that paths which strongly and primarily support nanotechnological development will be taken (Whitman 2006). Public regulation could then be confronted with difficulties or impossibilities of bringing protective measures into the design and application of technology, particularly when safeguards imply large implementation and compliance costs, and when they delay technological development. In this situation we are facing the difficulty that an enormous effort is required to break through locked-in technology and to open alternative paths of development.

What are the implications of these regulatory challenges for the relations between the state's legislature and non-state law? The characteristics of nanotechnological risk problems, conflicting interests and undesirable lock-ins of nanotechnological development indicate that there is a need for collaboration between public and private regulators. Public regulators depend on the industry's and academics' knowledge of nanotechnological characteristics and risk problems in establishing regulation, while the industry's preparedness to invest is dependent on a predictable institutional structure that can be provided by the state's legislature. In nanotechnological regulation state law and non-state law are intertwined.

3. FRAME OF ANALYSIS

3.1 Soft Law within Non-state Law and State Law

Above we mentioned Francis Snyder's definition of soft law. 'Soft law' is a very general term, and it has been used to refer to a variety of features. It has been discovered in international law (Kindred et al. 1993; Cutler 2003, p. 23; Hondius 1984; Tammes 1983) and international relations theory (Abbot and Snidal 2000). Soft law has drawn growing attention in the debate about global law (Teubner 1997) and new EU governance (Trubeck et al. 2006, p. 66; Trubek and Trubek 2005). The only common thread among the various accounts is that while soft law instruments have effects in legal practice they are not formally legally binding (Trubeck et al. 2006, p. 65). According to *narrow* approaches, soft law comprises either rules of conduct *or* principles and values, while a *broad* view includes rules of conduct *and* principles and values.[8] To reduce the complexity of our inquiry a narrow approach will be used. Where soft law is identified and assessed the focus lies on rules of conduct that can be derived from policy documents and regulatory practice.[9]

Soft law is more than non-state law. It is produced and enforced by non-state actors and state actors.[10] Public and private organizations deploy similar and different instruments of soft law. Instruments of public soft law that regulators may use are action plans, mission statements, communications, opinions and guidelines. Examples of soft law that private organizations may deploy are action plans, mission statements, guidelines, standards and codes of conduct.[11] Soft law can be found in all stages of the regulatory life cycle, including the stages of norm development, implementation, control, enforcement and conflict solution (Dorbeck-Jung et al. 2006). Referring to stages of the regulatory life cycle, Senden distinguishes between various categories of soft law instruments (Senden 2004, pp. 111–113). In this view soft law has an autonomous steering role, as well as the role of preparing the ground for hard law and contributing to the interpretation of hard law.

3.2 What is the Hardness and Softness of Law About?

Why is soft law used in regulatory practice? Which benefits are expected of its use compared with hard law? Proponents of soft law are primarily building on critical remarks on the effectiveness and efficiency of hard law (Trubek et al. 2006, pp. 67, 74, 75, 78; Trubeck and Trubeck 2005; Cutler 2003, pp. 23–25; Abbot and Snidal 2000; Teubner 1997, p. 21). In their view, the role of soft law is to improve the effectiveness of public regulation. They assume that soft law is more effective because, unlike hard law:

1. It can cope with situations of uncertainty, which may demand constant experimentation and adjustment in allowing minimum levels of adherence to be established and formalize progressive advancement towards higher standards. By experimentation progressively more coherent regulation can be developed.
2. It is capable of responding to the demands for frequent change of norms to achieve optimal results ('flexibility').
3. Its capacity of adaptation to changing circumstances makes it more suited to the unification of law.

4. It allows a range of possibilities for interpretation and trial and error processes without the constraints of uniform rules and threat of sanction. This makes soft law relatively resistant to symbolic destruction in the case of deviance. As Teubner put it: 'Stability comes from softness' (Teubner 1997, p. 21).
5. It allows for diversity in regulation, tailored to the needs of specific circumstances (since the forms of soft law are not strictly fixed).
6. It allows for simplicity and speed of regulation (since the procedure for establishing soft law is simple and not formalized).
7. It allows for regulatory sovereignty and autonomy and it supports the internalization of norms, as actors usually will accept rules of conduct they agreed upon, making it easier to achieve support for its implementation ('social basis of legitimacy').
8. It reduces negotiation costs, because non-binding norms lower the stakes for the parties involved.

According to these assumptions, the *hardness of soft law* lies in its capacity for openness, flexibility and simplicity, which is expected to foster the coherence, unification, stability and diversity of rules of conduct, as well as speed of regulation, empirical legitimacy and low negotiation costs. Regarding the regulatory challenges of nanotechnological development, soft law seems to be well equipped to cope with the uncertainty, complexity and ambiguity of nanotechnological risk problems, because it allows for reflective learning processes. Unlike hard law, soft law seems to be capable of facilitating constant experimentation and adjustment of regulation in response to new insights into nanotechnological risks.

However, in scientific debates on soft law its presumed benefits have been countered and contrasted with particular deficiencies. Opponents of soft law argue that, unlike hard law:

1. Soft law lacks the clarity and precision needed to provide predictability and a reliable framework for action that is essential for investment and innovation.
2. Soft law is not robust in its ability to constrain behaviour through credible threats of enforcement.
3. Soft law cannot forestall 'races to the bottom' in social policy. Compromises will lead to lower quality, efficacy and safety standards.
4. Soft law bypasses basic requirements of legitimacy of regulation (among them the requirements of legality, due process and accountability).
5. Soft law implies high transaction costs because of the constant adaptation and change of rules of conduct.

According to these statements, the *weakness of soft law* is related to deficiencies in providing acceptability, effectiveness and efficiency of regulation because of its unpredictability, unreliability, poor due process and accountability facilities, as well as low level of safeguards and high transaction costs. In view of these possible drawbacks special attention should be paid to the enforcement of soft law related to nanotechnological regulation and to the various aspects of legitimate regulation. Thus, while soft law poses many opportunities, it also represents limitations. Regarding the regulatory challenges of nanotechnological development hard law seems to be better equipped to cope with undesirable lock-ins of technological development, which may require legal sanctions to break through. Moreover, hard law seems to evoke another kind of certainty than soft law. Legal certainty aims to provide predictability and by doing so often can stimulate technological innovation and investment, while soft law deals with uncertainty by providing the flexibility necessary to allow for renegotiation and modification. Hence, a first conclusion is that a 'smart' combination of soft and hard law may optimize the effectiveness and legitimacy of nanotechnological regulation (Gunningham and Grabovsky 1998, p. 95). Where beneficial capacities of soft law are combined with beneficial capacities of hard law, optimal effectiveness and legitimacy can be expected.

3.3 A Constructivist Perspective

Our study of the interplay between soft and hard law in emerging nanotechnological governance refers to basic notions of social constructivism.[12] Nanotechnological governance is conceived as a 'project under construction'. Following this approach, the role of soft law will be explored in the context of the social structure that evolves in nanotechnological governance.[13] A genesis of the present social structure related to nanotechnological regulation can provide rich insights into the interdependencies of soft and hard law, as well as into their strengths and weaknesses regarding legitimate, effective and efficient regulation. These insights may also contribute to a theory of hard and soft law which social theory is calling for (Trubek et al. 2006, p. 91).

According to social constructivism, the social world is constructed by intersubjectively and collectively meaningful structures and processes. Social beings ('actors') are constituted by the social structure in which they interact.[14] They interact in the context of power relations, in which influence and change can build on certain pressures. Actors are interrelated through autonomous and coherent sets of rules, principles and values ('institutions') (Dorbeck-Jung 2003; Dorbeck-Jung and De Jong 2000, pp. 113–114; De Jong and Dorbeck-Jung 1997, p. 100), which are communicated to them by the 'significant others' (Berger and Luckman 1991, p. 66). By 'significant others' we understand a community of actors, which exert influence on regulatory activities.[15] Concurrently, by interacting in daily practice social actors are creating, reproducing and modifying rules, values and principles. Consequently, social structure is viewed as both a medium for, and an outcome of, the practices it repeatedly organizes (Giddens 1984, p. 25). Hence, actors and structures are regarded as two interdependent sets of phenomena, a duality. As a consequence, structure is not equated with constraint, but is always seen as both constraining and enabling. In social constructivism, the focus lies on how institutions facilitate constitutive processes such as learning, socialization, argumentation and persuasion. A basic assumption underpinning this theory is that these constitutive processes, with sustained interaction over the course of time, eventually result in the creation of new rules, values and principles based on intersubjective knowledge.

In the social constructivist view law is regarded as a broad social phenomenon deeply embedded in the practices, beliefs and traditions of societies, and shaped by interaction among societies (Finnemore and Toope 2001). Hard and soft law are created, reproduced and changed in the event of constitutive events, which comprise or lead to regulatory acts. Constructivism draws attention to the regulatory activities of policy professionals and of local, national and transnational communities, which facilitate or constrain the development and dissemination of social structures.[16]

Following the social constructivist approach, our case study tries to illuminate the multi-layered interactions between the regulatory structure, constitutive events, significant actors and regulatory activities. The exploration of the role of soft and hard law in UK nanotechnological regulation starts with an overview of the current regulatory structure. This overview addresses rules of conduct, relevant principles and values. Values refer to common moral judgments ('common public concerns'), as well as to judgments about the rightness of nanotechnological development ('legal and policy values'). We explore the development of activities leading to the role of constitutive events, significant actors and regulatory activities.

4. EMERGING NANOTECHNOLOGICAL REGULATION IN THE UNITED KINGDOM[17]

4.1 Overview of the Current Regulatory Structure

Rules of conduct

In the United Kingdom no specific *legislation* has been established with regard to nanotechnologies. In an overview of the framework of current regulation affecting the development and marketing of nanomaterials, 86 examples of current legislation have been identified.[18] These examples have been grouped, according to their scope and purpose, into the categories of introduction/notification, health and safety, producer responsibility–product quality and safety, consumer protection, environmental protection and waste. Rules of conduct laid down in *soft law* instruments can be found in:

- the recommendations of the Report of the Royal Society and the Royal Academy of Engineering (RS/RAEng) 'Nanoscience and Nanotechnologies: Opportunities and Uncertainties';[19]
- the response of UK Government to these recommendations;
- the Voluntary Reporting Scheme for industry and research organizations to provide Government with information on potential risks;
- the Government's research programme and its programme of stakeholder and public engagement;
- the responses to the Council for Science and Technology's Call for Evidence regarding the evaluation of the progress of regulatory action;
- the reviews of the adequacy of the current regulatory regimes of the Health and Safety Executive, the Office of Science and Innovation and the Department of Trade and Industry;
- the regulatory work of the Nanotechnology Industries Association (NIA);
- the regulatory work of the Nanotech Governance Code Initiative;
- public and private standardization activities;
- the minutes of the meetings of the various coordination groups and advisory committees.

Furthermore, UK policy on nanotechnologies refers also to rules of conduct that are included in the European Commission's Communication on Nanosciences and Nanotechnologies (COM(2005)243 final) and the Opinion of the European Economic and Social Committee on this Communication (INT/277).

Principles

UK regulatory initiatives are guided by three main principles. UK policy documents related to nanotechnological governance mention the principle of responsible development. Furthermore, UK policy on nanotechnologies refers also to rules of conduct that are included in the European Commission's Communication on Nanosciences and Nanotechnologies (EC 2005, p. 11), and to the opinion of the European Economic and Social Committee on the EC Communication on Nanosciences and

Nanotechnologies (EC 2005 INT/277). Another relevant principle is the precautionary principle, which is a highly debated notion in international, European and national politics on nanotechnologies.[20] According to the EU Communication on the Precautionary Principle (COM(2000)1 final), this principle points out that scientific uncertainty about technological risks is no reason for inaction if there might be immense adverse effects. Nevertheless, its implementation in the UK is guided by an evidence-based approach (Garrod, interview, 2007). Finally, the principle of 'shared responsibility' shapes governmental policy. This notion entails that in order to be successful, the responsible development of nanotechnology needs not to be solely the task of government, but also of industry and other relevant stakeholders (Garrod, interview, 2007).

Policy goals, legal values and public concern

Main objectives of the UK Government's regulatory measures are to safeguard responsible nanotechnological development and to shape international global development in the context of the benefits of nanotechnology. International engagement and national coordination are the cornerstones of the regulatory strategy. In the words of the UK Government's 'Response to the Council for Science and Technology's Call for Evidence' (Defra 2007) the overall objective is that 'the UK remains at the forefront of the development of these new technologies'. According to the consulted policy documents, health, safety, environmental and (more general) consumer rights, as well as property rights and scientific freedom, are the crucial legal values at stake. In line with the recommendations of the Royal Society and the Royal Academy of Engineering a main focus of the UK Government's work is to gather the necessary evidence to enable appropriate controls to be determined. The UK Government considers that it is essential for the emerging regulatory regimes to be internationally agreed and harmonized to realize the benefits of nanotechnologies more quickly and cost effectively. Public concern about the benefits and risks of nanotechnologies should also be taken seriously into account. In this regard the UK Government expressed its willingness to learn from the BSE crisis and the regulation process related to biotechnology (Oakedene Hollins 2007, p. 79).

4.2 Constitutive Events, Significant Actors

The emerging UK social structure related to nanotechnologies has been constituted by certain events that took place in the UK, the EU and other countries. The willingness of the British Government to engage with nanotechnological regulation was triggered by the publication of Prince Charles' alleged nanotech views and fears in British newspapers in April

2003.[21] When earlier in 2003 the Better Regulation Taskforce recommended that the British Government create nanotechnological regulatory controls, in line with the precautionary principle, it failed to follow up this recommendation. However, taking up the publication of the Prince of Wales' concerns, a debate on nanotechnological risks and regulation emerged in British newspapers and other societal spheres, resulting in calls for appropriate regulation (Van Amerom and Rip 2006). The UK Government initially responded with risk denial, and noted once more that existing regulation sufficed to protect the public from possible risks of nanotechnologies. Nevertheless, following ongoing debates on nanotechnological risks (Anderson et al. 2005), the British Government commissioned the RS/RAEng to investigate the opportunities and uncertainties of nanoscience and nanotechnologies.

Regulatory institutions emerged in reaction to the conclusions and recommendations of the RS/RAEng Committee's report, which was published in 2004.[22] It stated that nanotechnology, in particular nanoparticles, could represent considerable risks, highlighting several potential health and environmental risks of free engineered nanomaterials, including in relation to occupational safety. The committee also set priorities for research, a main conclusion being that the overall lack of available scientific data on health and safety and environmental hazards arising from free nanoparticles hindered the development of an effective UK policy in this area. A need for stronger public 'upstream engagement' was also identified. In its Response to this report the UK Government launched an action plan including regulatory measures (2005).[23] This plan can also be regarded as a response to the European Commission's Action Plan related to nanosciences and nanotechnologies, which was published in the same year. Another constitutive event was the 2005 formation of the Nanotechnology Industries Association (NIA), which has been active in standardization, best practices and other soft law activities, and which is supported through government funding. Early in 2006, the Royal Society, Insight Investment and the NIA founded the Nanotech Governance Code Initiative. At the end of 2006, the UK Government sponsored the Safe Nano initiative. Facilitated by the Institute of Occupational Medicine it offers industry information on how to develop and handle nanomaterials safely, through a website and consultancy services (Aitken, interview, 2007).

4.3 Soft Law Activities of State and Non-state Actors

In line with the cornerstones of the UK regulatory policy, regulatory activities refer to evidence gathering, metrology, characterization and standardization, regulatory review, funding of research and development, public and international engagement, and the coordination of regulatory activities. To reduce the complexity of our analysis we focus on major soft law activities of state and non-state actors. These regulatory activities mainly concern evidence gathering, standardization and a specific nanotech governance code. With regard to hard law, 86 pieces of current legislation apply to nanomaterials. As noted above, the UK Government has not taken specific legal action to cope with the regulatory gaps that have been discussed in the reviews of current regulations.[24] According to the UK Government, no significant gaps have been detected. In its view, the nano-specific regulatory problems which have been identified with regard to thresholds, definitions, scope and interpretation of current regulations must primarily be solved by soft law activities of international standard setting and evidence gathering.

Evidence gathering the Voluntary Reporting Scheme and risk assessment schemes[25]

Regarding evidence gathering the Voluntary Reporting Scheme (VRS) for engineered nanoscale materials is an important soft law instrument. Its purpose is to develop a better understanding of the properties and characteristics of 'free' engineered nanoscale materials, so as to enable a consideration of potential hazards and risks and to make decisions about necessary controls to protect human health and the environment. More specifically, the scheme is expected to deliver information through which the applicability of existing legislation can be tested. It is being run by the Department for Environment, Food and Rural Affairs (Defra) and will operate until September 2008. From March 2006 to June 2006 the proposed scheme was under consultation. In this process 120 relevant stakeholders were addressed[26] and a workshop was held. Following some new input Defra has modified the proposal. The scheme refers to free and deliberately engineered nanoscale materials (dimensions to 200 nm). It is targeted at any company or organization involved in manufacturing, using, importing or managing wastes consisting of those nanoscale materials. Data submission follows a certain format that has been set out in the annex to the scheme. However, the format is not mandatory. The scheme is subject to six-monthly reviews. Quarterly updates are made public, and a six-monthly summary report was published in Spring 2007, at which time the scheme was subject to its first review.

According to the quarterly reports covering the period 22 September 2006 to 22 June 2007 nine submissions were received (seven from industry and two from academia). Fear of disclosure of confidential commercial data on the side of companies is a main constraining factor (Donaldson, interview, 2007; Stark, interview, 2007). The UK's Freedom of Information Act and environmental regulations legally oblige Defra to disclose information on its policy plans and schemes where asked to do so in writing by third parties. In the first review of the scheme, the Advisory Committee for Hazardous Substances also felt that the current low level of response to the scheme, and the variable quality and relevance of data submitted, were due, in part at least, to shortcomings in the scheme guidance, particularly in defining how the data submitted would be used and what data might be relevant. The committee has recommended some changes to aid clarity in the data reporting form. In its response, Defra stressed that these recommendations will be taken forward. The European Nanotechnology Trade Alliance has offered to act as a 'broker', through whom submissions to the scheme may be made to afford anonymity to anyone wishing not to disclose company, personal or other details in their submission (Stark, interview, 2007). Additional support for the VRS comes from the NIA, which is offering its members assistance with the completion of the required data sheet.

To provide insights into nanotechnological risks other soft law instruments refer to the methodology of risk assessment. One of the corporate members of the Nanotechnology Industries Association has developed *Oxonica*.[27] This is a Proforma Scheme for a Prelimary Risk Assessment of Nanoparticulate Materials. It is characterized as a 'proposed ideal regulatory system' to evaluate the risks of nanomaterials. It is based upon a number of parameters (among which are the potential for exposure and intrinsic biological reactivity). *NanoSURE* is another scheme the NIA has developed for the precautionary assessment of nanotechnology-enabled products.

Standardization and metrology

Regarding the soft law instrument of standardization, UK Government and industry are displaying various regulatory activities. The UK is also playing a prominent role in the development of international standards related to nanotechnologies. More specifically, regulatory activities concern the development of standards related to the vocabulary of nanoparticles and the strong support for nano-standardization activities of the EU, the OECD, the ISO and the International Electrotechnical Commission. Moreover, the British Standards Institute is working on a Good Practice Guide on handling and disposal of free engineered nanomaterials, a guide to specifying nanomaterials and a Good Practice Guide for labelling of nanoparticles. These guides will be submitted to the ISO as base documents for standards development. According to the UK Government, standards for nanotechnologies are important, because they will help to ensure that nanotechnology is developed and commercialized in an open, sage and responsible manner by providing agreed ways of naming, describing and specifying nanotechnological properties, as well as of measuring and testing nanoproducts.

With regard to metrology, private actors are developing measurement protocols to detect and measure the most important class of nanoparticles. According to the UK Government, well-characterized reference materials are crucial in order to be able to interpret studies and to compare results with other experiments carried out in laboratories across the world. From the toxicological point of view, well-characterized materials are essential to know exactly the exposure of the cell, tissue or animal, in order to identify the most appropriate dose metric for a given type of nanomaterial, and thus interpret the results in a meaningful way.

Nanotech Governance Code[28]

The Nanotech Governance Code is a soft law instrument which is being developed by non-state actors. To aid the development of responsible nanotechnology the Royal Society and the Royal Academy of Engineering, Insight Investment and the Nanotechnology Industries Association are drafting a code of good practice for business involved in nanotechnologies. The governance principles include an overall commitment to responsible nanotechnology, as well as guidance on research and testing, workplace facilities, product information, corporate disclosure and public engagement. The code is intended to be voluntary. The adoption and implementation of principles will be monitored through a 'comply or explain' mechanism (e.g. companies report annually on how they comply with the code). A first version of the code was ready in September 2007. After a period of international consultation and amendment the final version was launched in February 2008.

Funding

Although there is no direct government funding available for nanotechnology risk research, to the dismay of the Council for Science and Technology and the Royal Society (Donaldson, interview, 2007; Green, interview, 2007), nanotechnology risk research has been identified as a priority by the Medical Research Council. In 2008, the Department of Innovation, Universities and Skills, while not creating a separate funding source for nanotechnology risk research, will increase funding for nanotech risk research through the research councils (Garrod, interview, 2007).

5. ANALYSIS

5.1 The Roles of Soft and Hard Law, State and Non-state Actors

In the UK's regulatory activities related to nanotechnologies, autonomous steering seems to be the main role of soft law. Soft law, not hard law, is used as a means to support the UK regulatory strategy with its focus on evidence gathering, standardization, public dialogue, funding of research and development, and international and national collaboration. Since soft law has not primarily been identified as a means to prepare legislation, we assume that the focus lies on its autonomous steering capacity. Evidently, the qualities of soft law are well suited for the current stage of nanotechnological development, in which huge profits are expected and technological risks are uncertain. Regarding the UK objective to remain at the forefront of nanotechnological development, the focus on open, flexible and informal regulatory instruments is understandable.

However, in the case of UK regulatory activities related to nanotechnological development, the steering role of soft law is only partly autonomous. In the examples of the voluntary self-reporting scheme and standardization soft law functions as a means to prepare the ground for legislation. These regulatory activities are also intended to support legislation and to deliver information about nanotechnological properties and risks, through which the applicability of existing legislation can be tested. The regulatory frame of the voluntary self-reporting scheme the UK Government has set leaves room for regulatory activities of non-state actors. According to Defra's policy, this regulatory space will, however, be restricted if the scheme is deemed not to have met its objectives.[29] Regulatory autonomy seems to be present in the case of the Nanotech Governance Code, measurement protocols and risk assessment schemes, which are developed by non-state actors. Even in these examples there are interdependencies with public regulation, which are indicated by public funding of the NIA's regulatory activities and the attention of the initiators of the Nanotech Governance Code, who are eager to stress that their regulatory activities are not intended to replace legislation.[30] State and non-state are extensively collaborating in UK nanotech regulatory activities. The UK case is an interesting example of co-evolutionary governance in which regulatory structures evolve in processes of collaboration and mutual shaping of state and non-state actors (Rip 2006a). It nicely illustrates the constructive perspective we discussed above.

What is the role of hard law and state actors in UK nanotech regulation? In the current regulatory stage hard law seems to be in the background. It is primarily viewed as a constraint to desirable innovation. It is intended to be used only where 'hard' evidence of harmful effects has been proved. As regards legislation, the UK Government has taken an incremental approach. This means that existing legislative structures are used to the maximum, reviewed and are amended only where regulatory gaps have been detected. According to this approach, hard law is viewed as a steering instrument in a later stage of nanotechnological development, in which there is more certainty about the properties and risks of nanotechnologies.

Considering the UK focus on enabling technological innovation, it is likely that in the future development of nanotechnologies the focus will still lie on soft law of state and non-state actors to keep the regulatory structures open and flexible. It will depend on such factors as the kind of hazards that will be detected, public concern and the power of stakeholders whether the regulation of nanotechnologies will be entrusted to soft or hard law.

5.2 Hardness or Weakness of Soft Law?

In the introduction to this chapter we related the 'hardness' of soft law to the regulatory focus of the UK's steering activities related to nanotechnologies. At a first glance, soft law seems to be of great importance in the current UK regulatory structure. In the regulatory activities of the past years only soft law instruments have been used. On closer observation, however, we realize that there is much legislation that is effective with regard to nanotechnologies. In the regulatory review of the Department of Trade and Industry 86 examples of current legislation were identified. According to the review, this regulatory framework will remain of great importance, even if it has to be adapted to the properties and implications of nanomaterials. Additionally, if the EU chemicals regulations (REACH[31]) are extended to nanomaterials, this legislation could be relevant in the future.

Regarding the assumptions about the hardness of soft law we mentioned in the second section, the case study indicates that soft law seems to be better equipped to cope with the current uncertainties of technological development, nanotechnological properties and risk problems. As the regulation process around the voluntary reporting scheme shows, soft law does allow for experimentation and adjustment to develop progressively more effective and coherent regulation. This instrument, however, also indicates the weakness of soft law. Above we saw that by now nine submissions have been received. According to some critical accounts, the voluntary scheme will not be effective because of the open character of the data-submitting format and the voluntariness of data submission. As interests of commercial confidentiality and intellectual property seem to be strong in this case, it is questionable whether soft law will be appropriate to provide reliable insights into the risks and properties of nanotechnologies. If the voluntary scheme is deemed not to have met its objectives, the UK Government will probably revert to the 'hardness' of hard law by imposing compulsory measures.

Considering the conflicts with secrecy interests we doubt that soft law, as proponents of soft law assume, generally supports the internalization of norms. Considering the great amount of time that the regulation of the voluntary reporting scheme has already taken up without being completed, it is questionable whether soft law allows for much more speed than hard law, especially in cases in which contradictory interests have to be accommodated. Regarding the deficiencies of legitimacy opponents ascribe to soft law, the early stage of regulatory activities allows only for some preliminary remarks. Obviously, the principle of legality is bypassed in the UK focus on soft law facilities. It is not yet clear whether democratic decision-making and control are provided for in current UK nanoregulation. Stakeholder consultation that has been provided in the regulatory process of the self-reporting scheme and in the review of the UK Government's regulatory activities does indicate that there is some participation, notably of industry and academic experts, in regulatory decision-making. Above we saw that much information on UK Government action related to nanotechnologies is published on various websites, which are easy to access. This is why we assume that transparency of the outcomes of regulatory activities is provided. It remains to be seen, however, whether these information disclosures are effective to empower stakeholders to participate and to control regulatory decision-making and whether they support the acceptance of soft law.

6. CONCLUSION

According to our analysis, soft law *and* hard law are important in nanoregulation. To cope with undesirable lock-ins and potential risk problems that may accompany nanotechnological development, complementary roles of soft and hard law seem to be appropriate. Nanotechnological regulation is faced with difficult and potentially contradictory imperatives. Public regulation is entitled to enable technological innovation, but by the same token must protect constitutional rights. Hence, the regulation of nanotechnological development calls for emerging hybridity of soft and hard law.[32] Regarding the deficiencies of soft law, our case study indicates that hard law can be useful to support the effectiveness of soft law instruments (like the voluntary reporting scheme), particularly in the case of strong and contradictory interests. In the example of the voluntary reporting scheme, hard law can also compensate for the lack of precision of soft law. Due to the characteristics of legal certainty, hard law can provide predictability and a reliable framework for action that are essential for investment and technological innovation. With regard to the principles of legality and sovereignty of Parliament, the legitimacy of soft law can only be provided through a 'surrogate' political process (Vos 1999, p. 94). This would require compensatory facilities that include stronger participation of citizens in the regulation process and robust transparency of regulation, as well as increased accountability and effective control of regulators. Hence, the most important issue of future nanotechnological regulation will be whether a 'smart' hybridization of soft and hard law can be achieved.[33] To meet the requirements of effective and legitimate regulation, 'smart' hybridization necessitates regulatory collaboration between state and non-state actors, but also regulatory distance to safeguard the impartiality of regulatory decision-making.

NOTES

1. 'Governance' is conceived of as a broader term than 'regulation' (see, Editors' Introduction to the Journal *Regulation and Governance* (2007), p. 3). Governance is about providing, distributing and regulating. In this view, regulation is conceived of as a large subset of governance that is about steering or controlling the flow of events and behaviour, as opposed to providing and distributing (Black 2002). In this contribution we focus on regulatory activities.
2. See the British Royal Society and the Royal Academy of Engineering's report (2004), available at: www.nanotec.org.uk, accessed 15 May 2007. Nanotechnology is described as an emerging engineering discipline that applies methods from nanoscience to create products. A clear and consistent definition of 'nano' is still missing. Nanotechnology is an interesting example of converging technologies, which connect diverse disciplines of science. In the case of nanotechnology, physics, chemistry, genetics, information and communication technologies, and cognitive sciences are connected.
3. An interesting overview of regulatory action is provided by the OECD Environment Directorate Report on Current Developments/Activities on the Safety of Manufactured Nanomaterials (ENV/JM/MONO (2006) p. 35). The first meeting of the OECD Working Party took place in London, 26–27 October 2006.
4. See Nanoforum, www. nanoforum.org, accessed 15 May 2007.
5. However, recently scientific instruments to assess exposure to engineered nanomaterials in air and water, to evaluate their toxicity and to predict their impact on the environment and human health have been discussed (Maynard 2006).
6. In literature the numbers of estimated existing nanoproducts vary from 300 to 500 (Woodrow Wilson International Center 2006, available at http://www.nanotechproject.org, accessed 15 May 2007; Information Society 2006, available at http://www.innovationsociety.ch, accessed 15 May 2007; Maynard et al. 2006). Although nanotechnology is still in an early stage of development, applications already exist in paints, food additives, cosmetics and other consumer products (Jopp 2003).
7. See note 4.
8. Many accounts of soft law focus on rules of conduct. According to Teubner, soft law is more a law of values and principles than a law of structures and rules (1997, p. 21). Teubner pointed out that in global law rules lose the strategic position they once had as core elements of law. In the switch from structure to process, the central elements of a legal order are communicative events, legal acts and not legal rules (1997, p. 13). In Teubner's view the strength of communicative links between regimes of soft law is essential for the stability of soft law. Stability and a certain normative consistency determine the evolutionary influence of soft law (1997, p. 18). Strong communicative links are produced by coordination and integration activities.
9. This includes rules of conduct that refer to regulatory debates on principles.
10. In this context we refer to public and private regulation. Public regulation is defined as sustained and focused control exercised by a public agency, on the basis of a legislative mandate, over activities that are generally regarded as desirable to society (Selznick 1985, p. 363). By private regulation we understand sustained and focused control of social

conduct and states of affairs exercised by a private organization, on the basis of its statutory mandate.
11. These examples fall into the category of Field A, as described in Chapter 2. Other examples of private soft law may fall into the other Fields.
12. Social constructivists are interested in how social phenomena became what they are (Adler 2002; Searle 1995; Berger and Luckman 1991; van der Veen 1990). As noted by Trubek et al. (2006, p. 75), constructivists have done surprisingly little to engage directly in debates over the merits of soft law and the conditions in which soft law can be effective. Nevertheless, constructivism has much to offer in this regard.
13. It must be noted that for constructivism soft law is not primarily viewed as being 'chosen', but as part of an evolution of the social structure.
14. A social structure is composed of common rules, principles and values (van der Veen 1998). In the broad view, soft law is treated synonymously with the term 'social structure'.
15. Another term we are using is that of a 'stakeholder'. Stakeholders are the group of social beings which is affected by nanotechnological development.
16. According to Mead, a community is defined as 'particular shared bodies of meaning that bind people together' (1934, p. 261). See also Dorbeck-Jung (2000).
17. The case study is based on policy documents and interviews with R. Aitken, Director SafeNano, Institute of Occupational Medicine, Edinburgh, 13 November 2007; K. Donaldson, Professor of Respiratory Toxicology, University of Edinburgh, 31 October 2007; J. Garrod, Science Policy Adviser to the UK Department for Environment, Food and Rural Affairs (DEFRA), London, 9 November 2007; N. Green, Team Leader, Science Policy Section, London, 7 November 2007; P. Hatto, Director of Research, Ionbond Ltd, Durham, 5 November 2007; D. Stark, CEO, ENTA, Glasgow, 19 November 2007.
18. Available at http://www.dti.gov.uk/science, accessed 30 September 2007.
19. Available at http://www.nanotec.org.uk/finalReport.htm, accessed 30 September 2007.
20. See also European Environment Agency (2001); European Commission (2004); Ladeur (2003); Rip (2006b).
21. Prince Charles was alleged by the *Mail on Sunday* (27 April 2003) to have serious concerns over nanotechnologies, because of 'Grey Goo fears', a scenario whereby self-replicating nano-machines consume the entire biosphere (see, Drexler 1986). Greenpeace UK expressed similar concerns.
22. See note 23.
23. Available online at http://www.dti.gpv.uk/science/, accessed 30 September 2007.
24. Several reviews have been commissioned to analyse and document how current regulations accommodate nanoparticles, as well as to identify any significant existing or future likely regulatory gaps, inadequacies or inconsistencies (see, section 4.1).
25. Information about the VRS is available at http://www.defra.gov.uk/environment/nanotech/research/meetings/index.htm, accessed 30 September 2007.
26. Only 37 stakeholders replied.
27. See the website of the NIA (http://www.nanotechnica.co.uk, accessed 30 September 2007).
28. Information about the Nanotech Governance Initiative and the Governance Code is available at http://www.defra.gov.uk/environment/nanotech/research/meetings/index.htm, accessed 30 September 2007.
29. See Update on Defra's Voluntary Reporting Scheme, available at http://www.defra.gov.uk/environment/nanotech/research/meetings/index.htm, accessed 30 September 2007.
30. See The Royal Society's involvement in the development of the code of conduct of industries, available at http://www.defra.gov.uk/environment/nanotech/research/meetings/index.htm, accessed 30 September 2007.
31. Registration, Evaluation, Authorisation and Restriction of Chemicals.
32. See Trubek et al. (2006, p. 93). Following Trubek et al., by 'hybridity' combinations of hard and soft law are understood.
33. In this context we refer to the idea of 'smart' regulation (Gunningham and Grabovsky 1998).

REFERENCES

Abbott, K. and D. Snidal (2000), 'Hard and Soft Law in International Governance', *International Organization*, **54**, 421–422.
Adler, E. (2002), 'Constructivism and International Relations Theory', in W. Carlsnaes, T. Risse and B. Simmons (eds), *Handbook of International Relations*, London: Sage Publications, pp. 93–107.
Anderson, A., S. Allan, A. Petersen and C. Wilkinson (2005), 'The Framing of Nanotechnologies in the British Newspaper Press', *Science Communication*, **27** (2), 200–220.
Berger, L. and Th. Luckman (1991), *The Social Construction of Reality*, London: Penguin Books.
Black, J. (2002), 'Critical Reflection on Regulation', *CARR Discussion Paper Series*, 4 (London: The London School of Economics and Political Science).
Colvin, V.L. (2003), 'The potential environmental impact of engineered nanomaterials', *Nature Biotechnology*, **21** (10), 1166–1170.
Cutler, A.C. (2003), *Private Power and Global Authority. Transnational Merchant Law in the Global Political Economy*, Cambridge: Cambridge University Press.
Defra (2007), 'Response to the Council for Science and Technology's call for evidence', www.defra.gov.uk, accessed 27 February 2007.
De Jong, H.M. and B.R. Dorbeck-Jung (1997), *Jurisdiche staatsleer*, Bussum: Coutinho, p. 100.
Dorbeck-Jung, B.R. (2000), 'Overtuigende wetgevingskwaliteit', in B. van Klink and W. Witteveen (eds), *De overtuigende wetgever*, Deventer: W.E.J. Tjeenk Willink, pp. 87–104.
Dorbeck-Jung, B.R. (2003), *Beelden over de wetgevingsadvisering van de Raad van State*, Den Haag: Boom Juridische uitgevers.
Dorbeck-Jung, B.R. and H.M. de Jong (2000), 'Legitimate Governance within the State', in H. Wagenaar (ed.), *Government Institutions: Effects, Changes and Normative Foundations*, Dordrecht: Kluwer Academic Publishers, pp. 109–127.
Dorbeck-Jung, B.R., M.J. Oude Vrielink-van Heffen and G.H. Reussing (2006), *Open normen en regeldruk – Een onderzoek naar de kosten en oorzaken van irritaties bij open normen in de kwaliteitszorg*, Enschede: Universiteit Twente/IGS.
Drexler, E. (1986), *Engines of Creation: The Coming Era of Nanotechnology*, New York: Anchor Books.
Editors' Introduction to the Journal *Regulation and Governance* (2007), **1**, 1–7.
European Commission (2004) (Community Health and Consumer Protection), 'A Preliminary risk analysis on the basis of a workshop organized in Brussels on 1–2 March 2004', Report.
European Commission (2005), *Communication on Nanosciences and Nanotechnologies: An action plan for Europe 2005–2009*, COM (2005) 243 final.
European Environment Agency (2001), *Late Lessons from Early Warnings: The Precautionary Principle 1996–2000*, Copenhagen, http://www.eea.eu.int, accessed 21 May 2007.
Finnemore, M. and S. Toope (2001), 'Alternatives to Legalization: Richer Views of Law and Politics', *International Organization*, **55**, 746–750.
Giddens, A. (1984), *The Constitution of Society*, Cambridge: Polity Press.
Gunningham, N. and P. Grabovsky (1998), *Smart Regulation. Designing Environmental Policy*, Oxford: Clarendon Press.

Haum, R., U. Petschow and M. Steinfeldt (2004), *Nanotechnology and Regulation within the Framework of the Precautionary Principle*, Berlin: IÖW.
Hondius, E.H. (1984), 'The Neo-corporatist Approach. Non-legislative Means of Consumer Protection: The Dutch Perspective', *Journal of Consumer Policy*, **7**, 137–156.
IRGC (2006), *Nanotechnology. Risk Governance*, white paper no. 2, Geneva: IRGC.
Jopp, K. (2003), *Nanotechnologie – Aufbruch ins Reich der Zwerg*, Wiesbaden: Gabler.
Kindred, H.M., J.-G. Castel, W. Graham, A. De Mestral, L. Reif, I. Vlasic and S. Williams (1993), *International Law: Chiefly as Interpreted and Applied in Canada*, 5th edn, Toronto: Edmond Montgomery Publishers Ltd.
Krämer, L. (2003), 'The Genesis of EC Environmental Principles', *Research Papers in Law* **7**.
Ladeur, K.H. (2003), 'The Introduction of the Precautionary Principle into EU Law: A Pyrrhic Victory for Environmental and Public Health Law? Decision-Making under Conditions of Complexity in Multi-level Political Systems', *Common Market Law Review*, **40** (6), 1455–1479.
Lyall, C. and J. Tait (2005), *New Modes of Governance*, Aldershot: Ashgate Publishing House.
Macnaghten, P., M. Kearnes and B. Wynne (2005), 'Nanotechnology, Governance, and Public Deliberation: What Role for the Social Sciences?', *Science Communication*, **27** (2), 1–24.
Majone, G. (2002), 'What Price Safety? The Precautionary Principle and its Policy Implications', *Journal of Common Market Studies*, **40**, 89–109.
Maynard, A.D. (2006), 'Safe Handling of Nanotechnology', *Nature*, **444**, 267–269.
Mead, H. (1934), *Mind, Self and Society. From the Standpoint of a Social Behaviorist*, Chicago, Ill: University of Chicago Press.
Oakdene Hollins (2007), *Environmentally Beneficial Nanotechnologies: Barriers and Opportunities*. Report for the UK Department for Environment, Food and Rural Affairs (DEFR01 098 report.doc).
Oberdörster, G., Z. Sharp, V. Atudorei, A. Elder, R. Gelein and W. Kreyling (2004), 'Translocation of inhaled ultrafine particles to the brain', *Inhalation Toxicology*, **16** (6–7), 437–445.
Oberdörster, G., E. Oberdörster and J. Oberdörster (2005), 'Nanotoxicology: An Emerging Discipline Evolving from Studies of Ultrafine Particles', *Environmental Health Perspectives*, **113** (7), 823–839.
Rip, A. (2006a), 'A Co-evolutionary Approach to Reflexive Governance – and its Ironies', in J.P. Voss, D. Bauknecht and R. Kemp (eds), *Reflexive Governance for Sustainable Development. Incorporating Unintended Feedback in Societal Problem-Solving*, Cheltenham, UK and Northampton, MA, USA: Edward Elgar, Chapter 4.
Rip, A. (2006b), 'The Tension between Fiction and Precaution in Nanotechnology', in E. Fisher, J. Jones and R. von Schomberg (eds), *Implementing the Precautionary Principle*, Cheltenham, UK and Northampton, MA, USA: Edward Elgar, pp. 270–283.
Searle, J.R. (1995), *The Construction of Social Reality*, New York: The Free Press.
Selznick, P. (1985), 'Focusing Organizational Research on Regulation', in R.G. Noll (ed.), *Regulatory Policy and the Social Sciences*, Berkeley, CA: University of California Press.

Senden, L. (2004), *Soft Law in European Community Law*, Oxford: Hart Publishing.
Snyder, F. (1995), 'The Effectiveness of EC Law', in T. Daintith (ed.), *Implementing EC Law in the UK*, Chichester: John Wiley, pp. 78–98.
Sørensen, K.H. (2002), 'Social Shaping on the Move? On the Policy Relevance of the Social Shaping of Technology Perspective', in K.H. Sørensen and R. Williams, *Shaping Technology, Guiding Policy*, Cheltenham: Edward Elgar pp. 19–36.
Sørensen, K.H. and Williams, R. (2002), *Shaping Technology, Guiding Policy*, Cheltenham: Edward Elgar.
Tammes, A.J.P. (1983), *Soft Law: Essays on International and Comparative Law in Honour of Judge Erades*, Den Haag: Nijhoff.
Teubner, Gunther (ed.) (1997), *Global Law without a State*, Aldershot: Dartmouth.
Trubek, D.M. and L.G. Trubek (2005), 'Hard and Soft Law in the Construction of Social Europe: The Role of the Open Method of Co-ordination', *European Law Journal*, **11** (3), 343–364.
Trubek, D.M., P. Cottrell and M. Nance (2006), 'Soft Law, Hard Law and EU Integration', in G. de Burca and J. Scott (eds), *Law and New Governance in the EU and the US*, Oxford: Hart Publishing, pp. 65–94.
Van Amerom, M. and A. Rip (2006), 'Actor-Strategies & Actor-Constellations in the Nanotech Risk Debate', paper presented at the EASST 2006 Conference, 23–26 August, Lausanne, Switzerland.
Veen, R.J. van der (1990), *De sociale grenzen van beleid. Een onderzoek naar de uitvoering en effecten van het stelsel van sociale zekerheid*, Leiden: Stenfert Kroese.
Veen, R.J. van der (1998), 'Intensieve benadering. Onderzoek naar rechtshulp en armoede', in W. Derksen, A.F.A. Korsten and A.F.M. Bertrand (eds), *De praktijk van onderzoek. Problemen bij onderzoek van politiek, bestuur en beleid*, Groningen: Wolters-Noordhoff, pp. 143–160.
Vos, E. (1999), *Institutional Frameworks of Community Health and Safety Regulation – Committees, Agencies and Private Bodies*, Oxford: Hart Publishing.
Whitman, J. (2006), 'Governance Challenges of Technological Systems Convergence', *Bulletin of Science, Technology & Society*, **26** (5), 398–409.

9. Barristers beyond the law: state and non-state actors work in partnership to enforce legal and moral norms

Jenny Job

1. INTRODUCTION

It can come as something of a surprise when so-called pillars of society break the rules and choose non compliance. This was the situation in the Australian state of New South Wales (NSW) in the late 1990s and early 2000s when many barristers chose to ignore their obligations to comply with taxation law by using bankruptcy law to nullify their debts to the Australian Taxation Office (ATO). In doing so, they also chose to ignore the rules of their profession about behaving ethically. Even more surprising, the Bar Association chose not to enact the sanctions in its rules and, initially, did not deal with the non compliance of its members. The tax office, its peers and the community trusted and expected the Bar Association to self regulate. The actions of the barristers concerned broke state and non-state laws, denied the community the use of millions of dollars in taxes, exposed their culture to public scrutiny and tarnished the reputation of the profession. The challenge for the tax office was in securing compliance in such a situation. Prosecution was an option, one typically used by taxation administrations, but this problem was not confined to just a few individuals. As well, bankruptcy law is not administered by the tax office. Other options for ensuring compliance were needed.

Despite the supposed clarity that has been given to the definition of law through distinguishing legal and moral norms (Tamanaha 1995), it has by no means provided clarity in the workings of state and non-state law in practice. The focus of this chapter is on the weaknesses of Field C in the map of non-state law as indicated in Chapter 2 – the inability of non-state actors to enforce their norms of decision in the world of business. This is where state law should take over, as it has the socially recognized role of enforcing legal norms. It would be nice if it was as simple as that, but the case study used in this chapter shows that just as the weakness for non-state law is in Field C, state law also has an inability to enforce legal norms in circumstances where people play the rules for their own gain. This chapter will consider whether, in a situation of blatant non-compliance, state and non-state actors can work together to enforce compliance, and the consequences of this for compliance and for the role of state actors. Rather than the role of state law declining, the case study used in this chapter illustrates that state and non-state law can work together as partners to enforce moral and legal norms. Close and ongoing cooperation between state and non-state actors resulted in a resolve by the legal profession to improve its self-regulation, the emergence of several new state laws and the refinement of the non-state law governing the legal profession.

In this chapter I examine the change which has occurred in regulatory style, both generally and within taxation administration. I explore the idea of regulation by governance (Burris et al. 2005; Hutter and Jones 2007; Parker and Braithwaite 2003). Rather than regulation being the role of government, the notion of governance assumes that many actors play a part in ensuring compliance. My aim is to show how weaknesses in the ability to enforce state and non-state law are being alleviated by a shift in regulatory approach. Rather than the role of the state in the enforcing of legal norms being overtaken by non-state actors, the ideas of decentred regulation using a nodal governance approach show how both state and non-state law and actors can work together to overcome their weaknesses in a complex situation of non compliance.

2. BEYOND STATE AND NON-STATE LAW

During the 1990s, the ATO noticed a growing trend among NSW barristers of large taxation debts and non-lodgement of taxation returns. Some of the debts amounted to several million dollars. In fact, 'the rate of debt default by NSW barristers was ten times higher than that of the rest of the Australian population' (Braithwaite 2005, p. 178). However, recovery was not possible as some barristers had bankrupted themselves, effectively negating their debts to the tax office.

The 2000–2001 ATO Annual Report shows the extent of the problem. In 2000, 590 barristers owed $AU52 million in income tax. Sixty-two practising barristers were bankrupt, or had entered into bankruptcy arrangements during the 1990s. The ATO was the only creditor in 90 per cent of these cases, with 56 individuals owing $AU20 million in tax. Not only did barristers have unusually large debts to the tax office, in mid-1999 nearly half of the NSW Bar had not lodged their tax returns on time. By January 2001, 38 more barristers were approaching bankruptcy, and there was a growing tendency towards serial bankruptcies. Despite earning six figure incomes, the barristers had no assets, but their families did. Yet bankruptcy did not stop barristers from practising in their profession.

3. REGULATING THE PRACTICE OF LAW IN NSW

Professional organizations are not newcomers to regulation. They are part of the civil sector which comprises many sources of regulation and includes organizations which are neither government nor business (Hutter 2006). For decades professional organizations have regulated the conditions of entry to the profession and stipulated standards of conduct which members of the profession are expected to honour (Hutter 2006; Hutter and Jones 2007).

The practice of law in the Australian state of NSW is regulated by both state and non-state law. The NSW Bar Association is a professional organization. It is a public company limited by guarantee, does not have a share capital and is registered as a club under the *New South Wales Registered Clubs Act 1976*. The NSW Bar Association states that it is a 'voluntary association of practising barristers'. It has its own Constitution, or in other words, its own rules. Part 3 of its Constitution sets out the objects or aims of the NSW Bar Association. Of particular relevance is Part 3.1.6:

> to promote fair and honourable practice amongst barristers; to suppress, discourage and prevent malpractice and professional misconduct; to inquire into so far as the law permits and decide questions as to professional conduct and etiquette of barristers; to make rules (including rules for the imposition on members of penalties, including expulsion, suspension or fines; with regard to the foregoing to the extent the law permits and in the absence of other rules and regulations made under the Act for breach of such rules; and if deemed necessary, to report any of such rules or decisions to the Supreme Court of New South Wales and to the Members of the Bar Association and to the public as the Bar Council sees fit.

This part of the Constitution sets out the expected requirement of ethical and professional behaviour or conduct by barristers. It makes clear that the rules include penalties and that the Bar Association will self-regulate by imposing penalties on members who behave inappropriately. There are two issues to note: that reporting of misconduct will only happen if the Bar Council *sees fit*; and it is not clear how far the expectation of ethical behaviour applies. Does it only apply when a barrister is practising the law, or does it apply to all aspects of their lives? Prominent Australian judge, Sir Anthony Mason, has been cited as saying: 'professional codes of conduct prescribe pursuit of high standards of both professional conduct and ethical conduct without drawing a distinction between the two' (D'Ascenzo

2007). This would seem to indicate that barristers themselves expect that their fellow members should behave appropriately in all aspects of their lives; ethical conduct seeming to apply beyond their workplace. The normative dimension of modifying behaviour is regarded as one of the main advantages of non-state regulation (Hutter 2006, p. 13).

These informal rules or non-state laws are reflected in state law. The current NSW Bar Association web page also states that: 'All barristers in New South Wales are bound by the Legal Profession Act 2004, the Legal Profession Regulation 2004 and the New South Wales Barristers' Rules.' Bedrossian (2004, p. 2) noted that to be admitted to the legal profession in NSW: 'Section 11 of the *Legal Profession Act 1987 (NSW)* ("the Act") provides: A candidate, however qualified in other respects, must not be admitted as a legal practitioner unless the Admission Board is satisfied that the candidate is of good fame and character and is otherwise suitable for admission.' The Act also deals with professional misconduct, referring to failure to reach reasonable standards of competence and diligence or conduct which justifies a finding that a legal practitioner is not of good fame and character or is not a fit and proper person to remain on the roll (Bedrossian 2004). The 1987 Act was in place when the NSW barristers chose to disregard their taxation obligations. The problem with this piece of state law was its lack of precision or specific criteria by which to judge fitness and rightness, and the lack of explicit sanctions.

> Under the system of self-regulation . . . the core tests of 'good fame and character' and 'fit and proper person' are open to wide interpretation. The history of the regulatory system entitles the public to think that the interpretations of these terms overwhelmingly influenced by the lawyers in the system have been absurdly stretched, such as, for example, excusing a barrister's failure to file tax returns as a result of 'involuntary inertia'. (Sydney Morning Herald 2001a)

Interestingly, court cases dealing with drug smuggling and sexual assaults by legal practitioners illustrate that the definition of professional misconduct was not clear in this Act which made it difficult to determine if a practitioner was fit to practise (Bedrossian 2004).

While there was non-state law in place, and it was supported by state law, it appeared that the non-state actors would not self-regulate for a number of possible reasons: they were protective of their own and did not 'see fit' to report improper behaviour so that it could be dealt with by state law; if improper behaviour did result in state enforcement in the courts they chose to apply leniency towards their own; they had no mechanism or criteria in place to know that members were behaving improperly; their rules were not clear about the type of behaviour which was improper; and state law was similarly unclear about what was improper or what behaviour might render members unfit to practise. Given the lack of clarity, how could state and non-state laws be used to regulate problem behaviour like that displayed by the bankrupt barristers?

4. A CHANGING STYLE OF REGULATION

Regulation is generally understood to mean the enforcement of both legal and moral rules declared by supranational (for example, the European Union) and subnational (for example, professional associations) bodies (Parker and Braithwaite 2003, p. 119). Nevertheless, self-regulation by professional bodies is an important aspect of the market (Ayres and Braithwaite 1992; Hutter 2006). Many industry associations and professional bodies self-regulate by developing agreements, accreditation schemes, codes of conduct, codes of practice and standards (Hutter 2006; OECD Working Party on Regulatory Management and Reform 2006). These rules guide the behaviour of those who belong to these industry or professional groups and make it clear to outsiders what is expected of members. The groups monitor the compliance of members and enforce compliance with the rules (OECD Working Party on Regulatory Management and Reform 2006). Thus:

> [i]n the present context the term 'regulation' may be taken to refer to the control of corporate and commercial activities through a system of norms and rules which may be promulgated either by government agencies (including legislatures and courts) or by private actors, or by a combination of the two. The direct involvement of the state is not a necessary condition for the existence of regulation in this sense, since rules may be derived from the activities of industry associations, professional bodies or similarly independent entities. (du Plessis et al. 2005, pp. 108–9).

Regulation is increasingly carried out by different 'classes' of private regulator. Scott (2002) has highlighted the growing role of private regulators where statutory powers are contracted out to non-state organizations. Nevertheless, not all private regulators have a legal mandate, meaning they lack that feature of the law that separates state and non-state law – the ability to impose sanctions (Scott 2002). However, '[a] regulator with no formal power to apply sanctions can nevertheless invoke competitive pressures and community disapproval, for example, by publishing information' (Scott 2002, p. 61). Scott (2002, p. 66) has classified a group of 'mandateless regulators' who hold 'governance power' through their ability to oversee other bodies, and possess and release information in the public interest. One such regulator is the media: 'Where the media maintains effective systematic oversight (as with some investigative journalism . . .) then it may come within this third class of mandateless regulators' (Scott 2002, p. 68). Scott (2005) has argued that the changing understanding of the regulatory state conceives of a 'loosening' of the divide between the state and the market and the public and the private. This changed understanding of the role of the state and state law has been described as 'decentred regulation' (Black 2002; Kingsford Smith 2004), where the act of regulating is 'diffused throughout society' (Black 2002, p. 2). Thinking more broadly about regulation has occurred along with the view that state law has its limitations (Black 2002; Scott 2005; Hutter 2006; Hutter and Jones 2007). There were demands by the community for the state to be more responsive in its approach to regulation, with non-state actors increasingly becoming involved in regulation (Osborne and Gaebler 1992; Hughes 1994; Sparrow 2000; Black 2002; Scott 2005; Hutter and Jones 2007). Hutter and Jones (2007, p. 27) argue that because state law is insufficient in regulating business, 'regulatory space is occupied by the state *and* a variety of non-state players'. The different classes of regulator described by Scott (2002) reinforce the notion of decentred regulation and the changed expectation of more dynamic and effective regulation (Kingsford Smith 2004).

5. REGULATION BY GOVERNANCE

The 'dispersal of capacities and resources relevant to the exercise of power among a wide range of state, non-state and supranational actors' has been defined by Scott (2005, p. 45) as governance. Governance is regarded as the management of the course or flow of events in a social system (Parker and Braithwaite 2003; Burris et al. 2005). Regulating the social system requires a focus on and understanding of the complexities of the actors and the mechanisms of that system (Burris et al. 2005). However, 'the complexity of governance in practice has evaded capture in the models that are commonly deployed in legal and regulatory theory' (Burris et al. 2005, p. 31). To understand how complex systems work in practice, Burris et al. (2005, p. 33) have proposed the theory of nodal governance: 'an elaboration of contemporary network theory that explains how a variety of actors operating within social systems interact along networks to govern the systems they inhabit'. Governance is an 'adaptive response' to complexity (Burris et al. 2005, p. 34). This implies that a social system includes many and different actors who interact as institutions in the governance of a system (Burris et al. 2005).

This framework is useful in understanding how the bankrupt barristers were successfully regulated. The situation being examined here is complex.

It crosses two tiers of government (Commonwealth and State levels of government); it includes state and non-state actors; it overlaps business and private worlds; it includes legal and moral norms; and the professional culture of the legal profession appeared to be having an influence. Each part of this complex system had a role to play in regulating the barristers.

On its own, the tax office could not have achieved compliance because the barristers had creatively used bankruptcy laws to put themselves beyond its reach. The Bar Association had moral rules which it was expected to monitor and regulate but this had not happened. The barristers could not be sanctioned for breach of the state-level Legal Practitioners' Act unless the Bar Association saw fit to abide by the rules of their profession and report their non-compliant behaviour to the courts, to the other members of the Association and/or to the public. It appears that it was the networks operating within the smaller social system of NSW barristers which realized the spread of the non-compliance rather than being a monitoring system to ensure compliance. It seems that the moral suasion aspect of non-state regulation had fallen down here – the rules of the legal profession which highlighted ethical behaviour were not enough to persuade members to comply.

6. A MORE RESPONSIVE STYLE OF TAXATION REGULATION

The role of state organizations is norm enforcement: 'the test for law is based upon the severity (coercion/force) and nature (publically approved and executed) of the sanction imposed upon infraction' (Tamanaha 1995, p. 507). As well, state organizations have clearly defined boundaries around their areas of responsibility which prevent them from regulating law beyond their own jurisdiction. While this is a strength, it can also act as a weakness, as in the case being explored in this chapter.

Until recently, taxation administrations have operated in the manner expected of state organizations. They have kept the door firmly shut when designing new law and administered the law with a command-and-control approach to regulation – a very resource intensive and demanding style of regulation. Since the late 1990s, an alternative approach to taxation compliance has increasingly been used in taxation administration: responsive regulation (Braithwaite 2003, 2007; Job and Honaker 2003; Braithwaite 2005; Job et al. 2007). A responsive regulatory approach shows an attitude by the regulator that is open to the use of a varied range of regulatory responses to gain compliance depending on the situation at hand (Ayres and Braithwaite 1992). The ATO adopted a responsive regulatory approach to taxation compliance in 1998. The aim was to: understand taxpayer behaviour; build a cooperative relationship with the community; encourage and support compliance; introduce a range of sanctions escalating in severity and known to taxpayers; and reduce complaints about procedural justice (ATO 1998; Job et al. 2007). The goal was to work cooperatively with taxpayers to build community ownership of the system and encourage taxpayers to take responsibility for their own actions.

But what happens when the ethical appeal in self-regulatory codes of conduct fails, or when a professional body fails to either monitor compliance or to enforce compliance? This appeared to be the situation with the bankrupt barristers in NSW who were ignoring their own professional rules. Moral suasion did not seem to work. Their ethical obligations to their fellow barristers and their profession were forgotten, as were their legal obligations to the tax office and the Australian community. However, there was no specific mention within their professional rules about any requirement to meet one's personal taxation obligations.

There were a number of ways to remedy the barristers' non compliance. Legal obligations are enforceable through the judicial system. The ATO could pursue that option and seek to punish the particular individuals. In this situation, faced with a less than enthusiastic response from the NSW Bar Association about self-regulation, the tax office took several of the worst offenders to court. However, resorting to this approach for all offending barristers would have been expensive and unlikely to achieve the desired result in most cases, as the past lenient treatment of barristers by the courts and tribunals had demonstrated. This was a rapidly growing problem spreading not only through the NSW legal profession but across the legal profession in Australia.

Something more was needed – a system of governance where each part in the system forms a node (Burris et al. 2005). Rather than being a network, where decision making is shared, nodal governance emphasizes the steering of the situation. In this case the steering was done by the media and by the tax office, which worked in cooperation with other members of the social system to regulate barristers through enforcing self-regulation, and strengthening state and non-state law.

7. ENFORCING COMPLIANCE THROUGH A SYSTEM OF NODAL GOVERNANCE

The challenge for the tax office was to achieve a change in this non-compliant behaviour and to encourage the Bar Association to be more active in self regulating its members. In this case the idea of fair and ethical behaviour which had appeared in the NSW barristers' Constitution had been left open. It could apply to everything a barrister did, or it might have been interpreted to mean only in relation to their work as a barrister and have no reference to their personal life. There were no criteria by which to judge the behaviour of members.

Initially, the ATO approached the NSW Bar Council about the problem of barristers bankrupting themselves to avoid paying their debts to the tax office, expecting it to deal with these barristers through a self regulatory process. However, its response was not quite what the tax office wanted to hear:

> The Bar Council took the view that making practising certificates conditional on tax compliance was not a matter of self-regulation, but a matter of regulation by the NSW Legal Services Tribunal. The Bar Council had taken a tax complaint to the Tribunal just once before, in 1997: Mr Tom Harrison had been convicted of 30 offences of failing to lodge a tax return over 14 years. The three senior lawyers on the Tribunal found Harrison not guilty of professional misconduct on the basis that 'his omissions were the result of an involuntary inertia rather than an attempt to avoid his responsibilities'. They were caused by 'a psychological block' which he had tried but failed to overcome (*Sydney Morning Herald*, 27 February, 2001, p. 4). (Braithwaite 2005, p. 179)

The Bar Association and the Law Council believed that the tax office should have come to them with details of the barristers involved (Haslem 2001; D'Ascenzo 2007). However, secrecy and privacy laws prevent the tax office from revealing an individual's taxation details to another person.

As a next step, the taxation commissioner highlighted the problem of the bankrupt barristers in speeches and in his annual reports. Doing so attracted the interest of journalists who began to investigate the problem and print detailed reports on the bankrupt barristers, their families, their assets and their extravagant lifestyles. It became even clearer that the NSW Bar Association appeared to be less than enthusiastic in its use of self-regulation:

> This newspaper revealed that some barristers had become bankrupt on more than one occasion as a way of 'managing' their tax liabilities. . . . In relation to bankrupt member Robert Somosi, the Bar had apparently been 'investigating' for five years his conviction for tax offences. 'You can't assume we're doing nothing,' Ruth McColl, the president of the Bar, reassured the Herald. (Ackland 2001)

Newspaper stories about the bankrupt barristers attracted the attention of Australian Attorneys-General at both Commonwealth and state levels who began to examine bankruptcy law (Braithwaite 2005). The Attorneys-General took the problem seriously and decided to introduce a suite of measures so that barristers could not declare bankruptcy to avoid paying tax. Rules across the country would be tightened up, including 'changes to the Bankruptcy Act aimed at stopping unscrupulous debtors using bankruptcy to defeat the legitimate claims of their creditors (such as the tax office)' (The Australian 2001), there would be tests to determine fitness to continue practising the law and the onus was put on barristers to notify their association of their tax or other serious offences (Farrant 2001).

> The regulations in force from today will require barristers and solicitors to notify the Bar Association or the Law Society if they become bankrupt or if they apply 'to take the benefit of any law for the relief of bankrupt or insolvent debtors'. Further changes to the Legal Profession Act will specify that bankruptcy falls within the definition of professional misconduct and so, possibly, lead to a practitioner being disciplined or struck off. A practitioner who is declared bankrupt will be suspended and will subsequently lose the right to practise unless she or he is able to show cause why she or he is still fit to practise. (Sydney Morning Herald 2001b)

It was then that the NSW Bar Association began to take more of an interest and take some action against its own. 'Facing the spectre of a law prohibiting any recent bankrupt from practicing law, the NSW Bar Association became interested in dealing with the problem' (Braithwaite 2005, p. 180). The NSW Bar Association took several of its legal practitioners to court. At least three were found unfit to practise law and their names were removed from the roll. Others were suspended from practising. As well, the Bar Association began to show a different public face, more in support of its own rules which were supposed to deal with improper behaviour. Ruth McColl, former president of the NSW Bar Association said: 'the Bar Association deplores persons who deliberately flout and avoid their legal and financial obligations. It strikes at the community and public interest. It undermines the reputation of the Bar and is a slur on the overwhelming majority of barristers who pay their taxes' (D'Ascenzo 2007). However, the lack of self-regulation on the part of the Bar Association resulted in the Attorneys-General taking changes to state law much further in an effort to ensure compliance in the future. The Legal Profession Act 2004 repealed the Legal Profession Act 1987, with its commencement being preceded by three new pieces of legislation. The Legal Profession Act 2004 adapted the National Legal Profession Model Provisions developed by the Attorneys-General which aimed to achieve improved national consistency and uniformity in the regulation of the legal profession (Webster 2006). Included in the Act was a chapter specifically dealing with the handling of complaints and conduct that may be the subject of complaint:

> Chapter 4 expressly applies to conduct of a local legal practitioner where there is a 'conviction' for a 'serious offence', a 'tax offence' or an offence involving dishonesty, conduct of the practitioner 'as or in becoming' an 'insolvent under administration' and 'in becoming' disqualified from managing or being involved in the management of a corporation. (Webster 2006, p. 66)

Specific definitions in the new Act included: serious offence; tax offence; insolvent under administration; unsatisfactory professional conduct; and professional misconduct; as well as suitability matters. Of most interest is the 'show cause event' definition which specifically includes 'being "convicted" of a "serious offence" or a "tax offence" whether or not in New South Wales' (Webster 2006, p. 70). These changes to state law dealt with the problem mentioned earlier of the lack of specificity and clarity in both the state and non-state laws about what type of behaviour was improper. If non-state law did not spell out specific criteria, the Attorneys-General decided that the new state law would do so. Another problem mentioned earlier which had to be dealt with by the Attorneys-General was the apparent reluctance of the NSW legal profession to self-regulate:

> No matter how much the Bar Association may insist that the system of regulation and discipline is not one of self-regulation, but co-regulation, it is essentially still one aptly characterised by the expression 'Caesar judging Caesar'. As Mr Debus says, those who practise law have an obligation to uphold the highest standards of lawful conduct. Mr Debus's task remains formidable. He has to produce legislation tough enough not only to close every loophole against every clever tax-shy lawyer, but also tough enough to overcome the bias inherent in an essentially self-regulatory system of professional standards. (Sydney Morning Herald 2001b)

The 2002–2003 ATO Annual Report showed a marked improvement in the barristers' compliance with their taxation obligations. There was improvement in the lodgement on time of tax returns, with 81 per cent lodging on time. By 2003, debt levels for barristers had declined, with 116 barristers in debt, and NSW barristers were showing a greater willingness to enter into arrangements with the ATO to pay their debts. Bankruptcies had declined. Nationally, tax collections from barristers had increased from $AU231.4 million in 2000–2001 to $AU346.2 million in 2002–2003, partly attributed to improved compliance.

The ATO credited these improvements to several factors: expanding its focus on barristers from NSW to barristers nationally; working closely with relevant parties such as trustees to obtain access to assets; its referral of barristers for prosecution; the management of their relationships with legal professional bodies; and the information sessions the ATO held for members on compliance.

Through the cooperation of state and non-state actors (two levels of government – the Commonwealth of Australia and the State of NSW – the media and the NSW Bar Association), Commonwealth tax and bankruptcy laws were strengthened and non-state law regarding the ethical behaviour of barristers was reinforced.

In using a nodal governance approach to deal with this problem, the tax office demonstrated its ability to be responsive in achieving compliance rather than relying on commanding and coercing. However, it was the media which played a prominent role in the steering of this situation to generate action from the nodes in this system – both state and non-state actors. It has been argued that the media can encourage taxpayer compliance by appealing to civic virtue, although the success of such an appeal depends on an individual's attitude towards the duty of paying tax (Mason and Mason 1992). It is the idea of moral suasion, or ethical behaviour, that is implicit in the informal law of non-state actors in regulating behaviour. The strength of non-state law is often based on an appeal to the moral or ethical side of a person's character which is the basis of Part 3.1.6 of the NSW Bar Association's Constitution. However, that appeal does not appear to have achieved the compliance of the individual barristers. Rather, by putting pressure on the profession, the media brought into play the idea of the 'social licence to operate' (Gunningham et al. 2003; Hutter and Jones 2007). The stories in the media did not only threaten the reputation of the legal profession. These stories made the profession face up to the prospect that their reluctance to self-regulate would result in changes to state law which might prohibit barristers from practising. It was this that prompted action from the NSW Bar Association and encouraged it to become an active node in the governance system.

8. CONCLUSION

It has not been revealed why so many NSW barristers decided to use the law in such a creative way to remove their taxation obligations. It could be that they, like so many others, are increasingly being caught up in the changing times which emphasize the economic over the ethical.[1] Some thought the closed culture of the profession was the main reason for its inability to self-regulate:

> As the tax debacle shows, the legal system's self-regulatory nature is largely to blame for such blatant abuses being allowed to continue for so long. The closed nature of the legal profession – the archaic airs and graces, the convoluted language, those pretentious wigs and gowns – lead to a mindset of indifference to the public interest and accountability. . . . unless and until a culture that turns a

> blind eye to abuses is reformed, legislators will have a hard time keeping ahead of those determined to ignore their obligations, to their own advantage. (The Australian 2001)

These barristers not only flouted state law but they ignored the rules of their profession and their social responsibility to behave ethically and to be a fit and proper person. While the rules in their Constitution are voluntary, they are built on and embedded in established social norms about the right way to behave and the way in which professional persons such as barristers should behave. These social norms are further reflected in state law.

The state and non-state laws governing the behaviour of barristers combined to form a 'network' or 'web' where different actors each played a part in the governance of the system (Sahlin-Andersson 2004, p. 143; Burris et al. 2005) In this case, the network regulating the legal system included non-state actors (the Bar Association, the barristers and journalists) and state actors (several government organizations at different levels of government and legal tribunals). Systems of rules which are not backed by legal sanctions rely on voluntarism (Sahlin-Andersson 2004). The assumption of these systems is that members will voluntarily follow the rules and will self-regulate by monitoring behaviour and sanctioning those who ignore the rules. The problem comes when voluntarism and self-regulation do not occur. This has been noted as one of the main problems of self-regulation when clear, known sanctions are not in place (Hutter 2006). In the case of the bankrupt barristers, the Constitution of the Bar Association was backed up by legal sanctions. And yet, the courts often seemed to be reluctant to enforce sanctions on those who were non compliant, preferring instead to make excuses for them, as demonstrated earlier in the Tom Harrison court case. A problem of organizational culture where members see fit to protect their own?

Coercion alone could not have achieved the desired result in this situation. Possession of a legal mandate by the tax office was insufficient to gain compliance. Nor were the norms of decision which should have been enforced by the Bar Association sufficient. Hutter and Jones (2007) posed the question of whether the regulated recognize regulation beyond the state. This appeared to be the issue here. These barristers understood not only the moral rules and norms but also the legal rules and norms so well they were able to play on the weaknesses in both state and non-state law to put themselves beyond the law. They recognized neither non-state nor state regulation.

The weakness in Hertogh's Field C of non-state law as described in Chapter 2 – the norms of decision and the inability of non-state law to enforce – is mirrored in state law. Each state organization has responsibility for different facets of the law and the power of state institutions is constrained so that they may only act within their own mandated area. A tax office can only enforce tax laws. Such constraints are a good thing; however, as this case study demonstrates, they can be a weakness by preventing state actors from crossing their own boundaries, even to the point of inability to share information about non-compliant individuals, as was the situation in this case. The narrow view of law and its enforcement is that it is the role of the state. This view has more recently been challenged by the notion of decentred regulation (Black 2002). However, even a decentred approach to regulation is insufficient in cases like this. More was required to enforce compliance – governance (Scott 2005; Hutter and Jones 2007) and a nodal governance regulatory approach (Burris et al. 2005) where state and non-state actors worked not alone but as a networked system.

These recent ideas about regulation are not challenging state law, or the role of the state in the making and enforcing of law. Rather, they are examining the role of both state and non-state law and actors, and the relationships between them. State and non-state actors can work together to make and enforce rules in a way that makes up for their respective weaknesses. Government organizations like a tax office must operate within state law. They can limit their role to seeing the role of state law as one of coercion. Or, they can broaden the role of state law and their ability to enforce it by allowing space for interaction with non-state actors to enable a more dynamic and effective system of enforcing the law.

This study illustrates the focus of this book on the interaction between the state legislature and non-state law. In this instance, non-state law did influence the state legislature at two levels of government to change several pieces of legislation, not necessarily because non-state law was inadequate but because the non-state actor would not, or could not, enforce its own rules. In the face of this action by the state, the non-state actor chose to strengthen its own rules and to finally self-regulate by investigating the behaviour of its members.

It would seem that non-state law works when things are going well but is not effective on its own in the business world when there is deliberate non-compliance. State law is needed in these situations to enforce where non-state actors cannot. Rather than seeing a declining role for the state, the issue is more one of state and non-state actors needing to work in cooperation to ensure compliance. Where there is 'genuine conflict' or widespread and deliberate non-compliance, as there was with the bankrupt barristers, non-state law has weaknesses which may prevent its ability to achieve compliance. This is where a nodal governance approach to compliance can bring state and non-state actors together in a web of influence to achieve what has been argued as the preferred regulatory mix of state and non-state regulation (Hutter 2006). This change has occurred in the way state actors think about and conduct regulatory activity. What was once a state activity, with each government organization seeing its role as separate from other regulators, is changing to a governance system where several state and non-state actors may work together.

The consequences for the role of the state would appear to be twofold. First, as this case study has demonstrated, there is the need to ensure that explicit sanctions are reflected in state law to ensure compliance when the enforcement of moral norms in the business world fails to occur. Then, there is the realization that the state does not have to bear the sole brunt of enforcing the law. It increasingly works as an essential part of a larger system where state and non-state actors can work in an enforcement partnership when necessary to enforce state and non-state law.

NOTE

1. See the speech, 'Legal Professional Ethics in Times of Change', by The Hon. Justice Michael Kirby at The St James Ethics Centre Forum on Ethical Issues, Sydney, 23 July 1996 on The New South Wales Bar Association website.

REFERENCES

Ackland, Richard (2001), 'Lowering the Bar in a Year that Speaks for Itself', *Sydney Morning Herald*, 28 December.

ATO (1998), *Improving Tax Compliance in the Cash Economy*, Canberra: Commonwealth of Australia.

The Australian (2001), 'No Leniency when Judging Tax-Dodgers', *The Australian*, 8 June.

Ayres, Ian and John Braithwaite (1992), *Responsive Regulation: Transcending the Deregulation Debate*, New York: Oxford University Press.

Bedrossian, Vahan (2004), 'Regulation of Admission, Fitness to Remain on the Roll of Legal Practitioners and the Retention of Rights to Practise: Obligations Owed to Professional Colleagues', NSW Bar Association, www.nswbar.asn.au/docs/professional/pcd/bedrossian. pdf, accessed 21 April 2007.

Black, Julia (2002), 'Critical Reflections on Regulation', *Australian Journal of Legal Philosophy*, **27**, 1–37.

Braithwaite, John (2005), *Markets in Vice, Markets in Virtue*, Annandale, NSW: The Federation Press.

Braithwaite, Valerie (1998), 'Communal and Exchange Trust Norms: Their Value Base and Relevance to Institutional Trust', in Valerie Braithwaite and Margaret Levi (eds), *Trust and Governance*, New York: Russell Sage Foundation, pp. 46–74.

Braithwaite, Valerie (ed.) (2003), *Taxing Democracy: Understanding Tax Avoidance and Evasion*, Aldershot: Ashgate.

Braithwaite, Valerie (2007), 'Introduction to Responsive Regulation and Taxation, Special Issue of Law & Policy', *Law & Policy*, **29** (1), 3–10.

Burris, Scott, Peter Drahos and Clifford Shearing (2005), 'Nodal Governance', *Australian Journal of Legal Philosophy*, **30**, 30–58.

D'Ascenzo, Michael (2007), 'Barristers Who Look the Wrong Way', *Lawyers Weekly*, http://www.lawyersweekly.com.au, accessed 22 April 2007.

Du Plessis, Jean, James McConvill and Mirko Bogaric (2005), 'Regulation of corporate governance', in *Principles of Contemporary Corporate Governance*, Cambridge: Cambridge University Press, Chapter 6, pp. 108–109.

Farrant, Darrin (2001), 'Lawyers Face Tax Crackdown', *The Age*, 26 July.

Gunningham, Neil and Peter N. Grabosky (1998), *Smart Regulation: Designing Environmental Policy*, Oxford: Oxford University Press.

Gunningham, Neil, Robert A. Kagan and D. Thornton (2003), *Shades of Green: Business, Regulation, and Environment*, Stanford, CA: Stanford University Press.

Haslem, Benjamin (2001), 'Bankrupt Barristers to Face National Crackdown', *The Australian*, 1 March.

Hughes, Owen E. (1994), *Public Management and Administration*, London: HarperCollinsBusiness.

Hutter, Bridget (2006), 'The Role of Non-state Actors in Regulation', *CARR Discussion Paper No. 37*, The London School of Economics and Political Science, London.

Hutter, Bridget and Clive Jones (2007), 'From Government to Governance: External Influences on Business Risk Management', *Regulation & Governance*, **1**, 27–45.

Job, Jenny and David Honaker (2003), 'Short-Term Experience with Responsive Regulation in the Australian Taxation Office', in Valerie Braithwaite (ed.), *Taxing Democracy: Understanding Tax Avoidance and Evasion*, Aldershot: Ashgate Publishing Limited, pp. 111–129.

Job, Jenny, Andrew Stout and Rachael Smith (2007), 'Culture Change in Three Taxation Administrations: From Command-and-Control to Responsive Regulation', *Law & Policy*, **29**, 84–101.

Kingsford Smith, Dimity (2004), 'Beyond the Rule of Law? Decentered Regulation in Online Investing', *Law & Policy*, **26** (3&4), 439–476.

Mason, Laurie and Robert Mason (1992), 'A Moral Appeal for Taxpayer Compliance: The Case for a Mass Media Campaign', *Law & Policy*, **14**, 381–399.

OECD Working Party on Regulatory Management and Reform (2006), 'Interim Report on Alternatives to Traditional Regulation: Self-regulation and Co-regulation', *GOV/PGC/REG(2006)3*, Paris: Organization for Economic Cooperation and Development.

Osborne, David and Ted Gaebler (1992), *Reinventing Government: How the Entrepreneurial Spirit is Transforming the Public Sector*, New York: A Plume Book.

Parker, Christine and John Braithwaite (2003), 'Regulation', in Peter Cane and Mark Tushnet (eds), *The Oxford Handbook of Legal Studies*, Oxford: Oxford University Press, pp. 119–145.

Sahlin-Andersson, Kerstin (2004), 'Emergent Cross-sectional Soft Regulations: Dynamics at Play in the Global Compact Initiative', in Ulrika Morth (ed.), *Soft Law in Governance and Regulation*, Cheltenham: Edward Elgar, pp. 129–53.

Scott, Colin (2002), 'Private Regulation of the Public Sector: A Neglected Facet of Contemporary Governance', *Journal of Law and Society*, **29** (1), 56–76.

Scott, Colin (2005), 'Regulation in the Age of Governance: The Rise of the Post-regulatory State', in Jacint Jordana and David Levi-Faur (eds), *The Politics of Regulation: Institutions and Regulatory Reforms for the Age of Governance*, Cheltenham: Edward Elgar Publishing Ltd, pp. 145–176.
Sparrow, Malcolm K. (2000), *The Regulatory Craft*, Washington DC: Brookings Institution Press.
Sydney Morning Herald (2001a), 'Lawyers and Tax', *Sydney Morning Herald*, 3 March.
Sydney Morning Herald (2001b), 'Checks On Barristers', *Sydney Morning Herald*, 9 March.
Tamanaha, Brian (1995), 'An Analytical Map of Social Scientific Approaches to the Concept of Law', *Oxford Journal of Legal Studies*, **15** (4), 501–535.
Webster, Carol (2006), 'Legal Profession Act 2004: Complaints Procedures and Show Cause Requirements', *Bar News*, Summer, 65–74.

10. In a world without a sovereign: native title law in Australia

Francesca Dominello

1. INTRODUCTION

In *Mabo v Queensland (No. 2)*[1] the High Court of Australia held, by a six-member majority, that the Meriam people, the recognized indigenous inhabitants of the Murray Islands, were entitled, as against the whole world, to possession, occupation, use and enjoyment of the lands of the Murray Islands.[2] For the first time in Australian law a form of indigenous native title was found not only to exist, but also to have pre-dated and to have survived the acquisition of British sovereignty over the Australian territories. The Court's formulation was grounded in the common law: the common law recognized that native title did exist; however, the content of native title would arise from the traditions and customs of the indigenous peoples themselves.

In order to facilitate the common law recognition of native title, the Court first considered it necessary to reject the *terra nullius* doctrine as forming any part of Australian law.[3] The Court found that the *terra nullius* doctrine had operated to deny any indigenous rights to land through the characterization of Australia at the time of first settlement as a land belonging to no one. This legal characterization had found support from a line of judicial pronouncements that had declared the continent to be in effect 'desert and uncultivated'[4] at the time of British settlement.

Before *Mabo* indigenous customary law only had the status of what could be described as a form of non-state law. It had been generally accepted that indigenous peoples had their own systems of laws; however, these laws were not officially recognized or endorsed by the state's legal institutions. In the area of property law this lack of official status had rendered indigenous property interests as practically non-existent. Thus the significance of *Mabo* was that it was the first time that an indigenous legal precept had been recognized by Australian law, and with its recognition came the promise of indigenous property rights being treated equally with other interests. It was a positive recognition of difference, where normally throughout Australian colonial history the indigenous peoples had been discriminated against because of their difference.[5]

However, despite the promises held out by *Mabo*, indigenous peoples are still being discriminated against, even in the native title context. In this chapter, I will explore the reasons for this, and consider how to overcome the obstacles still in the way of the equality of treatment that *Mabo* had seemed to foreshadow.

In the first part of the chapter, it is argued that the problems that indigenous peoples still face stem from perceptions of their difference, which are in turn translated into their treatment as inferior. Throughout Australian colonial history there has been little inclination to accommodate indigenous interests in law or in society more generally (Webber 1995). Specifically in relation to native title, its inferior treatment stems from the High Court's perception of its own institutional history and that of Australian law as grounded in British origins. Australian law has its origins in English law, and indigenous customary law does not. A tension exists within the *Mabo* decision between preserving Australian law, and the English law from which it derives, and changing the law in order to give effect to contemporary conceptions of justice and human rights. Ultimately, the more recent High Court cases have shown that deference to the British legal heritage now stands in the way of further change beneficial to indigenous peoples. In this respect indigenous customary law retains its status merely as a form of non-state law simply because it does not originate from English law.

What is particularly problematic with this construction is that indigenous peoples are still accorded an inferior status through the way that their laws are not recognized as having their own legal force, but are mediated through and thus remain under the control of Australian law. Initially this control was exerted through the *Mabo* decision itself. But the effects of that decision were partly adopted and partly modified by the *Native Title Act 1993* (Cth) ('*NTA*'), and further remodelled by statutory amendments in 1998.[6] Although both versions of the *NTA* were intended to provide a framework for the implementation of the common law concept of native title enunciated in *Mabo*,[7] the statutory prescriptions have turned out to operate in a way that effectively excludes any continued influence of the common law. In effect the differences in origin between Australian law and indigenous customary law have led the High Court to conclude that native title cannot be understood in terms of common law precepts, and may only be understood in terms of the provisions of the *NTA*.[8] Thus the focus has shifted from a common law understanding of native title to a statutory approach.

On this approach, it is argued in the second part of the chapter that what is crucial to the maintenance of Australian legal control over indigenous peoples' native title claims is the line that the Court continues to draw back to its origins in British legal traditions, and in particular the acquisition of British sovereignty over the Australian territories.

In the third part of the chapter ways of addressing the High Court's approach to native title will be considered. As against the approach that the Court has taken, I will focus on the issue of giving state recognition to Aboriginal sovereignty and law as a means to redress the effect that invocations of British sovereignty have had in the native title context. I will conclude by arguing that in the current Australian legal system the status of indigenous customary law as a form of non-state law continues to contribute to the perpetuation of the colonizer–colonized relationship in Australia, and to the unequal treatment of indigenous peoples that arises from that relationship. However, if change to the law is to occur there needs to be a corresponding change in attitude towards indigenous peoples in Australian society.

2. AUSTRALIAN LAW AND NATIVE TITLE

In *Mabo* the High Court for the first time in Australian legal history gave legal recognition to an indigenous property precept, which it called native title. In the process the High Court rejected the so-called *terra nullius* doctrine as forming any part of Australian law. Whether it was in fact necessary for the Court to reject the *terra nullius* doctrine in order to recognize indigenous peoples' native title rights and interests is a matter of continuing controversy (Ritter 1996; Connor 2005). As Ritter has argued, it may not have been the doctrine of *terra nullius* as such that precluded the legal recognition of indigenous laws, but rather what may fairly be called the 'discourse of *terra nullius*' that informed the legal treatment of indigenous peoples throughout the period of colonization (Ritter 1996, p. 12). According to Ritter's analysis of the law in Australia, the doctrine of *terra nullius* was a doctrine that had emerged at the international legal level. There were no direct authorities in the Australian common law declaring the Australian territories as *terra nullius* in those precise terms. Furthermore, in the early colonial period there were no cases establishing a nexus between the doctrine of *terra nullius* and the absence of any common law recognition of native title. But in the absence of such a nexus, the discourse surrounding the nature of Aboriginal society (what Ritter has described as 'discourses of power')[9] was to an extent reflected in the existing authorities (Ritter 1996, p. 10). Among these discourses Ritter has identified the contribution that law played in the expropriation of the original owners:

> When the courts addressed the existence of the indigenous population at all, Aboriginal peoples were described as 'wandering . . . without certain habitation and without laws'; 'not in such a position with regard to strength as to be considered free and independent tribes'; without sovereignty; and wasteful of arable land. The Aboriginal people that were found on land were seen as 'physically present, but legally irrelevant'. (Ritter 1996, p. 12)[10]

The images depicted in these authorities were consistent with scientific opinion prevalent at the time on human evolution and the nature of indigenous peoples more generally. Indigenous peoples were readily identified as hunters and gatherers and as such were deemed to be at the bottom of the scale of civilization. Moreover, as they were considered to be in a perpetual state of nature they were denied recognition of their property rights, since they had no concept of property as understood in Western terms. According to Locke, for instance, the notion of 'property' was derived from the 'mixing' of land and labour made possible through the application of reason (Locke [1690] 1967, pp. 317–319). In this regard the 'absence of cultivation' on the Australian landscape came to reflect the indigenous peoples' own lack of reason.

Of course these attitudes, although dominant, were not universal. In *R v Bonjon*[11] Willis J accorded the status of domestic dependent nation to the indigenous peoples of New South Wales, as had been done in relation to the native populations in the United States.[12] He found that Aboriginal customary law and jurisdiction survived the introduction of the common law to the colony of New South Wales (Hookey 1984, p. 5).[13] This was consistent with the position that had been taken by Forbes CJ in relation to inter se matters arising between indigenous persons.[14] More generally, these positions were consistent with the understanding that the Imperial authorities had of the legal entitlements of the indigenous inhabitants to their lands (Reynolds 1987, pp. 139–140). However, these entitlements were never fully acknowledged by the colonists: at most indigenous peoples were entitled only to 'blankets, rations and protection from cruder forms of violence' (Reynolds 1987, p. 151). The dominant view of the colonists was that the indigenous inhabitants were 'too primitive, nomadic, savage' to have any legal entitlement to land (Reynolds 1987, p. 150) and these perceptions appear to have prevailed in the case law at the time.[15]

It would only be in the twentieth century, with the rise of anthropological studies of indigenous peoples, that this dominant view would begin to change. It was the anthropologists who would find that indigenous peoples did in fact have a culture: 'a social, economic, legal, political and religious organization by which they are able to adapt themselves to their geographical and social environment' (Elkin 1934, p. 15). Consequently the study of indigenous peoples would come to be dominated by the discourse of ritual and kinship, and by conceptions of the traditional Aborigine as impervious to historical change. As Wolfe has argued, 'Australia's anthropology's heterotopia *par excellence* is the Dreamtime, an ethnographical invention whose Edenic resonances have commended it to a global imagination' (Wolfe 1994, p. 109). But if indigenous peoples were seen as adaptable, their adaptability was understood as solely in terms of their own traditional culture. Aboriginality, from this anthropological perspective, was timeless and homogenous so that once the traits that were proof of Aboriginality were exposed to and tainted by British civilization, it was thought they were lost forever.

Legal acceptance of this perception of Aboriginality and the effect such perceptions have had on indigenous peoples has been patchy.[16] In the area of land rights the question of whether native title had survived the acquisition of British sovereignty was first considered in *Milirrpum v Nabalco*.[17] In that case Blackburn J accepted the evidence that showed the claimants had

> a subtle and elaborate system highly adapted to the country in which the people led their lives, which provided a stable order of society and was remarkably free from the vagaries of personal whim or influence. If ever a system could be called 'a government of laws, and not of men', it is that shown in the evidence before me.[18]

Nevertheless, he ultimately rejected the native title claim on the basis that 'the doctrine does not form, and never has formed, part of the law of any part of Australia'.[19] According to Blackburn J, if there was to be any recognition of such a title it could only be enshrined by 'express statutory provisions'.[20]

Despite the statutory provision of land rights (and because of their failure to fully deliver land rights to indigenous peoples) the result in *Milirrpum* was unsatisfactory. According to Blackburn J's own findings, it showed that a gap existed between Australian history and law: the indigenous claimants were found to be socially organized with their own system of laws and government that pre-dated the British arrival, yet there was no legal acknowledgement of that fact. It was only in *Mabo* that this gap was finally bridged through the legal recognition of native title in that case. But had the gap between law and history been completely filled?

If the law could be modified in *Mabo* in order to overturn the *terra nullius* doctrine and give legal recognition to native title it depended, in part, on bringing Australian law into line with developments in international law (most notably the rejection of the *terra nullius* doctrine by the International Court of Justice,[21] and developments in Australian domestic law (most notably the enactment of the *Racial Discrimination Act 1975* (Cth) ('*RDA*')). In this way Australian law was brought into 'conformity' with what Brennan J described as 'contemporary notions of justice and human rights'.[22] However, this was not of paramount importance to him. In determining whether modification of the law was possible in the first place: 'it is necessary to assess whether the particular rule is an essential doctrine of our legal system and whether, if the rule were to be overturned, the disturbance to be apprehended would be disproportionate to the benefit flowing from the overturning'.[23] That assessment was to be made by reference to the body of law (or at least its 'skeleton')[24] inherited from England. Thus, according to Brennan J's view in *Mabo*, the Court has a responsibility to declare the law for Australia in a way that does not undermine the legal system of which it is a part.[25] In this way, protecting that legal system becomes paramount – modifying the law to adhere to contemporary notions of justice and human rights is of secondary importance.

By maintaining continuity between Australian and English law in this way, Brennan J in *Mabo* reinscribed Imperial–colonial relations between Australia and Britain in spite of the level of independence now enjoyed by Australian law from English law.[26] However, to the extent that his judgment maintains the link between English and Australian law, rather than simply modifying the law to conform to contemporary notions of justice and human rights, it has also reinforced the colonizer–colonized relationship as between the Crown and the indigenous peoples. While the Court can transform English law into Australian law to form part of the fabric of Australian law, native title cannot be so transformed. To that extent native title remains foreign to Australian law, but unlike other foreign laws (including English laws) it does not have its own Court to offer it protection – 'no dual system of law, as such is created by *Mabo*'.[27] Justice Kirby's observations in *Wik* illustrate the difference in status between English law and Aboriginal customary law – the difference lies in the fact that the Court 'established by the Constitution, operates within the Australian legal system. It draws its legitimacy from that system. Self-evidently, it is not an institution of Aboriginal customary law.'[28]

For the Court, the unity of origin that it maintains between Australian law and English law cannot be paralleled by any similar unity between Australian law and Aboriginal customary law. Nonetheless, in the absence of any legal system of their own to protect their native title rights and interests, indigenous peoples are left to depend on the High Court (and now the *NTA* and the High Court's interpretation of that Act). As Hughes and Pitty have observed:

> The very act of affirming indigenous law asserts the jurisdiction of the High Court over the indigenous law of the continent. By assuming the power to affirm the continuing force of indigenous law in a severely restricted context . . . the High Court

> affirmed its jurisdiction and authority over indigenous laws. The Court may have contributed to the capacity of some indigenous peoples to live independently of the Australian state by securing their access to traditional land, but by making traditional land ownership dependent on the Court itself, the judicial arm of the state paradoxically asserts its jurisdiction over native rights. (1994, p. 14)

The formal recognition of native title by the common law could have advanced the development of legal pluralism in Australia: of two separate and distinct streams of law flowing through the Australian legal system, each having an equal status in its own right (Hocking 1993). Support for this interpretation of *Mabo* derives from the *sui generis* character ascribed to native title in the judgment of Deane and Gaudron JJ.[29] And, as Brennan J observed,

> [n]ative title has its origin in and is given its content by the traditional laws acknowledged by and the traditional customs observed by the indigenous inhabitants of a territory. The nature and incidents of native title must be ascertained *as a matter of fact* by reference to those laws and customs. (Emphasis added)[30]

Even so, it may be that as a matter of fact native title must be ascertained by reference to the laws and customs of indigenous claimants; but, as a matter of law it is the High Court that determines native title claims that come before it and the conditions that need to be met by indigenous claimants in order to succeed in their claims.

This is just one of the ways in which colonial relations in Australia are perpetuated in the *Mabo* decision, insofar as the control for deciding native title issues remains in the hands of non-indigenous legal institutions, and subject to non-indigenous laws. This is nowhere more obvious than in the effect that the doctrine of extinguishment has on native title. As McNamara and Grattan have observed:

> there appears to be no evidence that extinguishment – at least in the ways now recognised as part of the Australian common law – was possible under Aboriginal laws. And yet, the rules on extinguishment form a crucial part of the law of native title. Indeed . . . the concept of extinguishment 'functions to cancel out' the concept of native title. (1999, p. 146)

The perpetuation of colonialism is also evident in the Court's insistence on extending legal recognition only to native title, and not to any other indigenous customary laws, so that these laws remain unenforceable in Australian law.[31]

Ultimately, the different sources of Australian law and native title have justified their differential treatment. Thus, while English law may still share the same status as Australian law in Australia, native title does not. Instead it has an inferior status: it cannot be 'incorporated' completely and to the extent it is inconsistent with the common law it is void. And even though it has derived from a relationship of inequality, both the Court and the legislature have been reluctant to translate this into a requirement of protection within the legal framework of a fiduciary relationship. In any event, the limitations in *Mabo*, exacerbated by the outcomes of subsequent cases including in particular *Western Australia v Ward*[32] and *Members of the Yorta Yorta Aboriginal Community v Victoria*,[33] have eliminated any possibility of 'equal protection' for native title and compounded its inferior status. A wide swathe of native title is found to have been extinguished,[34] and once extinguished, native title cannot be revived; and no compensation can be paid for past acts of extinguishment prior to the enactment of the *RDA*. To the extent that native title may coexist with other titles to land, native title survives, but will be extinguished to the extent of any inconsistency with non-indigenous titles. As for the content of native title, in *Ward* the Court has endorsed a 'bundle of rights' approach, rather than an 'occupation' approach, which militates against any claim to exclusive possession of land. Moreover, both in *Ward* and *Yorta Yorta*, the Court has emphasized the traditional aspect of native culture in a way that limits both the kind of rights that can be claimed and the kind of people that can claim them. And, in *Ward* and *Yorta Yorta* the High Court has decidedly rejected any reference to the common law in determining native title claims under the *NTA*. This is particularly unfortunate for indigenous claimants, as the provisions in the *NTA* have in many ways contributed to compounding the inferior status of native title law in Australia (Tehan 2003, p. 555). In the next section particular attention will be given to the issues arising in *Ward* and *Yorta Yorta*.

3. THE BRITISH SOVEREIGN AND INDIGENOUS LAWS

The way in which native title is constructed – as different, but inferior – is underpinned by the Court's emphasis on the acquisition of British sovereignty and its consequences for the exercise of the Court's jurisdiction. 'The acquisition of territory by a sovereign state for the first time is an act of state that cannot be challenged, controlled or interfered with by the courts of that state.'[35] In stating the Court's position on the non-justiciability of the question of sovereignty in Australia, Brennan J quoted from Gibbs J's judgment in *NSW v Commonwealth*;[36] but the source of this principle in fact lies in the Privy Council decision in *Post Office v Estuary Radio Ltd*.[37] Thus as a statement of principle this position illustrates the continued adherence of the High Court to the English common law. More importantly the exercise of such judicial restraint effectively retains the British sovereign to the exclusion of any traditional indigenous law-making bodies that may have existed at the time that sovereignty was acquired. This view was expressly endorsed by the joint judgment in *Yorta Yorta*: 'the assertion of sovereignty by the British Crown necessarily entailed . . . that there could thereafter be no parallel law-making system in the territory over which it asserted sovereignty. To hold otherwise would be to deny the acquisition of sovereignty and . . . that is not permissible.'[38] The result in the end seems quite odd. While adhering to English precedents on the question of sovereignty in this way, so that British sovereignty cannot be subject to any possibility of judicial disturbance, the *Mabo* decision goes on to create an anomaly, so that in fact the overall result does not accord with the English position on the establishment of British colonies at all. According to Blackstone there are three ways that new territories could be acquired by the British Crown: conquest (which implies a clash of arms between two sovereigns), cession (which implies a treaty between two sovereigns) and settlement (which implies that the land is uninhabited, or at the very least uncultivated). It was the third category that had been applied to the Australian territories, on the understanding that they were 'desert and uncultivated'. Arguably, insofar as the Court in *Mabo* rejected the *terra nullius* doctrine and was able to give recognition to native title, that should have meant that the Australian territories would have to be reclassified as either 'conquered' or 'ceded', and on either basis the sovereignty of the peoples in pre-existing occupation would have been acknowledged (although the existing laws would be subject to modification or replacement by the Crown or by Parliament) (Blackstone 1773, pp. 106–108). However, the Court has now constructed its own anomalous category whereby native title is recognized but the territories are still classed as 'settled'. The implication is that indigenous peoples presumably did have laws, at least in respect of property in land, but did not have sovereignty.

However, what makes it even odder is that clearly by the time the Court decided *Yorta Yorta*, the analysis of the joint judgment in that case depended on a recognition that the indigenous peoples did have sovereignty after all: but only in a lost pre-history which the arrival of the British brought to an end. Thus, the end result in these cases is that native title survived the change in sovereignty, but Aboriginal sovereignty (and other indigenous customary laws) did not. And, as the case law reveals, even in relation to native title, the effects of the change in sovereignty are still being felt.

First, as the reasoning of the joint judgment in *Yorta Yorta* has made clear, the incidents of native title must now be determined as at the date of the acquisition of sovereignty by the British Crown, since this is the date on which indigenous sovereignty was brought to an end. It is on the basis of this logic that the joint judgment has understood the nature of the laws and customs from which native title derives as 'traditional' within the definition of native title in section 223(1) of the *NTA*. According to this understanding, only the native title rights and interests that were rooted in the traditional laws and customs of the pre-existing Aboriginal sovereignty, and have continued to be acknowledged and observed by the indigenous claimants, and who, by such adherence, have maintained their connection to their lands and waters since the acquisition of British sovereignty, are capable of legal recognition by Australian law.

In *Commonwealth v Yarmirr*[39] and *Ward*, this understanding of 'traditional' entailed dissecting the domestic use of rights to land and waters to the exclusion of economic rights, as these were found not to have been in existence at the time of the acquisition of sovereignty. In addition the reasoning in *Yorta Yorta* has allowed only some scope for change to, or adaptation of, traditional law or custom or interruption of enjoyment or exercise of native title rights or interests in the period between the Crown asserting sovereignty and the present.[40]

Thus the emphasis on the role of the British Crown in these cases has effectively served to confine the area over which native title can be claimed, the kinds of rights and interests that may be exercised over that area, and the people who may actually claim them. In fact in *Yorta Yorta* the joint judgment went so far as to find that the 'society'of the *Yorta Yorta* community 'which had once observed traditional laws and customs had ceased to do so and, by ceasing to do so, no longer constituted the society out of which the traditional laws and customs sprang'.[41] The result has been particularly unfortunate for indigenous peoples as it could lead to being subjected to discrimination: the drawing of distinctions between them (and worse still the possibility of a finding that their societies no longer exist) according to how well they present as 'traditional' Aborigines. In this way the emphasis given to the acquisition of sovereignty as the 'date' at which native rights and interests are to be recognized gives preference to the anthropological understanding of Aboriginality as immutable so that legal acceptance of indigenous laws and customs as traditional depends on how well indigenous communities have been able to resist change. In turn the emphasis on the date of the acquisition of sovereignty and the image of the 'traditional Aborigine' become interdependent. However, such an approach fails to acknowledge how the construction of the 'traditional Aborigine' has more recently come under challenge within the social sciences (Byrne 1996, pp. 82–84; Murray 1992; Attwood 1996a, p. xv) and by indigenous peoples themselves (Dodson 1994). Moreover, such an approach fails to account for change that has been wrought upon indigenous peoples against their will as a consequence of colonization practices and policies.[42]

Secondly, the binary opposition created by the Court's insistence that the two systems of laws have different sources, means that native title cannot be incorporated into Australian common law. Indigenous peoples have thereby been denied any of the potential positive benefits available in the common law doctrines relating to native title (Pearson 2003). The difference is one of origin: the source of Australian law and sovereignty is derived from British sovereignty, whereas indigenous laws have no such derivation. By adhering to this construction of the different laws, native title has been excluded from the common law. As the Court opined in *Yorta Yorta*, any continuing interaction between the two now lies in the *NTA*.

In *Ward* the stark contrast between indigenous law and Australian law effectively meant that common law property precepts (tacitly constructed as economic)[43] could not be used to give substance to indigenous peoples' conceptions of property (explicitly constructed as 'spiritual');[44] and this has meant that indigenous peoples' conceptions of property must always fall short of what would be considered as property at common law, and may never be given the same status and protection as common law property rights. If the underlying reasoning is circular, its effect in cases such as *Ward* has been none the less devastating. In the end result in *Ward* the Court took a 'bundle of rights' approach to native title, as the Court understood this approach as arising from the *NTA*. This means that native title rights and interests can be separated from each other and hence extinguished one by one, depending on whether the claimant group has continued to acknowledge and observe each of these fragmented rights since the acquisition of sovereignty. Arguably, the approach in cases like *Ward* is neither consistent with indigenous peoples' conception of property, nor commensurate with the conceptions of occupation and exclusive possession ascribed to such 'property' by the common law in other jurisdictions.[45] Rather, it has been argued:

> The construction of native title as a bundle of rights and interests, confirmed in the *Miriuwung Gajerrong* [*Ward*] decision . . . reflects the failure of the common law and the [*NTA*] to recognise Indigenous people as a people with a system of laws based on a profound relationship to land. Native title as a bundle of separate and unrelated rights with no uniting foundation is a construction which epitomises the disintegration of a culture when its law-making capacity, that is its sovereignty, is neatly extracted from it. (Aboriginal and Torres Strait Islander Social Justice Commissioner 2003, p. 27)

On the one hand, there may be an element of the inevitable in the way that the Court maintains its link to the British Crown and British legal traditions as the source of Australian law. So long as the legitimacy of the Australian nation is traced back to the acquisition of British sovereignty, the judicial emphasis on the time at which British sovereignty was acquired can be understood. Moreover, since the Australian colonies were perceived (at least at that time) as 'settled', there was no room for an acknowledgment of indigenous sovereignty, nor any requirement for the received common law to incorporate any doctrines of indigenous customary law. Thus, so long as the Court continues to focus on what happened at the time of acquisition, the exclusion of indigenous customary laws from Australian common law can also be understood.

On the other hand, it is also true that the complete independence now enjoyed by Australian law from English law, means that it can no longer be said that it has its foundation solely in English law. And, to the extent that native title was recognized by the Australian common law, it is a product of the processes of that system and in that respect has its origin in the Australian common law. So much appears to have been accepted by Parliament when it referred to native title as 'the rights and interests . . . recognised by the common law of Australia' in the definition of 'native' title in section 223(1) of the *NTA*. In the absence of legislative provisions explicitly purporting to override the common law, the scope for the common law to continue to inform developments in the area of native title law remains.

But even at the time of the acquisition of sovereignty the English common law, as received by the Australian colonies, could have been adapted to suit the local conditions where the circumstances were exceptional enough to warrant modification. Such modification in order to incorporate indigenous customary laws may not have been acceptable to the colonists during the early period of colonization; but now that there has been recognition at least in relation to native title, it is difficult to see why the same recognition should not be extended to other aspects of Aboriginal customary law, even though this might entail an acknowledgment of pre-existing Aboriginal sovereignty. If the common law can be modified to accommodate native title, there is no reason why it could not be similarly modified in other respects, although it may be a question that only Parliament and the Australian people can now answer. In light of the more recent native title cases it would seem that recognition of some form of Aboriginal sovereignty has now become imperative, as the symbolism of such recognition could serve to promote technical changes to the High Court's construction of native title in cases like *Ward*, and to accommodate the diversity and adaptability of indigenous peoples' experiences of colonization that cases like *Yorta Yorta* have ignored. In short, recognition of Aboriginal sovereignty may align Australian law and history more closely together.

4. SOVEREIGNTY REVISITED

Calls for the recognition of Aboriginal sovereignty and the implementation of the policy of self-determination in relation to issues concerning indigenous peoples have been high on the agenda of indigenous activists in Australia (Behrendt 2003). Such calls are understandable considering the level of discrimination experienced by indigenous peoples who remain subject to Australian law. Evidently, while indigenous peoples have their own systems of laws, these laws have not been incorporated into the state's legal institutions. As a form of non-state law, indigenous customary law does not have the protection of Australia's legal institutions and, as the case law in native title reveals, even when such laws are legally recognized they still are not fully protected. Moreover, the case law in native title also reveals how indigenous culture in the legal context continues to be essentialized and rendered ahistorical. Achieving the status of sovereign peoples could assist indigenous peoples to overcome these problems.

It is important to recognize, however, that sovereignty as understood by indigenous peoples is not necessarily the same as 'sovereignty' as understood in international law. While there are some indigenous activists who envisage establishing separate states or nations (Mansell 1989; Gilbert 1999), for others the term connotes sovereignty at the grass roots level: a form of sovereignty that will provide indigenous peoples, whether as groups or as individuals, with independence and autonomy in the decision-making processes that impact on them the most. In this respect 'sovereignty' is more akin to the notion of self-determination. Even on this understanding, however, while 'sovereignty' may transform indigenous experiences at the grass roots level, its transformative spirit may have to start at the top with the state.

Behrendt (2003) is among those indigenous activists and scholars who take this more moderate line. The most important change that Behrendt has proposed in relation to law reform is the introduction of legal pluralism to Australian legal institutions and legal norms. This model of legal pluralism would reflect indigenous experiences and values and include the recognition of indigenous sovereignty and laws. However, there are problems that need to be addressed in making these suggestions.

Notably, Behrendt has avoided altogether the more difficult issues of accommodating aspects of indigenous customary laws that are potentially incommensurate with Australian law (and international human rights standards), particularly in the areas of criminal law and marriage law[46] and, for that matter, the dilemmas involved in establishing the content and substance of the customary laws that are to be accommodated in the first place.[47] In this regard she may too readily sidestep some of the problems that plague indigenous communities – they too are sites of inequality of power between individuals and groups.[48]

Moreover, contemporary arguments for legal pluralism may not escape the problems associated with pluralism as a political movement. For example, Wolff (1969, pp. 40–49) has argued that in any attempt at intergroup pluralism, the established groups will always be favoured over those struggling for recognition; and similarly that the more powerful groups will always be favoured over the weaker, so that legitimate interests lacking organizational strength will continue to be disadvantaged. Both points are relevant to the Australian experience and indeed to the experience of indigenous peoples across the world who historically have not enjoyed the conditions of equality with their non-indigenous counterparts due to their conditions of powerlessness. There are lessons to be learned from the experiences of indigenous peoples in other parts of the world, including the United States, New Zealand and Canada. Those lessons are not always encouraging.

However, that is not to deny that benefits can be derived from such reforms. In particular the degree of recognition given to indigenous rights in such countries has led to a ready understanding (or at least more ready than has hitherto been achieved in Australia) of the relationship between cultural rights and economic rights: 'an appreciation of the connection between land and aspirations to self-government and economic self-sufficiency' (Brennan et al. 2005, p. 99). In Australia, development towards this approach is lagging behind. As far as the case law on native title is concerned, movement towards this approach has been further obstructed. In *Ward* the Court rejected the proposition that control of traditional cultural knowledge was a native title right: the 'recognition' of this right would extend beyond denial or control of access to land held under native title.[49] Moreover, in both *Croker Island* and *Ward* the economic potential of a positive finding of native title was effectively undermined – only the native title rights and interests that existed at the time of the acquisition of sovereignty and have survived to the present time will be given legal recognition. And yet a trend is being set towards this approach by the increased use of agreement-making between indigenous and non-indigenous bodies.[50] In fact native title recognition has led to a greater willingness by non-indigenous bodies to engage in negotiations with indigenous peoples than ever before.[51] Undoubtedly agreement-making has its shortcomings (not least that such agreements are subject to law and the inherent shortcomings of the current legal system).[52] Paradoxically, however, these agreements could bypass some of these problems and alleviate others that have arisen in the native title context.[53]

Even so, Behrendt's analysis has failed to address the issue of how genuine conflict between competing rights is to be resolved. In practice (at least in the native title context) it may be that one solution is for stakeholders to engage in agreement-making whereby 'rights' to land are negotiated, while also acknowledging the shortcomings of such an approach. More broadly, however, the theoretical problem of 'rights' which are conceived of as absolute, but must nevertheless be reconciled with other conflicting absolute 'rights', has no satisfactory solution, especially for indigenous peoples whose attempts at achieving rights due to the conditions of inequality have been less than successful.

Yet, while criticisms of pluralism illuminate the problems that may arise due to the inequality of power between the players within such a system, such criticisms are not reason enough to abandon it entirely. Inequality of power between state institutions is a problem that could plague any model of government. An advantage that a legal system based on a model of pluralism would have over the present model is that at least it would address a structural problem inherent in the present one – the failure to incorporate indigenous laws and sovereignty in Australia's legal and political institutions. This may not overcome the issue of inequality of power, but it could be a step in that direction. At the least it would serve a symbolic function – a reminder that indigenous peoples' interests should not be ignored and can be accommodated through reform of existing, and if need be the creation of new, institutional structures.

However, of more crucial concern to the prospects of introducing legal pluralism to Australia are the conservatives' claims that such reforms are divisive and undermine the unity of Australia as a sovereign nation (Markus 1996; Attwood 1996b). These concerns echo another criticism of legal pluralism advanced by Wolff (1969, pp. 49–52): namely, that its emphasis on group and inter-group interests excludes any overriding conception of 'the public interest' or 'the common good'. Arguably, however, such concerns ignore the dilemma surrounding the establishment of the Australian state in the first place. According to Behrendt, if Australian law and history are to be reconciled, Australians have to come to terms with the way that the Australian state was illegitimately founded – most notably in the treatment of Australian territory as *terra nullius* and the taking of possession of the territory without the 'consent of the natives' in a way that was contrary to the international legal precepts of the time. According to this understanding the legal recognition of Aboriginal sovereignty would place the legitimacy of the nation on a more secure foundation (Behrendt 2003, pp. 103–104, 141–145).

Moreover, underlying the conservatives' concerns are conceptions of Aboriginality as inferior, undeserving or, worse still, a threat to the nation. Such attitudes can be found at all levels of Australian social and political life (Markus 1996) and, as the discussion of native title law has revealed, even in the High Court. Once this is accepted then it becomes apparent that any structural obstacles in the way of recognition of Aboriginal sovereignty and laws in fact derive their legitimacy from a particular conceptual framework in which 'non-Aboriginality', or at least 'whiteness/maleness' (Pettman 1988, p. 3), continues to be set as the standard against which indigenous peoples are measured and found lacking. In this regard if a recognition of Aboriginal sovereignty and the establishment of legal pluralism that it will entail is to take place, it requires a rethinking of the images of 'Aboriginality' and 'Australian-ness' upon which exclusion of indigenous interests has historically been legitimized.

Thus, what is also needed is successful promotion of respect for cultural difference in Australia so that it becomes accepted as part of Australian cultural life. For Patton three things are necessary in order to achieve this outcome:

> First, we must become capable of thinking of cultural differences in positive terms, as specific differences between distinct ways of life, none of which is singled out as the standard by which others are unilaterally judged. Second, we should expect and welcome movement and cross-fertilisation between the different forms of social life. Third we need to appreciate the value of such differences within the larger networks of community and social life that make up a modern nation state. (1995, pp. 164–165)

The difficulty remains that any assertion of difference attributable to the indigenous cultural identity as a basis for change is informed by assumptions of the settler culture even while it seeks to transcend them. Thus, while in theory a social order created out of 'cross-fertilization' is conceivable, it is not so easy to construct it in practice, especially as long as relations of power remain as they are. Even Behrendt (2003, pp. 131, 139) has conceded the extent to which indigenous identity is itself a product of colonial invention, at the same time as she reclaims this identity as potentially transformative of the prevailing institutional structures. The difficulty with this approach is that, by maintaining Aboriginality as the focal point for change, a trace of the colonial discourses surrounding Aboriginality may remain; and it is difficult to see how such a concept can now be used as a positive force in a way that would free it from the negative associations it has had in the past. This may be an inevitable shortcoming which it may not be possible or desirable to overcome, especially for those seeking a more culturally inclusive Australia. As indigenous peoples have also found:

> both Aboriginal and non-Aboriginal people create Aboriginalities. These constructions, however much we may wish to reject them, are the context in which we live. They inform not only the way others think about and react to us, but also the lived experience that we have of ourselves and of each other. They have also become the enemy within. (Dodson 1994, p. 6)

Questioning the perception of identities (whether of individuals, groups or institutions) as fixed and unified, and revealing them not to be so, may provide a framework for change. By contrast to the conservative vision of Australia as unified and cohesive, such a framework would reveal the extent of disunity already present in Australian society, not only in its institutional structures but in the racial tensions pervading its fabric. Paradoxically it is the persistent claim of the conservatives that any form of recognition of indigenous rights would divide the nation which perpetuates the racial divisions in Australian society. And it is through these racial divisions that control over indigenous peoples continues to be made possible. This particular form of 'divide and rule' strategy is known all too well to indigenous peoples:

> It is an historical fact that from the very inception of British colonisation, the indigenous people of this country have been treated as a separate society. However, when we project this fact in our aim of achieving sovereignty and of our struggle for compensation for dispossession and for economic independence that will allow us to run our own affairs, people say 'You can't do that – it's divisive'. (Behrendt 1995, p. 399)

Currently it would seem that racial tensions and divisions pervade all levels in Australia but as yet motivation to overcome these divisions is still lacking.[54] If change is to take place, the change needs to be perceived as positive and not as negative, as seems to be the mainstream view. In order for this change to take place it may require nothing less than breaking the cycle of a history of colonialism in Australia.

5. CONCLUSION

At the height of the debate over native title in the 1990s Murrandoo Yanner made the poignant observation:

> The farmers in their hysteria think they're going to lose their land. Our people in their error think they're going to get their land. They're both wrong. So you win native title on a pastoral lease, and then what happens? The pastoralist opens the gate and says, 'Murrandoo, go do your dance and song and catch a turtle – and close the gate when you leave tomorrow'. Native title is not sovereignty. It's not land rights . . . it gets us to the table, that's all. (Ivison 2002, p. 148)

The result in *Mabo* could have been worse for indigenous peoples. The High Court did at least affirm the common law's recognition of native title when it could have rejected the claim in *Mabo* altogether. However, it did not go as far as giving full legal protection to indigenous peoples' native title rights and interests. As McHugh J observed in *Ward*, '[t]he deck is stacked against the native-title holders whose fragile rights must give way to the superior rights of the landholders whenever the two classes of rights conflict.'[55] But if non-indigenous property rights must always trump those of indigenous peoples it is because of the way they have been constructed in Australian law. Native title, 'though recognized by the common law, is not an institution of the common law',[56] and thus it remains foreign to Australian law. However, as it has no legal system of its own to offer it protection, it remains under the control of Australian law. As other indigenous customary laws, its status remains as a form of non-state law and as such subordinate to Australian law and the interests it protects. As argued in this chapter, recognition of Aboriginal sovereignty could overcome these problems. Ultimately the success of such a strategy would depend on the good faith of the Australian state and its people.

NOTES

1. (1992) 175 CLR 1 ('*Mabo*').
2. Ibid 76 (Brennan J). This order related to the whole of the Murray Islands except for a parcel of land leased to the Trustees of the Australian Board of Missions and any parcels of land which had been validly appropriated for use for administrative purposes the use of which was inconsistent with the continued enjoyment of the rights and privileges of Meriam people under native title.
3. Ibid 41–42 (Brennan J); 108–9 (Deane and Gaudron JJ); 184 (Toohey J).
4. See especially *Attorney-General (NSW) v Brown* (1847) 1 Legge 312; *Cooper v Stuart (1889)* 14 App Cas 286; *Williams v Attorney-General (NSW)* (1913) 16 CLR 404; and *Randwick Corporation v Rutledge* (1959) 102 CLR 54. See generally *Mabo* (1992) 175 CLR 1, 102–4 (Deane and Gaudron JJ).
5. This discrimination was reflected in the *Commonwealth of Australia Constitution Act 1900* (UK) ('the Constitution'). For instance, originally s. 127 of the Constitution had provided that: 'In reckoning the numbers of the peoples of the Commonwealth, or of a State or other part of the Commonwealth, aboriginal natives shall not be counted.' This provision was repealed by referendum in 1967. Moreover, indigenous peoples were not entitled to vote at federal elections until the *Commonwealth Electoral Act 1918* (Cth) was amended in 1962.
6. *Native Title Amendment Act 1998* (Cth).
7. Commonwealth of Australia, 16 December 1993; Commonwealth of Australia, 2 December 1997.
8. *Yorta Yorta* (2002) 214 CLR 422.
9. See also Williams (1990, p. 6). This notion of 'discourses of power' has been adopted and adapted in colonial contexts from the work of Michel Foucault. See especially Foucault (1980, pp. 119–130); see also Foucault (1972), Foucault (1971) and Foucault (1979). See also Said (1978); Said (1985). In relation to the Australian context see especially Attwood and Arnold (1992).
10. The internal quotations are from *MacDonald v Levy* (1833) 1 Legge 39, 45; *R v Murrell* (1836) 1 Legge 72, 73; *R v Bonjon* (Unreported, Supreme Court of New South Wales, Willis J, 18 September 1841); and Simpson (1993, p. 200).

11. Unreported, Supreme Court of New South Wales, Willis J, 18 September 1841.
12. *Cherokee Nation v Georgia*, 30 US (5 Peters) 1 (1831); and *Worcester v Georgia* 31 US (6 Peters) 515 (1832).
13. See also Decisions of the Superior Courts of New South Wales, 1788–1899, www.law.mq.edu.au/scnsw/cases 1840-41/cases 1841/R%20v%20Bonjon,%201841.htm, accessed 12 June 2007.
14. *R v Ballard or Barrett* (Dowling, Proceedings of the Supreme Court, Vol. 22, Archives Office of New South Wales, 2/3205, 98–106, Decisions of the Superior Courts of New South Wales, 1788–1899, www.law.mq.edu.au/scnsw/Cases 1829-30/html/r_v_ballard_or_barrett__1829.htm, accessed 12 June 2007.
15. Most notably in *R v Murrell* (1836) 1 Legge 72, it was found that the 'aboriginal natives' were not sovereign and did not have their own laws. Burton J opined: 'although it be granted that the aboriginal natives of New Holland are entitled to be regarded by Civilized nations as a free and independent people, and are entitled to the possession of those rights which as such are valuable to them, yet the various tribes had not attained at the first settlement of the English people amongst them to such a position in point of numbers and civilization, and to such a form of Government and laws, as to be entitled to be recognized as so many sovereign states governed by laws of their own' (Supreme Court, Miscellaneous Correspondence relating to Aborigines, State Records of New South Wales, 5/1161, 210, 211, Decisions of the Superior Courts of New South Wales, 1788–1899, www.law.mq.edu.au/scnsw/cases 1835-36/html/r_v_murrell_and_bummaree__1836.htm#10a, accessed 12 June 2007).
16. Cf *Aboriginal Land Rights Act 1983* (NSW) ss 3, 4 and *Aboriginal Land Rights (Northern Territory) Act 1976* (Cth) s. 3.
17. (1971) FLR 141 ('*Milirrpum*').
18. Ibid 267.
19. Ibid 245.
20. Ibid 244. All Australian states and territories except Western Australia have since passed land rights legislation.
21. *Western Sahara (Advisory Opinion)* [1975] ICJR 12.
22. *Mabo* (1992) 175 CLR 1, 30.
23. Ibid.
24. Ibid.
25. Ibid.
26. Australian legal independence from English law culminated with the enactment of the *Australia Act 1986* (Cth).
27. *Wik Peoples v Queensland* (1996) 187 CLR 1, 214 ('*Wik*'). See also *Yorta Yorta* (2002) 214 CLR 422, 443–44.
28. *Wik* (1996) 187 CLR 1, 213.
29. *Mabo* (1992) 175 CLR 1, 89.
30. Ibid 58.
31. See *Coe v Commonwealth* (No. 2) (1993) 118 ALR 192; *Walker v New South Wales* (1994) 182 CLR 45; *Bulun Bulun v R & T Textiles Pty Ltd* (1998) 157 ALR 193; and *Western Australia v Ward* (2002) 213 CLR 1 ('*Ward*').
32. (2002) 213 CLR 1 ('*Ward*').
33. (2002) 214 CLR 422 ('*Yorta Yorta*').
34. See, eg, *Wilson v Anderson* (2002) 213 CLR 401; *Yorta Yorta* (2002) 214 CLR 422; *Risk v Northern Territory of Australia* [2006] FCA 404; and *Jango v Northern Territory of Australia* (2006) 152 FCR 150, in all of which the native title claims wholly failed. For examples of partially successful claims see *Commonwealth v Yarmirr* (2001) 208 CLR 1 ('*Croker Island*'); *Ward* (2002) 213 CLR 1; *Daniel v Western Australia* [2003] FCA 666; *Neowarra v Western Australia* [2004] FCA 1092; *Sampi v Western Australia* (No. 2) (2005) 224 ALR 358; *De Rose v South Australia* (No. 2) (2005) 145 FCR 290; and *Bennell v Western Australia* (2006) 153 FCR 120.
35. *Mabo* (1992) 175 CLR 1, 31 (Brennan J).
36. (1975) 135 CLR 337, 388 ('*Seas and Submerged Lands Case*').

37. [1968] 2 QB 740.
38. *Yorta Yorta* (2002) 214 CLR 422, 443–4 (Gleeson CJ, Gummow and Hayne JJ).
39. (2001) 208 CLR 1 ('*Croker Island*').
40. *Yorta Yorta* (2002) 214 CLR 422, 454–6.
41. Ibid 458 (Gleeson CJ, Gummow and Hayne JJ).
42. More recently this issue arose in *Risk v Northern Territory of Australia* [2006] FCA 404; aff'd [2007] FCAFC 46. In that case Mansfield J affirmed the High Court's decision in *Yorta Yorta*. In his summary of his reasons for decision Mansfield J noted (at para. [12]) some of the effects of colonization on the claimant group. These effects led him to conclude (at para. [13]) that 'the current Larrakia society, with its laws and customs, has not carried forward the traditional laws and customs of the Larrakia people so as to support the conclusion that those traditional laws and customs have had a continued existence and vitality since sovereignty'. Cf Lamer CJ in *Delgamuukw v Queen in right of British Columbia* [1997] 3 SCR 1010, 1103 ('*Delgamuukw*'), where he comments: 'To impose the requirement of continuity too strictly would risk "undermining the very purpose of s. 35(1) [of the *Constitution Act 1982*] by perpetuating the historical injustice suffered by aboriginal peoples at the hands of colonizers who failed to respect" aboriginal rights to land.' Gaudron and Kirby JJ (in dissent) took a similar view in *Yorta Yorta*, insisting that it had been the intention of Parliament when it enacted the *NTA* to acknowledge a history of dispossession and give protection to native title rights and interests: 'So much was impliedly recognised in the Preamble to the Act which "sets out considerations taken into account by the Parliament", including that Aboriginal people and Torres Strait Islanders had been "progressively dispossessed of their lands"' (*Yorta Yorta* (2002) 214 CLR 422, 463).
43. *Ward* (2002) 213 CLR 1, 395–7 (Callinan J).
44. Ibid 65 (Gleeson CJ, Gaudron, Gummow and Hayne JJ).
45. See especially *Delgamuukw* [1997] 3 SCR 1010, 1103.
46. This is an acute problem arising in the context of traditional customary marriages, particularly where there are allegations of violence. See *Amagula v White* [1998] NTSC 61 (7 January 1998) and *Ashley v Materna* [1997] NTSC 101 (21 August 1997). Cf *Jamilmira v Hales* [2004] HCATrans 18 (13 February 2004).
47. In *Ngatayi v The Queen R* (1980) 149 CLR 305, 13 Murphy J identified this as a concern: 'The existence of two systems of law side by side, the prevailing one and aboriginal customary law, with their very different attitudes to guilt and responsibility, creates serious problems and the question of how far our law should apply to aboriginals and how far their law should be allowed to apply to them is controversial.'
48. This dilemma has been highlighted most recently with revelations of high incidences of domestic violence and child abuse in remote areas of the Northern Territory. See Northern Territory Government, *Inquiry into the Protection of Aboriginal Children from Sexual Assault*, www.nt.gov.au/dcm/inquirysaac/report_summary.html, accessed 22 July 2007.
49. *Ward* (2002) 213 CLR 1, 84.
50. See, for example, Mildura Marina Indigenous Land Use Agreement (ILUA) (6 October 2005), www.atns.net.au/agreement.asp?EntityID=3118, accessed 29 August 2007; Ord Final Agreement, Indigenous Land Use Agreement (16 August 2006), www.atns.net.au/agreement.asp?EntityID=2654, accessed 29 August 2007; Eastern KuKuYalanji Indigenous Land Use Agreements (11 April 2007), www.nrw.qld.gov.au/nativetitle/dealings/yalanji.html, accessed 29 August 2007. Each of these agreements was made pursuant to the *NTA*.
51. Most notably this has occurred in Western Australia, where historically there has been the greatest resistance to acknowledge any pre-existing indigenous title to land.
52. For an overview of the problems facing indigenous peoples when engaged in agreement-making processes, see Tehan (2003, pp. 564–565, 569–570); Bradfield (2004, p. 12); Agius et al. (2002, p. 12); and Dolman (1999, pp. 8–9). See generally Godden and Dorsett (2000).
53. Notable examples include the Co-operative Management Agreement between the *Yorta Yorta* Nation Aboriginal Corporation and the State of Victoria and the Ord Final

Agreement Indigenous Land Use Agreement between the government of Western Australia, Miriuwung Gajerrong traditional owners and various private sector developers. Both agreements were entered into at the completion of the *Yorta Yorta* and *Ward* native title litigation in the High Court. The benefits of the agreement for the *Yorta Yorta* Corporation fall short of those that would have flowed from a positive finding of native title. Significantly, however, the agreement acknowledges that '[t]he State [of Victoria] recognises that the *Yorta Yorta* Peoples are the traditional owners of and have a unique relationship with and responsibility to their country' and that '[t]he State of Victoria acknowledges the cultural connection of the *Yorta Yorta* People to the Designated Areas', a recognition that no Australian court was prepared to make. (Quoted in Seidel and Hetyey 2004, pp. 15, 16.)

54. In Council for Aboriginal Reconciliation (2002), the Council for Aboriginal Reconciliation ('CAR') recommended the enactment of legislation to put in place a process which would unite all Australians by way of an agreement, or treaty, and which would enable outstanding issues of reconciliation to be resolved. These recommendations were rejected by the Howard Government at the time. In Commonwealth of Australia (2002), the Government reaffirmed its opposition to a treaty by insisting that (at 19) 'a legally enforceable instrument, as between sovereign states would be divisive, would undermine the concept of a single Australian nation'.
55. *Ward* (2002) 213 CLR 1, 241.
56. *Mabo* (1992) 175 CLR 1, 59 (Brennan J).

REFERENCES

Aboriginal and Torres Strait Islander Social Justice Commissioner (2003), *Native Title Report 2002*, Parliamentary Paper No. 41.

Agius, P., Jocelyn Davies, Richie Howitt and Lesley Johns (2002), 'Negotiating Comprehensive Settlement of Native Title Issues: Building a New Scale of Justice in South Australia', *Land, Rights, Laws: Issues of Native Title*, **2** (20), 1–12.

Attwood, B. (1996a), 'Introduction: The Past as Future: Aborigines, Australia and the (Dis)course of History', in B. Attwood (ed.), *In the Age of Mabo*, Sydney: Allen & Unwin, pp. vii–xxxviii.

Attwood, B. (1996b), '*Mabo*, Australia and the End of History', in B. Attwood (ed.), *In the Age of Mabo*, Sydney: Allen & Unwin, pp. 100–116.

Attwood, B. and John Arnold (eds) (1992), *Power, Knowledge and Aborigines*, Melbourne: La Trobe University Press.

Behrendt, L. (2003), *Achieving Social Justice: Indigenous Rights and Australia's Future*, Sydney: Federation Press.

Behrendt, P. (1995), 'Aboriginal Sovereignty: Australian Republic: A Catalogue of Questions and Answers', in I. Moores (ed.), *The Voices of Aboriginal Australia: Past, Present, Future*, Springwood: Butterfly Books, pp. 398–405.

Blackstone, William (1773), *Commentaries on the Laws of England*, Volume I, Introduction, sect. 4, Oxford: Clarendon Press.

Bradfield, S. (2004), 'Agreeing to Terms: What is a "Comprehensive" Agreement', *Land, Rights, Laws: Issues of Native Title*, **2** (26), 1–16.

Brennan, S., Larissa Behrendt, Lisa Strelein and George Williams (2005), *Treaty*, Annandale: Federation Press.

Byrne, D. (1996), 'Deep Nation: Australia's Acquisition of an Indigenous Past', *Aboriginal History*, **20**, 82–107.

Commonwealth of Australia (1993), *Parliamentary Debates*, 5097, (Gareth Evans, Leader of the Government in the Senate), Senate, 16 December.
Commonwealth of Australia (1997), *Parliamentary Debates*, 10171, (Nicholas Minchin, Special Minister of State and Minister, Assisting the Prime Minister): *Members of the Yorta Yorta Aboriginal community v Victoria* (2002) 214 CLR 422, 467–8 (McHugh J) ('*Yorta Yorta*'), 2 December.
Commonwealth of Australia (2002), *Commonwealth Government Response to the Council for Aboriginal Reconciliation Final Report – Reconciliation: Australia's Challenge*.
Connor, M. (2005), *The Invention of Terra Nullius: Historical and Legal Fictions on the Foundation of Australia*, Sydney: Macleay Press.
Council for Aboriginal Reconciliation (2002), *Reconciliation: Australia's Challenge*.
Dodson, M. (1994), 'The Wentworth Lecture. The End in the Beginning: Re(de)finding Aboriginality', *Australian Aboriginal Studies*, **1**, 2–13.
Dolman, K. (1999), 'Native Title Mediation: Is it Fair?', *Indigenous Law Bulletin*, **4** (21), 8–10.
Elkin, A.P. (1934), 'Anthropology and the Future of the Australian Aborigines', *Oceania*, **5**, 1–18.
Foucault, Michel (1971), *Order of Things*, New York: Pantheon Books.
Foucault, Michel (1972), *The Archaeology of Knowledge*, New York: Pantheon Books.
Foucault, Michel (1979), *The History of Sexuality, Volume 1: An Introduction*, London: A. Lane.
Foucault, Michel (1980), 'Truth and Power', in Michel Foucault, *Power/Knowledge: Selected Interviews and Other Writings 1972–77*, C. Gordon (ed.), Brighton: Harvester Press, pp. 109–133.
Gilbert, K. (1999), '*Aboriginal Sovereignty: Justice, the Law and Land.* A draft written in consultation with Aboriginal Members of the Sovereign Aboriginal Coalition at Alice Springs on 19–21 June 1987', in B. Attwood and Andrew Markus (eds), *The Struggle for Aboriginal Rights: A Documentary History*, St. Leonards: Allen & Unwin, pp. 310–313.
Godden, L. and Shaunnagh Dorsett (2000), 'The Contractual Status of Indigenous Land Use Agreements', *Land, Rights, Laws: Issues of Native Title*, **2** (1), 1–12.
Hocking, B. (1993), 'Aboriginal Law Does Run in Australia', *Sydney Law Review*, **15**, 187–205.
Hookey, J. (1984), 'Settlement and Sovereignty', in P. Hanks and Bryan Keon-Cohen (eds), *Aborigines and the Law*, Sydney: Allen & Unwin, pp. 1–18.
Hughes, I. and Roderic Pitty (1994), 'Australian Colonialism after Mabo', *Current Affairs Bulletin*, **71** (1), June/July, 13–22.
Ivison, D. (2002), *Postcolonial Liberalism*, Cambridge: Cambridge University Press.
Locke, John [1690] (1967), *Two Treatises of Government*, P. Laslett (ed.), London: Cambridge University Press.
Mansell, M. (1989), 'Treaty Proposal', *Aboriginal Law Bulletin*, **2** (37), 4–9.
Markus, A. (1996), 'Between Mabo and a Hard Place: Race and the Contradictions of Conservatism', in B. Attwood (ed.), *In the Age of Mabo*, Sydney: Allen & Unwin, pp. 88–99.
McNamara, L. and Scott Grattan (1999), 'The Recognition of Indigenous Land Rights as "Native Title": Continuity and Transformation', *Flinders Journal of Law Reform*, **3**, 137–162.

Murray, T. (1992), 'Aboriginal (Pre)History and Australian Archaeology: The Discourse of Australian Prehistoric Archaeology', in B. Attwood and John Arnold (eds), *Power, Knowledge and Aborigines*, Melbourne: La Trobe University Press, pp. 1–19.
Patton, P. (1995), 'Post-structuralism and the Mabo Debate: Difference, Society and Justice', in M. Wilson and Anna Yeatman (eds), *Justice & Identity: Antipodean Practices*, Sydney: Allen & Unwin, pp. 153–171.
Pearson, N. (2003), 'The High Court's Abandonment of "The Time-Honoured Methodology of the Common Law" in its Interpretation of Native Title in *Mirriuwung Gajerrong* and *Yorta Yorta*', *Newcastle Law Review*, **7**, 1–14.
Pettman, J. (1988), 'Whose Country is it Anyway? Cultural Politics, Racism and Politics, Racism and the Construction of Being Australian', *Journal of Intercultural Studies*, **9**, 1–24.
Reynolds, H. (1987), *The Law of the Land*, Melbourne: Penguin.
Ritter, D. (1996), 'The "Rejection of *Terra Nullius*" in *Mabo*: A Critical Analysis', *Sydney Law Review*, **18**, 5–33.
Said, Edward (1978), *Orientalism*, London: Routledge.
Said, Edward (1985), 'Orientalism Reconsidered', *Race and Class*, **XXVII**, (2), 1–15.
Seidel, P. and Julian Hetyey (2004), 'Summary of the *Yorta Yorta* Nation Aboriginal Corporation/State of Victoria Co-operative Management Agreement', *Indigenous Law Bulletin*, **6** (4), 15–17.
Simpson, G. (1993), '*Mabo*, International Law, *Terra Nullius* and the Stories of Settlement', *Melbourne University Law Review*, **19**, 195–210.
Tehan, M. (2003), 'A Hope Disillusioned, an Opportunity Lost? Reflections on Common Law Native Title and Ten Years of the *Native Title Act*', *Melbourne University Law Review*, **27**, 523–571.
Webber, J. (1995), 'The Jurisprudence of Regret: The Search for Standards of Justice in *Mabo*', *Sydney Law Review*, **17**, 5–28.
Williams, R.A. (1990), *The American Indian in Western Legal Thought*, New York: Oxford University Press.
Wolfe, P. (1994), 'Nation and MiscegeNation: Discursive Continuity in the Post-Mabo Era', *Social Analysis*, **36**, 93–152.
Wolff, R.P. (1969), 'Beyond Tolerance', in R.P. Wolff, Barrington Moore Jr and Herbert Marcuse (eds), *A Critique of Pure Tolerance*, Boston: Beacon Press, pp. 3–52.

11. Regulating the living will: the role of non-state law at the end of life

Oliver W. Lembcke

1. INTRODUCTION

It is the contribution of legal positivism that state and law are seen as a unit. The representatives of natural law positions achieved their greatest success when the standards for human rights were internationalized; but the legal positivists should not only pride themselves in having concisely summed up the logics of the legal system. They also summed up the legal profession's self-description in a concise manner. Their point of view governs the dogmatic daily routine of the legal system, at least in states founded on the rule of law. Seen from this perspective, it must come as a 'culture shock' when there is an encounter with other political communities where law is not (exclusively) 'positively' determined by the state but is formed in a social context in everyday worldly situations from which it draws its effectiveness. It is precisely this 'other hemisphere of the legal world', as described in Chapter 2, that legal pluralism refers to (e.g. Griffiths 2002), therefore stirring up a controversy which is still going on today (Woodman 1998) and which is, in a fundamental sense, by no means less intense than the controversy over the relationship between law and morals.

Legal pluralism has characteristically gained its insight by dealing with other cultures (e.g. Merry 2003). These anthropological and sociological studies have promoted, among other things, the belief that law cannot be categorically distinguished from other forms of social control. Indeed, the dividing lines are blurred, which is due, in part, to the phenomenon that the sources motivating people to follow rules are similar if not the same (Griffiths 2001). While questions concerning motivation are of no significance to a legal positivistic position, the gradualized distinction between legal and social norms, which is intended by legal pluralism, encounters even greater resistance.[1] It seems impossible to reach an agreement on this problem, because legal positivism, as described in Chapter 3, rejects all legal sources with the exception of the authority of the state, whereas the representatives of legal pluralism do not view it as a theory but as an 'ideology of legal centralism' (Griffiths 1986). According to their conviction, legal systems can develop independently from a state and exist side by side (Galligan 2007, p. 162); and not only in those former colonial societies whose regimes are now in transformation. It is also possible in states founded on the rule of law among the West's (post-)industrial societies.

Within this context, the regulations for passive euthanasia seem to provide us with insights that may go beyond this dichotomy and often ideologically driven controversies about the 'nature' of (state) law. Of course, the topic of euthanasia itself is ideologically controversial and moreover characterized by a number of particular circumstances (Dworkin et al. 1998). Among other aspects, it means that there is a conflict of values in which two fundamental principles of a state founded on the rule of law – autonomy and the protection of life – are juxtaposed, both on behalf of human dignity (Lembcke 2007). At first sight, this case study may encumber comparative and insightful statements but, on second thought, this normative 'mixture' proves to be quite revealing when the relationship between state law and non-state law is examined. In legal history as well as in the history of political ideas the Hippocratic Oath appears to be embedded in a tradition of self-commitment, which depicts, to a certain extent, a kind of prototype of non-state law. But its 'counterpart', the living will, also deserves close consideration because, in a legal sense, it demands a great deal: in a life-and-death situation, the living will is designed to permit the patient to have the last word, even though he is no longer conscious. The one-sidedness of this legal declaration of intent resembles a last will; but since it is frequently rejected by the doctor in charge of the patient, it raises the question of practicability (Gehring 2006, pp. 208–210) as well as the question of its relationship to state law.

2. TYPES OF LEGALITY

Distinguishing between state law and non-state law is only helpful when the terms are defined as precisely as possible. Law is understood as legal regulations which are of a generally compulsory nature.[2] By adding the word *state* to law, it does not refer to a specific legal area (e.g. public law), but it refers to the justification upon which all general obligations are based, i.e. state authority. On the surface, state law is characterized by its authority to use force, as stated by Kant ([1797] 1907, p. 231). And that is the main difference from non-state law, which is unable to implement the state's monopoly on the legitimate use of physical force to fulfil its obligations. But the fact that non-state law develops from a social agreement should not mislead one to believe that disobedience will be accepted without any consequences. Whenever someone violates accepted rules of behaviour, the 'perpetrator' should always be prepared to experience various forms of social isolation as an outsider. In sum, the validity of non-state law is based on the general acceptance that certain forms of behaviour are right.[3]

2.1 The Hippocratic Oath

The Hippocratic Oath[4] is given credit for being the first oath to lay down the basic ethical principles for physicians (Wilmanns 2000, p. 205). Among other things, it establishes the fundamentals of the relationship between the physician and the patient; those passages in particular are of lasting validity. Three specific passages are of special significance to our present topic: In the first paragraph, the subsequent statements of the Hippocratic Oath are subject to the experience of day-to-day practice, where only that which is possible is valid practice. A physician's duty is to cure patients, a technique which can only be exercised under the conditions of what is actually possible on the basis of systematic experience; to do less would be negligent, fraud. In the third paragraph, the principle is put forward that what is useful for an individual patient is of utmost priority. The standard is not determined by Plato's and Aristotle's polis but by the individual who serves as the standard for judging a physician's treatment. In the fourth paragraph, there are some very remarkable statements which postulate that killing a patient is absolutely forbidden; a physician is neither allowed to actively aid or to advise someone to die when they are tired of living nor to assist in abortion.

What the Oath introduces is essentially a set of professional ethics for physicians (Jouanna 1996, p. 72). Its continued significance today is due to the description of the relationship between the physician and the patient, which should be characterized, according to the Oath, by trust (Wilmanns 2000, p. 206). The considerations on euthanasia are astonishingly relevant, perhaps because arguments are given for both sides. Those who want to protect life can cite the passages that reject (active) forms of euthanasia and refer to the spirit of the text, which is absolutely incompatible with the idea of killing. The other side, the representatives of a patient's autonomy, find arguments based on the principle that what is useful for a patient is of utmost priority and that a physician must act on the basis of his own ability and knowledge (Admiraal 2003, p. 36). Whatever interpretation of the text is accepted depends primarily on the interpretive power of the persons involved as well as the specific cultural framework of the situation.

In regard to German physicians, for whom the Hippocratic Oath serves as the nucleus of their professional standards (Taupitz 1991), the picture is by no means clear, but certain structures are recognizable: A large majority rejects the idea of active euthanasia, which includes the idea of assisting someone to commit suicide. German physicians see themselves as protectors of life – especially against the background of euthanasia during the Nazi reign. They place terminal care above palliative care (Beleites 2003, pp. 44–50). This is also reflected in the principles of the German Medical Association (Bundesärztekammer) regarding palliative care. It is emphasized that a patient has the right of self-determination, but it is also stressed that a physician's role is to protect the life of a patient, especially towards the end of his life.

With reference to physicians' professional standards, there is a need to qualify this non-state law on the basis of legal theory. In this sense, the 'mapping' suggested in Chapter 2 has proven to be quite helpful. It distinguishes between a geographical and a methodological axis. In regard to the geographical axis, it is quite obvious: in modern societies physicians are members of the functionary elite in a political community; they act within the framework of laws and require this embeddedness in a state's jurisdiction, because otherwise their behaviour would be punishable due to their continued violation of objects protected by law: the life and well-being of their patients. At the same time, we should not forget that the Hippocratic Oath is older than every state on earth which was founded on the rule of law. So the oath can actually claim a validity which is normally only seen in connection with natural law.[5]

The classification is less obvious on the methodological axis. Undoubtedly both the Hippocratic Oath as well as professional standards for physicians have to do with rules of conduct; that is perfectly clear. But the medical function of a physician is also connected to an objective authority, a circumstance which has recently been critically discussed in association with the concept of 'paternalism' (Zude 2006). This, however, does nothing to change the situation that the physician who is treating a patient can often only rely on himself when it comes to making long-range decisions. Consequently, every standardization for physicians fulfils two functions: on the one hand, it relieves the physician when he makes a decision; on the other hand, it offers a concrete list of general normative steps which can be taken in any case, no matter whether the legislative power had been able to or will be able to foresee what might occur. These or guidelines for physicians take on the character of rules of conduct.

2.2 The Living Will

The basic idea of the living will is to anticipate the state of the patient's incapability to consent and to make binding arrangements for the extent and manner of medical care at one's own end. Authors of such regulations intend to draw an image of death in dignity according to their own ideas. The living will, then, has a twofold purpose: firstly, it should exclude circumstances in which the patient's will is disregarded or misinterpreted by a third party. The intention here is to minimize the risk not to receive attention in an adequate way or, even worse, to become a homo sacer – in Agamben's words – totally depending on the physician's sovereign decision about life or death (Agamben 1998, pp. 160–165). To prevent such situations, the concept of the living will aspires, secondly, to transform situations of incapability to consent, which tend to limit the euthanasia's catalogue of measures, through professed declarations, set down in voluntary situations in advance. Their maxim is to establish the patient's will as a primate with regard to the medical duty to save life. By that, patients who are no longer able to take decisions on their own come closer to the status of those who are in (full) possession of their mental powers and can express themselves appropriately. Moreover, the implementation of their own ideas about the death process becomes easier and the role of the appointed custodian – if necessary – to the guardianship court or the doctors in attendance is strengthened. Nevertheless, there are possible cases in which the will, that once formed the basis of the living will, becomes out-dated and does not correspond with the current treatment situation any longer.

3. THE LEGAL SITUATION IN GERMANY

Current debate on euthanasia in Germany, which is driven by the desire to strengthen patient rights, is urging the legislature to act. Yet the issues are complex. They begin with the conceptual distinction between active and passive euthanasia, which is of considerable significance legally but appears questionable ethically. The legal situation is marked by gradual transitions from one offence definition to another, which the courts and the academic literature tediously adapt to the challenges of individual fate in the world of the living while struggling to interpret presumed intent. Accordingly, the living will is the focal point of various draft bills in this area, but the requirement for and extent of its validity remain legally unclear even after two landmark decisions of the German Federal High Court (BGH).

3.1 Jurisdiction

In Germany, as in many other countries, the reference to the presumed will refers to the most difficult chapter of legal euthanasia. In principle, for the continuation of the treatment, it is legally assumed that an alleviation of pain complies with the patient's presumed will (Dölling 1987, p. 6). But within the framework of the will's interpretation this assumption can prove to be wrong. Since the German legislator has not taken any regulations on its own in this field so far, it had been up to the jurisdiction to develop principles for the status and for the scope of the patient's presumed will and to set criteria for its application in the field of euthanasia; in this connection the BGH's decisions of general principle of 1994 and 2003 are most relevant (Lembcke 2007).

In its verdict of 1994 the BGH decided on the question of whether the intended termination of the nasogastric feeding of a persistively appalic patient, on the son's initiative and already planned by the physician in the medical file, had been in accordance with the law (BGHSt 40, p. 257). As a result the court of justice judged the action as attempted homicide, but referred the case back to the district court with a number of stipulations which can be summarized in the following three points: Firstly, an 'admissible killing' is not to be ruled out a priori, as the district court mistakenly assumes, but rather, as the court argues, it depends on presumed consent (BGHSt 40, p. 257, p. 262). If such a consent is non-existent (as in the particular case), it can secondly be replaced by an effective consent of the custodian, for which (in analogy to § 1904 BGB) the agreement of a guardianship court is required. If the custodian has not obtained this agreement, it is thirdly, according to federal judges, necessary to reconstruct the presumed subjective will of the patient for discontinuing the treatment admissibly because only such a reconstruction can claim to do justice to the actual patient's will (BGHSt 40, p. 257, p. 263). In summa: due to the BGH the patient autonomy is shielded from different perspectives of the participants involved in two ways. The treatment can neither be stopped nor continued against the patient's will, even if the discontinuation is considered to be premature and therefore unreasonable (Dreier 2007, p. 323).

In a second verdict of 2003 the BGH made further ascertainments of its first decision (BGHZ 154, p. 205). Contrary to the verdict of 1994, in this case a living will was existent, though its implementation was threatening to fail due to the resistance of the attending physician. Among other things, the federal judges made clear that the formerly submitted expression of will is going to be persistent despite the incapability to consent that has occurred in the meantime (§ 130 Abs. 2 BGB) – provided that (as in this particular case) an appointed custodian enforces the will of the patient – and that furthermore, the continuation of the medical treatment is still dependent on the consent of the patient respectively of the appointed custodian.

That way the BGH strengthened the rights of patients as well as the role of the custodian; at the same time, in a volte of its own jurisdiction of 1994 the judiciary emphasized the difference between the patient who is incapable of consent and one who is capable of consent; and additionally to the (presumed but via provision confirmed) will the judiciary designated objective factors as a requirement for discontinuing a treatment: 'If a patient is incapable of consent and if his underlying disease turns out to be irreversibly fatal, life-sustaining and life-prolonging measures have to be ceased when this meets the pre-assigned will – for instance in the form of a so-called living will. This follows from human dignity' (BGHZ 154, p. 205; translation by Oliver W. Lembcke).

3.2 Legislative Drafts

It is in the nature of things that, on the basis of two cases, supreme court practice cannot (and neither should) fulfil the function of the legislator. A number of questions, especially with their focus on technical details, therefore remain open and face a legislative regulation of euthanasia: Is the irreversibly fatal course of the underlying disease, which the court is speaking about, a necessary requirement for discontinuing treatment? Or does patient autonomy, at least under these requirements which are on hand for the court's decision, have to be obeyed unrestrainedly? Reversed: despite the decisions of the supreme court, it continues to be open, whether and in which way the autonomy of the patient will be and can be restrained through the evaluation of physical condition and chances of recovery by the physician – proximity of death, extent of pain, chances of alleviation, and so on. Basically, it is this unsolved situation that has caused the increasing demand for the legislator in recent years.

Quite different drafts circulate in the present German debate on euthanasia. These different and partly very detailed drafts clarify the extent of legislative responsibility which requires the examination of the possibly essential legal regulations of omission, restriction and discontinuation of life-sustaining measures as well as the clarification of rather technical questions like the deposit of and the access to living wills. A comparative examination of the abundance of material makes just as clear that as yet there can be no question of an agreement on the fundamental problem which became apparent in the discussion about the decisions of the BGH. The representatives of an unrestricted self-determination of the patient's will still face those who speak up for the restriction of the will's scope. This is paradigmatically expressed in two parliamentary drafts:[6] on the one side the group bill around the representatives Wolfgang Bosbach, René Röspel, Josef Winkler and Otto Fricke; on the other side the draft of Joachim Stünker, all members of the German Parliament.

Stünker's draft on the part of the SPD starts out from the theoretically comparable position of patients who are capable of consent and patients who are incapable of consent. This position is established through the living will – and is hereby primarily based on the decision of the BGH in 1994. In this sense the obligatory nature of the living will is emphasized, in fact 'independently of type and stage of the illness'. In contrast, the group bill (Bosbach et al.) refers to the scope limitation of the living will:

> Also a living will has to stay within the limits of legal admissibility: contents of a living will which contravene the law or offend common decency are declared invalid. Active euthanasia, passive euthanasia without the availability of an infaust prognosis (or the social facts of the final loss of consciousness) as well as the exclusion of a basic health care are impossible by means of the living will (scope restriction). (Lembcke 2007, p. 515, own translation)

Corresponding to the diversity of views, the role of the guardianship court is built up in different ways. The draft of the SPD sees the function of the court mainly in dispelling existing doubts about the presumed will through court – and consistently reduces the access barriers to legal checks, when third persons have doubts. The other side however, wants to grant the state law the right to have further-reaching rights to control. In that view, the court's function is not limited to a kind of clearing regarding the presumed will, as it is seen in the discussion paper of the SPD. Instead it is, with regard to the participants involved, given the right to intervene in the quarrel and the regulatory powers in case of dissent (whose probability increases with the rising number of persons involved); moreover, the court holds a fundamental reservation of decision regarding the will of the person affected, expressed in the form of a living will – at least when the criterion of the proximity of death is lacking, despite the hopelessness of the disease.

4. CHARACTERISTICS AND COMPARISONS

4.1 The Relation of State Law and Non-State Law

The German regulations of the living will are structured by the legal distinction between active and passive euthanasia. According to the law in force § 216 StGB prohibits every form of direct euthanasia (killing on request). However clear the threat of punishment might appear at first sight, so difficult is the delimitation to the two concepts of assisted suicide and indirect euthanasia (Jakobs 1998) – with consequences for medical practice. The fear of physicians of being prosecuted for killing on request is comprehensible, for instance in cases in which medicinal alleviation of pain brings about life-shortening effects (Dreier 2007, pp. 320–321).[7]

As for 'assisted suicide' the logic is the following: since dying at one's own hands is, according to German law, not an intentionally illegal criminal act – as Hegel has already argued (1971, p. 350) – its assistance is in principle not subject to punishment. But this literally changes in the very second when the 'aid' begins to take its effects. This is when, according to German criminal law dogmatics, the power to act (*Tatherrschaft*) passes to the helping hand, with the result that he is committed to save life with the threat of punishment (homicide through omission). If it matters whether the physician who mixed barbiturates into the beverage is still present or not, the argument lacks convincing reasoning because all depends on chance, but not on the agreement of the people involved nor on the distinction of active/passive euthanasia.

For 'indirect euthanasia' the legal judgments meander similarly. These include measures for the alleviation of serious suffering which may be life-shortening due to their inevitable side effects. Depending on aim and form of action, these measures can therefore basically be classed as active euthanasia ('active-indirect euthanasia'), by which they are part of the norm of killing on request. It is still correct that a good pain therapy can be helpful for not letting rise the desire for a quick end in the moribund or to suppress the already existing death wish. But it is also true that the intentions for alleviating pain on the one hand and the life-shortening effects on the other can be very closely joined together. Anyhow, the border to active euthanasia, in fact also in the case of patients who are not capable of consent, is definitely crossed when the moribund cannot live to see the (intended) alleviation of pain because death appears immediately. Below this threshold, criminal law dogmatics offers numerous possibilities of solution (Lembcke 2007). The prevailing opinion basically tries to solve the problem by means of emergency measures (§ 34 StGB) in connection with the patient's consent. This legal interpretation is supposed to smooth the physician's way to weigh up between quality of life (qua alleviation of pain) and protection of life.[8]

This legal situation has raised an overall feeling of insecurity not only among German physicians but also among patients and their families (Beleites 2003, p. 44) to which the distinction between active and passive euthanaisa has contributed. However comprehensible this distinction might appear at first sight, it has been fundamentally criticized. The criticism is twofold: On the one hand, the relevance of the differentiation between active and passive euthanasia for the moral assessment of facts is being denied (Siep and Quante 1999, pp. 45–46); on the other hand, the difference between acting and failing to act is doubted (Quante 1998, p. 213). As far as the form of action is concerned (active/passive), it becomes obvious that both passive and active forms presuppose a decision-making process, and, as the case of a renunciation of therapy shows, it also requires activity (e.g. to turn off the equipment).[9] With that the comparison of life-prolonging and life-shortening measures as a criterion for the allocation of acting and failing to act begins to sway. Legally, at least according to German law, life-prolonging measures are requested and their omission is prohibited and the life-shortening measures are prohibited and their omission is requested. The explanation of passive euthanasia, with reference to the patient autonomy that emanates from human dignity, could indeed open up the scope for considering and justifying certain measures but, at the same time, suggests the question of why measures that allow an improvement of the patient's quality of life detrimental to his life expectancy, should be impossible. Looking at the corresponding case groups in criminal law dogmatics, it becomes ascertainable that such measures can be (exceptionally) justified (Lembcke 2007). Yet, this justification has less to do with the distinction between acting and omitting, but with the patient's consent and the responsibility of the 'helping hand'.

The problems with the forms of acting as a base for the differentiation between active and passive euthanasia seem to result from a misleading contrast: omission as non-action. This perspective is misleading because it fails to see the ethical and legal evaluations underlying the different forms of action. Usually, the motives and consequences (inasmuch as these are relevant) play an important role in the evaluation of actions. The question about the agent of the action seems to be less important, unless the person's capacity to act autonomously is in doubt (e.g. in cases of criminal offences committed by minors). In the case of omission, however, the order is reversed. Here, the crucial factor is who has omitted to act, whereby a constant examination of the consequences of the respective failure is followed. In connection with passive euthanasia this means that in the view of the physician, only his failing treatments on the patient are relevant for the evaluation; others are not. If some other person, like the neighbour in the next bed, stops the therapy through turning off the equipment, it is no longer necessary to consider passive euthanasia but murder and homicide. Acting and failing to act are not mutual negations but refer to other perspectives; they are therefore unsuitable to convey the serious valuation difference of active and passive euthanasia. Rather, they offer the reason for understanding that the forms of euthanasia can be differentiated but that they are related to each other by their gradual transitions. In this network of relations the forms of action (active/passive) are less recommending 'guideposts' than regulative 'traffic lights' that express an already existing evaluation of the respective measure of euthanasia: *active* is supposed to be the sign for actions that are prohibited, whereas *passive* is the sign for requested actions; it is a question of 'framing', and within the context of euthanasia it depends essentially on the patient's will, whether actions are requested or prohibited.

However, as such, framing is just an expression for a more serious problem. To put it in simple terms, there are three strategies which can be used in dealing with non-state laws: (1) The state can integrate non-state laws and equip them with sanctions; (2) the state can delegate its regulatory competence to non-state actors and steer results and standards by prior selection and education as well as by implementing after-the-fact control mechanisms; and (3) non-state laws can be respected by the state as independent laws and treated as such, whereas the duty of the state consists of leaving room for non-state regulations. German regulations regarding euthanasia are strictly determined and monitored by the state and sanctioned by state law. This, however, does not promote the relationship between the physician and the patient. Considered from a point of view determined by criminal law, the relationship of trust, as mentioned in the Hippocratic Oath, is, for the most part, factored out as a prerequisite for successful medical treatment.[10]

Yet, specific problems of age and ageing have become increasingly significant on the political agenda. Within this context, the topic of euthanasia has been attracting more and more public attention. An increasing number of Germans have been dealing with the problems of dying with dignity and with the possibilities offered by the living will (e.g. Kodalle 2003). This has not taken place without leaving an impact on German physicians. The public discussion has helped to change the self-conception of physicians; in the meantime, the profession of medical doctor has become less paternalistic. This change has been documented in the guidelines of the German Medical Association during the past 30 years: in 1979 the medical profession spoke of the precedence of keeping a patient alive no matter what the patient wanted. However, this original principle has been revised since 1998, ever since the meaning of the living will was emphasized as a major factor determining medical decisions (Beleites 2003, pp. 44–45).

4.2 Germany, USA, the Netherlands

Much like the German model, American regulations are also strictly influenced by jurisdiction, because the legislative power has refused to pass binding laws.[11] So, just as in Germany, American courts have been forced to develop general regulations based on individual cases. The first case considered to be a 'right to die' case was Karen Ann Quinlan in New Jersey. After falling into a coma (PVS) on 15 April 1976, without any hope of recovering, her father applied for court permission to have her life-support apparatus shut off. Based on the right of privacy, the New Jersey Supreme Court (Matter of Quinlan, 355 A. 2d 647) derived the right of self-determination, which could be exercised by a medical attendant to the best of his knowledge. Provided that the person concerned was incapacitated, substituted judgment could be carried out.[12] In 1990 the United States Supreme Court passed judgment on its first case of passive euthanasia (Cruzan v. Director, Missouri Dept. of Health, 497 U.S. 261 and passim). In that case, the court maintained the strict standards for evidence which had been previously applied by the lower courts in Missouri. Clear and convincing evidence of the patient's wishes was necessary to shut off the life-support apparatus. The protection of life was of utmost priority, because a life-sustaining mistake could always be corrected after the fact, whereas a mistake that ended a patient's life could not (Schmaltz 2001, pp. 88–93).

As the various examples point out, regardless of the different legal cultures, case law has become state law in both the USA and Germany. In terms of content, both cases have developed in the same direction with the difference between active (illegal) and passive (legal) euthanasia dominating. This is particularly clear in the court decision of Barber v. Superior Court of the State of California (195 Cal. Rptr. 484; Cal. App 2 Dist. 1983). In this case the court decided that terminating life-support measures as well as refusing to give the patient a manual IV (infusion) was not active treatment but negligence. But, on the other hand, there is no legal duty to act when the patient wants no further treatment and actually considers it to be 'pointless'. Nevertheless, neither in Germany nor in the USA has jurisdiction succeeded in gaining a consensus of the population to develop a legal awareness of the fine dividing lines between legal certainty and uncertainty. On the contrary, the attitude that prevails among judges in American courts is that cases dealing with passive euthanasia should not be made the object of courtroom decisions, as far as this is possible. Their aim is to reach a unanimous agreement among the actors involved beforehand;[13] incidentally, according to political appeals, Congress is responsible for establishing binding regulations (e.g. Conroy, 486 A. 2d 1209, 1220). Regarding this field, German courts, on the other hand, do not show any intention of retreating. On the contrary, the BGH has pointed out the significance of the 'guardianship' courts which are to be incorporated not only for lawsuits but also as a kind of structural pre-control system (see above).

Regardless of these differences, the same consequences have been observed in both countries for the relationship between a patient's autonomy and fiduciary medical duty. Formed by jurisdiction, i.e. through verdicts in individual cases, both legally relevant principles are seen as a collision and not as a moment of cooperation between the physician and the patient. Yet it is hardly remarkable that courts usually tend to upgrade the patient's declaration of intent, as it corresponds in a number of ways to the well-known legal figures of day-to-day jurisdiction. But this will not necessarily strengthen the autonomy of patients, because both American and German jurisdictions have especially implemented objective criteria for interpreting the living will (irreversibility of the illness, impending death, etc.). That way not only the patient's subjective concept of dying with dignity is hollowed out. Essentially the primacy of a physician's decision-making authority is secured and stabilized,[14] at least as long as the courts possess no professional competence of their own regarding their regulation of passive euthanasia. Indeed, they seem to confine their efforts to regulating malpractice.

In contrast, the Dutch have largely freed themselves from the 'myth' of an absolute murder ban for physicians. To them, it isn't a matter of deciding between active and passive euthanasia (Admiraal 2003, p. 40). It is a mutual process of decision-making between the physician and the patient. The physician must be able to trust the patient that his decision to cut his life short is meant seriously. The patient, on the other hand, must be able to trust that the doctor will support him in every way possible and take the utmost care. Considered together, these demands yield a catalogue of duties for both sides: among other things, the patient must have repeated his will several times and have depicted his suffering in a believable way. The physician, on the other hand, must have his diagnosis confirmed by another doctor that the patient's situation is hopeless and there is no way to free him of his suffering; in addition to this, he must be present during the process of dying and report the patient's death to the municipal coroner at the end. During the procedure, the physician is to follow the corresponding regulations of the Burial and Cremation Act, which specifically includes the physician's duty to report the case. The report will later become the object of an investigation by the ethics commission, whose results will determine whether the patient 'died in peace' or – in the case of a violation of the physician's obligation to take care – whether the district attorney will bring charges against the physician responsible for the patient (e.g. Wernstedt 2004, p. 109).

Dutch lawmakers became active in a way quite different from what had been done in the USA and Germany after the courts had already permitted (active) euthanasia in specific cases (Fischer 2004, p. 189).[15] Politics not only assimilated and positivized large sections of those regulations which had been established by medical practitioners beforehand. Politicians also made sure that a physician's area of action was removed from the radius of a criminal offence – though only under reserve. Therefore, the relationship between state law and non-state law is defined by the thought of deference which is supposed to facilitate self-regulation in the medical area of euthanasia (Griffiths 2000): if a relationship of trust exists between a physician and a patient and corresponds to the spirit of the Hippocratic Oath, the state limits its duty to a final procedural inspection. Within this constellation, the possible collisions between the autonomy of the patient and the physician's obligation to care are weakened; the living will integrates itself into a conception where both sides have to fulfil their obligations to ensure a mutual decision-making process.

5. CONCLUSIONS

Against the background of a legal comparison between the American and the Dutch models, the structure of German euthanasia regulations can be more clearly defined by taking a closer look at the difference between state law and non-state law: By assuming that 'physicians are not allowed to kill' one brings together a state law in the form of criminal law with the physician's self-conception according to the Hippocratic Oath which is also reflected as a non-state law in various guidelines of the German Medical Association. But this agreement has not been used to legally widen the area of action for physicians; and that will probably not change in the near future, as the short description of various drafts of new legislation has shown. A delegation of authorized regulations, ranging from state law to non-state law, can only be found within the narrow limits of jurisdictional inspection, because only in this way can the circumstances be justified – according to German (and also American) legal attitudes – that the necessary actions do not represent murder within the framework of 'passive' euthanasia.

The living will has become by virtue of jurisdiction a bona fide moment of decision-making recognized by state law within the framework of euthanasia. But the way the relationship between the patient's autonomy and the physician's obligation to care has been formed by the courts has led to a situation where both principles have ended up with a kind of zero-sum game: the patient's self-determination reduces the physician to the level of a security function who wards off abusive interpretations from third parties; on the other hand, the physician's expert knowledge threatens to patronize the patient. This contradictory point of view can only be redeemed by having the actors interact in a procedural context in which both the governmental actors (lawmaker, courts, experts) and the social actors (doctors, patients, family members, attendants) do not mutually demand too much of each other. Among other things, that includes the possibility of establishing a self-regulatory practice in which decisions are actually made in a decision-making process. In this sense, the Dutch model offers quite illustrative material.

The state law dealing with euthanasia within a German context which has been formed by court measures is subject to the self-deceptive belief that it can steer a process, although the state essentially lacks any instruments to actually steer the process. It has hardly any means at its disposal with which to establish incentive systems, so it must essentially rely on the control mechanisms of legal proceedings and the sanctions of criminal law. But, in accordance with common jurisdiction, it still fundamentally depends on the competence of physicians. The BGH decisions have not only revaluated the living will. They have also revaluated the objective factors needed to interpret the patient's will. This tilted treatment of the objective factors needed for the interpretation of the living will requires a judgment primacy which can only be redeemed by the doctors in charge of treatment whose regulations go beyond the character of behavioural norms and achieve the quality of decision-making norms.

NOTES

1. This became especially clear in the Kelsen–Ehrlich debate (Kelsen and Ehrlich 2003).
2. For example, contracts undoubtedly have to do with law, but they only oblige those parties who signed the agreement to abide by the contract.
3. As Max Weber (1980, pp. 122–124) clearly pointed out, the reasons for this belief can be varied, ranging from a dull habit to a conviction derived from intense reflection.
4. Named after Hippocrates of Kos (460–370 BC), who is generally known as the founder of scientific medicine.
5. It may be possible to interpret the Hippocratic Oath in many different ways, as mentioned above, but a violation of its norms or its spirit could cause negative 'emotional overtones' which might indicate a break in human rights standards. Ehrlich ([1936] 1975, p. 165) speaks in this sense of a 'feeling of revolt', 'indignation' and 'disgust'. See Brugger (1992) for the significance of an unlawful experience in justifying human rights.
6. For a detailed discussion of the several different legislative drafts see Lembcke (2007).
7. Also the base of legitimacy for the punishment of killing on request remains unclear, since in German law suicide is not subject to prosecution. It seems to be the danger that in the end it was not the will of the killed person but a sovereign decision of the 'helper' which led to death. But this could lead to the unsatisfactory solution of forcing a totally helpless person to continue a life that tortures him/her to live. A case in point is the example of Diane Pretty (EctHR, 2346/02, 29 July 2002). In such borderline cases assisted suicide is basically ruled out. The argument appears to be somewhat cynical: because of the complete physical dependence of the patient the power to act fundamentally lies with the assistant.
8. A construction which the BGH lent support to: 'Because the possibility of a death in dignity and in freedom of pain, in accordance with the patient's declared or presumed will, is a legally protected right of higher quality than the prospect to have to live under the most serious, in particular so-called excruciating pain any longer' (BGHSt 42, 301, 305; transl. by Oliver W. Lembcke).
9. In this regard, it is therefore consistent to talk about an 'omission through action', as Roxin (1987, p. 349) has suggested.
10. The German legislator seems to recognize the problem: the work group of the German Federal Ministry of Justice suggested an amendment to § 216 StGB to clarify that indirect as well as passive euthanasia are not included in the radius of homicide. The aim

of such a regulation is evident: The medical profession shall be prevented from being afraid of possible consequences of criminal law, so that everything within the available possibilities of medicine can be done to alleviate the most serious pain (Kutzer 2006, p. 37).

11. Oregon is an exception in this respect; see the Oregon Death with Dignity Act, Ore. Rev. Stat. §§ 127.800–127.995 (1995); Attach. B. Active euthanasia has not been dealt with by a law yet – as opposed to the situation in the Netherlands.
12. In later decisions, the courts developed more precise standards regarding the prerequisites for terminating treatment; see the cases of 'Matter of Conroy' (486 A. 2d 1209 New Jersey) and 'Matter of Peter by Johanning' (529 A. 2d 419 New Jersey 1987); Schmaltz (2001, pp. 81–88).
13. Although US courts consider a trial to be 'inexpedient', numerous physicians are still waiting for the decision of an American court before they participate in a case of passive euthanasia. The reason for this is an impending medical malpractice suit (Schmaltz 2001, p. 116).
14. This sense was clearly expressed in a statement by the Nordic Medical Council in 1998: 'The Nordic medical associations respect and appreciate the principle of a patient's right to decide for themselves if they will submit to treatment and choose between several different treatments. However, the respect for human rights should not lead to the fact that actions are put on doctors which are in conflict with the fundamental medical-ethical principles, to which doctors in the Nordic countries feel committed. Therefore, the Nordic medical associations would like to warn the governments of the Nordic countries against introducing the right to euthanasia in the Nordic countries' (quoted in Wernstedt 2004, p. 97).
15. For a more detailed view on the Dutch legal situation before the year 2002, especially on the 'requirements of careful practice', see Griffiths et al. (1998, pp. 104–107).

REFERENCES

Admiraal, Pieter (2003), 'Euthanasie - das niederländische Modell', in Klaus-Michael Kodalle (ed.), *Das Recht auf ein Sterben in Würde. Eine aktuelle Herausforderung in historischer und systematischer Perspektive* (Kritisches Jahrbuch der Philosophie, vol. 4), Würzburg: Königshausen & Neumann, pp. 31–41.

Agamben, Giorgio (1998), *Homo Sacer. Sovereign Power and Bare Life* (transl. by Daniel Heller-Roazen), Stanford, CA: Stanford University Press.

Beleites, Eggert (2003), 'Über die Diskussion in der deutschen Ärzteschaft zum Thema "Aktive Sterbehilfe" ', in Klaus-Michael Kodalle (ed.), *Das Recht auf ein Sterben in Würde. Eine aktuelle Herausforderung in historischer und systematischer Perspektive* (Kritisches Jahrbuch der Philosophie, vol. 4), Würzburg: Königshausen & Neumann, pp. 43–50.

Brugger, Winfried (1992), 'Stufen der Begründung von Menschenrechten', *Der Staat*, **31** (1), 19–38.

Dölling, Dieter (1987), 'Zulässigkeit und Grenzen der Sterbehilfe', *Medizinrecht*, **5** (1), 6–12.

Dreier, Horst (2007), 'Grenzen des Tötungsverbotes', *Juristenzeitung*, **62** (1/2), 261–270, 317–326.

Dworkin, Gerald, Raymond G. Frey and Sissela Bok (1998), *Euthanasia and Physician-Assisted Suicide*, Cambridge: Cambridge University Press.

Ehrlich, Eugen ([1936] 1975), *Fundamental Principles of the Sociology of Law*, New York: Arno Press.

Fischer, Elena (2004), *Recht auf Sterben?! Ein Beitrag zur Reformdiskussion der Sterbehilfe in Deutschland unter besonderer Berücksichtigung der Frage nach der Übertragbarkeit des Holländischen Modells der Sterbehilfe in das deutsche Recht*, Frankfurt a.M.: Peter Lang.

Galligan, Dennis J. (2007), *Law in Modern Society*, Oxford: Oxford University Press.

Gehring, Petra (2006), *Was ist Biomacht? Vom unzweifelhaften Mehrwert des Lebens*, Frankfurt a.M. and New York: Campus.

Griffiths, John (1986), 'What is Legal Pluralism?', *Journal of Legal Pluralism*, **24**, 1–50.

Griffiths, John (2000), 'Self-regulation of Medical Behavior that Potentially Shortens Life', in Hans Krabbendam and Hans-Martien ten Napel (eds), *Regulating Morality: A Comparison of the Role of the State in Mastering the Mores in the Netherlands and the United States*, Antwerp and Apeldoorn: Maklu, pp. 173–190.

Griffiths, John (2001), 'Legal Pluralism', in Neil J. Smelser and Paul B. Baltes (eds), *International Encyclopedia of the Social and Behavior Sciences*, vol. 13, Amsterdam: Elsevier, pp. 8650–8654.

Griffiths, John (2002), 'Legal Pluralism', in Reza Banakar and Max Travers (eds), *An Introduction to Law and Social Theory*, Oxford: Hart Publishing, pp. 289–310.

Griffiths, John, Alex Bood and Heleen Weyers (1998), *Euthanasia and Law in the Netherlands*, Amsterdam: Amsterdam University Press.

Hegel, Georg Wilhelm Friedrich (1971), *Der Geist des Christentums*, in Eva Moldenhauer and Karl M. Michel (eds), *Werke in 20 Bänden*, vol. 1, Frankfurt a.M.: Suhrkamp, pp. 317–418.

Heun, Werner (2006), '"The Right to Die" – Terri Schiavo, Assisted Suicide and ihre Hintergründe', *Juristenzeitung*, **61** (9), 425–431.

Jakobs, Günther (1998), *Tötung auf Verlangen, Euthanasie und Strafrechtssystem*, Munich: Bayerische Akademie der Wissenschaften.

Jouanna, Jacques (1996), 'Die Entstehung der Heilkunst im Westen', in Mirko D. Grmek (ed.), *Die Geschichte des medizinischen Denkens. Antike und Mittelalter*, Munich: Beck, pp. 28–80.

Kant, Immanuel (1797), *Metaphysik der Sitten*, reprinted in Königliche Preußische Akademie (ed.) (1907), *Kants gesammelte Schriften*, vol. 6, Berlin: Reimer u.a.

Kelsen, Hans and Eugen Ehrlich (2003), *Rechtssoziologie und Rechtswissenschaft. Eine Kontroverse (1915/1917)*, Baden-Baden: Nomos.

Kodalle, Klaus-Michael (ed.) (2003), *Das Recht auf ein Sterben in Würde. Eine aktuelle Herausforderung in historischer und systematischer Perspektive* (Kritisches Jahrbuch der Philosophie, vol. 4), Würzburg: Königshausen & Neumann.

Kutzer, Klaus (2006), *Patientenautonomie am Lebensende*, Baden-Baden: Nomos.

Lembcke, Oliver (2007), 'Sterben in Würde. Zur institutionellen Vermittlung zwischen Selbstbestimmung und Fürsorgepflicht', *Jahrbuch Recht und Ethik*, **15**, 501–523.

Merry, Sally Engle (2003), 'From Law and Colonialism to Law and Globalisation', *Law and Social Inquiry*, **28** (2), 569–590.

Quante, Michael (1998), 'Passive, indirekte und direkt aktive Sterbehilfe – deskriptiv und ethisch tragfähige Unterscheidung?', *Ethik der Medizin*, **10**, 206–226.

Roxin, Claus (1987), 'Die Sterbehilfe im Spannungsfeld von Suizidteilnahme, erlaubtem Behandlungsabbruch und Tötung auf Verlangen', *Neue Strafrechtszeitschrift*, **7** (8), 345–350.

Schmaltz, Christiane (2001), *Sterbehilfe, Rechtsvergleich Deutschland – USA*, Frankfurt a.M.: Peter Lang.

Siep, Ludwig and Michael Quante (1999), 'Ist die aktive Herbeiführung des Todes philosophisch zu rechtfertigen?', in Adrian Holderegger (ed.), *Das medizinisch assistierte Sterben. Zur Sterbehilfe aus medizinischer, ethischer, juristischer und theologischer*, Freyburg, Schweiz: Universitäts-Verlag, pp. 37–55.

Taupitz, Jochen (1991), *Die Standesordnungen der freien Berufe*, Berlin: Walter de Gruyter.

Weber, Max (1980), *Wirtschaft und Gesellschaft. Grundriß der verstehenden Soziologie* (ed. by Johannes Winkelmann), 5. rev. ed., Tübingen: Mohr.

Wernstedt, Thela (2004), *Sterbehilfe in Europa*, Frankfurt a.M.: Peter Lang.

Wilmanns, Juliane C. (2000), 'Ethische Normen im Arzt-Patienten-Verhältnis auf der Grundlage des Hippokratischen Eides', in Nikolaus Knoepffler and Anja Haniel (eds), *Menschenwürde und medizinethische Konfliktfälle*, Stuttgart: Hirzel, pp. 203–220.

Woodman, Gordon R. (1998), 'Ideological Combat and Social Observation: Recent Debates about Legal Pluralism', *Journal of Legal Pluralism*, **42**, 21–59.

Zude, Heiko (2006), *Paternalismus. Fallstudien zur Genese des Begriffs*, Freiburg i.B.: Alber.

12. The influence of court judgments on non-state law

Hans Peters

1. INTRODUCTION

The central question in this book is how the state legislature should react towards non-state law. What is or should be the influence of non-state law on the legislature? Should the legislature take forms of non-state law into account? Is it wise to participate in legislation on non-state law? Does it give the legislator more authority? Is an association with non-state law convenient for the legislator?

Because they are focused on the role of the legislature, these questions suggest that there is a clear difference between non-state law and state law and that it is for the legislator to decide whether a rule can be seen as state law or non-state law. That is only half the truth. Of course, by introducing non-state law into state regulation, the legislature can change non-state law into state law. However, it is mostly a ruling from a court that finally decides whether a rule can be seen as non-state law or state law. The legislature should be aware of that: the borderline between state law and non-state law is thin and relative. In this contribution, I would like to explore the borderline between state law and non-state law and how that line can shift. Therefore it is necessary to define the concepts of state law and non-state law in a legal sense.

Earlier in this book, non-state law was defined from the perspective of the author or the actor. For instance, in Chapter 2 non-state law is described as 'a body of norms produced and enforced by non-state actors'. Under that definition, non-state law contains all the examples of law of which the primary author is not the state legislature. This is more or less a legal sociological definition and in fact does not say much about the legal character of the rules.

From this legal character point of view, the difference between non-state law and state law is more complex. Of course, non-binding codes of conduct are an example of non-state law, but is it the same situation when a code of conduct is agreed upon and can be enforced under private law because it is part of a contract or a provision in the articles of association? The enforcement is then provided by the state legislature. However, in my opinion this code of conduct is still an example of non-state law. Concerning the legal character of the rules, the question is how the rule is given its legal effect. In that perspective, the force of law of non-state law is based on voluntary compliance by the participants, which can have its basis in private law or no law at all. The character of state law is crucially different because of the unilaterally binding force of the rules. This means that, concerning the character of the legal rules, the elements that distinguish non-state law from state law are, in one way, the same as those that distinguish public law from other – mostly private – law. Self-regulation, for example, is a form of non-state law that can have different legal manifestations, but as Julia Black (2001, p. 113) stated: 'Whatever self-regulation is, it is not state regulation!'

The Dutch legal system is a civil law system, so the distinction between private law and administrative law is important. However, similar problems may very well arise in common law countries, as my main finding is that courts use non-state law in a legal setting and thus draw non-state law into a state law context. From this point of view, the central question in this contribution is: *under what circumstances does the private nature of non-state law change into a public character and what effect does this have on non-state law?*

As said, it is the court that decides whether an arrangement of non-state law should be regarded as state law. For that decision, the court uses two criteria: firstly, the legal effect of a rule of non-state law and secondly, the institutional relationship with the government. Perhaps the last criterion needs some explanation. Every form of law is developed within a group of people. This is inherent in the function of law: the regulation of human relations to maintain peace and order. Pitlo (1988, p. 1, my translation) stated it beautifully: 'On the isle of Robinson Crusoe, there is no law until another human being arrives. Then law comes into existence, because Friday becomes the employee and Robinson the employer. It may be in a primitive or sophisticated form, but as soon as two humans make contact, law arises.' Not only is non-state law developed in a group, its binding character is often also limited to that group. From a legal point of view, the group is a legal entity governed by private law. A different legal form would change the non-state law immediately into state law. For the use of non-state law, the government can participate in that legal entity governed by private law and this entails institutional relations.

2. THE CONSEQUENCES OF INSTITUTIONAL RELATIONS

In the case law of the administrative courts, institutional relations between a legal entity governed by private law and the government have played a role especially for the application of the Central and Local Government Personnel Act 1929 (*Ambtenarenwet 1929*) and the Government Information (Public Access) Act (*Wet openbaarheid van bestuur*).

Under Dutch law an employee is a 'civil servant' and can rely on the Central and Local Government Personnel Act 1929 if he or she is (1) appointed in the public service as (2) a civil servant. In the eyes of the Central Appeals Tribunal (*Centrale Raad van Beroep*, a special appeals tribunal for cases involving civil servants and social security issues), a legal entity governed by private law can be considered part of the 'public service' if the government can exert a predominating influence on the management of that legal entity. It is settled case law that four conditions must be met in this context (Van Zutphen 1991, p. 92):

1. the government must have a predominating influence on the composition of the governing board and have the right to dismiss members of the board (right of appointment and right of dismissal of the governing board);
2. the government must have an important influence on the finances of the legal entity (for example, approval of the budget by the government and accountability to the government);
3. the government must play a role with respect to the personnel policy (competence to appoint or dismiss staff and influence on the labour agreement policy);
4. the government must approve a number of the decisions within the legal entity (substantive influence on the legal entity).

This case law shows that an institutional relation between the government and a legal entity under private law can bring an element of public law into the private domain of the legal entity governed by private law. That element only has consequences relating to labour law and does not interfere with the private law character of the legal entity governed by private law nor its activities. In other words, it does not affect the non-state law character of the legal person or its activities.

The Government Information Act is applied similarly. According to this Act, everyone can ask for disclosure of any governmental information held by an administrative authority. Section 3 of the Act provides this right of disclosure also regarding governmental information that is held by 'an agency, service or company carrying out work *for which it is accountable to an administrative authority*'.[1] The accountability referred to in this section has been interpreted by the courts as applying to institutions which, in pursuance of their private law or public law regulation, must follow (general) instructions of an administrative authority. According to the present case law of the Administrative Jurisdiction Division of the Council of State (*Afdeling bestuursrechtspraak Raad van State*), the influence of an administrative authority on the institution and the involvement of the government with the functioning of the institution already qualify as the accountability referred to in Section 3.[2]

In the system of the Government Information Act, it is still the government (the administrative authority) which takes the decisions about disclosure of the governmental information in possession of the private law entity, which decisions are public law acts under Article 1:3 of the General Administrative Law Act (*Algemene wet bestuursrecht*).[3] This means that the application of the Government Information Act as a public regulation does not affect the non-state law character of the private law entity and its activities.

3. THE APPLICATION OF NON-STATE LAW IN STATE LEGISLATION: REFERENCES

State legislation sometimes refers to non-state law. A good example is the use of certification by the state legislature. For instance, Article 7.6 of the Dutch Working Conditions Decree (*Arbeidsomstandighedenbesluit*) provides that a person operating a crane must have a certificate of professional competence. With respect to the content of the requirements, Article 7.7 refers to certification schemes from the Vertical Transport Certification Association (*Stichting Toezicht Certificatie Verticaal Transport*). This is an association – a legal entity governed by private law – in which employers and employees are united and in which professionals from both sides work on the certification schemes. They know what kinds of requirements are necessary and they are probably more knowledgeable on this subject than the authorities. It is a wise decision of the legislature to take advantage of such professional knowledge.

The method in the Working Conditions Decree to use these certification schemes is a so-called 'static reference': the legislature refers to specific certification schemes – for instance, 'TCVT W3-01/06-2002' – whose contents cannot be changed. It is essential to note that the legislature uses its own public authority and the association is not invested with any public authority. The Vertical Transport Certification Association is not an 'administrative authority' as referred to in Article 1:1 of the

General Administrative Law Act and its activities stay within the private domain.

This is an important issue for the legislature. The legal context is different when a 'dynamic reference' is used in legislation and the legislature refers to a certificate whose content is determined by an association. In that situation, the association can be defined as 'government' because it is invested with public authority. This means that the association concerning that specific activity qualifies as an 'administrative authority' and public rules like the General Administrative Law Act apply.

In the Dutch legal culture, there is an explicit preference for administrative authorities in a public law form. This preference – with the private legal form as an exception – is set out in Article 124b of the General Guidelines for Legislative Drafting (*Aanwijzingen voor de regelgeving*) and in Article 4 of the Autonomous Administrative Authorities Framework Act (*Kaderwet zelfstandige bestuursorganen*).[4] Because a dynamic reference results in a classification as an administrative authority, the General Guidelines reflect the preference for static reference in the event that non-public law standards are referred to.[5] Nevertheless, dynamic references to non-public law standards turn up now and then. For example, the minister granted a mussel fisherman a licence with a catchlimit. For the quantity that the fisherman was allowed to catch, reference was made in the licence to the partitioning in the regulation of the Cooperative Dutch Mussel Farmers' Organization (*Coöperatieve Producentenorganisatie van de Nederlandse Mosselcultuur U.A.*), a cooperative association. Unfortunately, the fisherman brought an appeal against the administrative decision of the minister and not against the regulation of the cooperative association.[6] Nevertheless, the Administrative Jurisdiction Division of the Council of State argued that no legal basis for delegation to the cooperative association existed in this case. This shows that a dynamic reference is concerned in the administrative decision of the minister, with the result that the cooperative association could be seen as an administrative authority and its regulation as an administrative decision.

4. THE APPLICATION OF NON-STATE LAW IN STATE LEGISLATION: THE OBLIGATION TO ASSOCIATE

Similar to the issue of certification is an arrangement in state legislation that can be characterized as 'an obligation to associate': the legislature prescribes connection at a certain organization. In Dutch legislation, such an obligation was introduced in the Seeds and Planting Materials Act

(*Zaaizaad- en plantgoedwet*). Article 87 provided that the trade in seeds and planting materials was only allowed by companies registered by a certification institute, indicated by the minister. The minister had indicated the Netherlands Inspection Service for Horticulture (*Stichting Nederlandse Algemene Kwaliteitsdienst Tuinbouw*, an association set up as a result of self-regulation in this sector of agriculture) and the question arose whether registration by the association was an act of a public authority. On that point, there was not much discussion: state legislation stipulated that trade was only allowed after registration by the association, and so registration was an administrative decision. But was the association only through that act an administrative authority? How should the decision about the membership fee be classified? The Administrative Jurisdiction Division of the Council of State also described that decision as a public law act as referred to in Article 1:3 of the General Administrative Law Act.[7] Therefore, not only the act of registration but also other acts qualified as administrative decisions.

The same goes for the duty to associate as stipulated in the Telecommunications Act (*Telecommunicatiewet*). A telephone company must be registered by an association indicated by the minister. One of the associations was the Information Services Code of Conduct Foundation (*Stichting Informatiedienstencode*). In order to register, a company had to sign a registration agreement with the association and this contract entailed financial penalties if the company failed to abide by the terms of the registration agreement. The question was: is a financial penalty an administrative decision or an act under private law? Although the basis of the penalty was found in regulations based on the articles of association, the Trade and Industry Appeals Tribunal (*College van Beroep voor het bedrijfsleven*, as the highest administrative court) identified an administrative decision and the Information Services Code of Conduct Foundation was classified as an administrative authority.[8]

In the case of the mussel fisherman, there was also an obligation to associate because, for a fish quota, a fisherman had to be a member of the cooperative association. The Administrative Jurisdiction Division argued that the fisherman could not be obliged to become a member of a private law organization (that is, the cooperative association). The difference with the obligations to associate in the other cases is that, in this case, the obligation was not laid down in legislation.

These cases, as well as those about certification, show that the legislature should be very careful in linking up with non-state law in state legislation. If the link is not made carefully in legislation, the non-state organization can easily be seen as an administrative authority to which all kinds of public regulations apply. Arrangements that were first known as non-state law change character as a result. A private law organization suddenly qualifies as an administrative authority and some of its activities can be classified as administrative decisions.

5. PUBLIC TASK CASE LAW

A special category of case law from the administrative courts is the so-called 'public task case law'. This case law started with the Former Miners' Silicosis Foundation (*Stichting Silicose Oud-mijnwerkers*). This foundation supplied lump sum payments to former miners suffering from silicosis or to their widows. The funds supplied for that purpose were private donations. The State Secretary had pronounced responsibility for this group, voiced support and appealed for cooperation with this existing foundation. The State Secretary provided funds out of the Treasury and determined conditions for payment. These conditions were laid down in the private law regulation of the foundation. The Administrative Jurisdiction Division of the Council of State reached the decision that this foundation fulfilled a government task and, as a result, the foundation was classified as an administrative authority and its decisions about the payments as administrative decisions.[9] The rationale behind this judgment is clear. As soon as funds originating from the government are paid by a foundation on the basis of criteria determined by the government, this foundation is simply an 'office window' and must legally be treated as if it were the government itself paying the money.

The public task as a result of which a legal entity governed by private law is classified as an administrative authority consists of two elements. There must be a financial relation (the money must come from the government) and a substantive relation (the government stipulates the criteria on the basis of which the money is paid). With those elements, a range of foundations in the Netherlands have meanwhile been classified as administrative authorities.

The criteria have evolved over time. The financial relation moved from only government financing to the government financing 'to a predominant degree'. As regards the substantive relation, it seems no longer necessary that the substantive involvement comes from the same governmental organization which also provides the money, as long as it is the government. Additionally, the binding character of the substantive influence seems to get weaker. In a recent case,[10] the internal regulation of a foundation contained the same criteria as formulated by the minister as a line of policy. This was enough to meet the element of substantive influence. This is not the strict, substantive influence which was formerly used in the case law as a starting point.

These shifts in the criteria used in the case law about the public task seem to be minor modifications, but they can have a large impact on public task case law because, with the new criteria, the classifications seem to have become detached from the original rationale behind this case law. Vigilance is in order here because, as a result of the evolving criteria, not only has the rationale of this case law disappeared but the courts do not deem to follow any clear policy in classifying private law entities as administrative authorities.

6. THE DUTCH SUPREME COURT AND THE PRIMACY OF PUBLIC LAW

So far, it has been the administrative courts that have placed non-state law organizations within the sphere of state law as administrative authorities. That is understandable because the competence of the courts and the legal protection in the system of the General Administrative Law Act depend on that classification.

A special case as regards the boundary between non-state law and state law was submitted to the Netherlands Supreme Court, the highest civil court in the Netherlands. It concerned the Foundation for Quality Guarantee of the Veal Sector SKV (*Stichting Kwaliteitsgarantie Vleeskalversector SKV*).[11] At the end of the 1980s, the Netherlands was rocked by growth hormone scandals in the veal sector. Consumer confidence in the quality of Dutch veal was considerably lowered and the sale of veal fell sharply. Naturally, the Product Board for Livestock and Meat (*Productschap voor Vee en Vlees*), a government organization under the Industrial Organization Act (*Wet op de bedrijfsorganisatie*) took measures and prohibited the use of certain substances. The branch as such, not only the farmers but also traders and slaughterhouses, also undertook action. In 1990, they established the SKV, which checks slaughtered calves for the presence and use of prohibited substances. Approved meat is given a quality certificate. The majority of companies can be checked by the SKV and nearly all slaughterhouses and importers accept only calves which have a certificate. Farmers can join the SKV if they sign a private law contract (the so-called 'connection agreement') with the foundation. The inspection procedure of the entire production chain has been laid down in a protocol, the SKV Control and Sanction Regulation 1991 (*Controle- en Sanctiereglement SKV 1991*), to which companies submit by signing the connection agreement.

A company which was a member of the SKV was fined because it had failed to observe the SKV regulations. This case involved private law aspects – the foundation with its regulation – and public law aspects – the

Product Board with its regulation. If a prohibited substance is found, conflicting (private and public) legal rules apply and the question arises: what rules prevail?

The Netherlands Supreme Court applies the so-called 'Two Ways Doctrine'. This is settled case law concerning the question of whether the government can use private law when also public law action can be taken. For example, a municipality has the possibility, on the basis of the law, to intervene and demolish a construction built illegally on municipality territory, but the municipality can also achieve that result by a private law action based on its right of ownership. According to the Two Ways Doctrine of the Supreme Court, the government must preferably use public law. Private law remedies are only permitted if they do not interfere with public law. One important criterion in this context is the degree of legal protection given by the public regulation.[12] In the SKV case, the Supreme Court used the Two Ways Doctrine and stipulated that the private law option interfered in an unacceptable way with public regulation.

The question arises whether the use of the Two Ways Doctrine is appropriate, because in this case it was not the government (the Product Board) but the SKV as a legal entity governed by private law that took the initiative to fine. However, the Supreme Court decided to apply the Two Ways Doctrine, arguing that the foundation should be looked upon as 'an extension of the Product Board'. This view is based on several circumstances:

- the establishment of the SKV had been welcomed by the State Secretary because the government was not able to tackle the problems;[13]
- the SKV had tried to fulfil its statutory goal by carrying out tasks which had been transferred to the SKV by the Product Board within the framework of the quality control in the branch;
- the charter and regulations of the SKV had been approved by the Product Board, which had also appointed a member to the board of the SKV;
- the SKV was nearly entirely financed by the government (Product Board and ministry);
- the standards from the Product Boards regulations were incorporated in the regulations of the SKV.

That led to the conclusion that the SKV, although a private law legal entity, actually functioned as an extension of the Product Board. This placed the SKV within the Two Ways Doctrine: because the government was involved in the SKV along institutional relations and because it had gradually developed more or less the same activities as the government, the SKV was seen as an application of private law by the government and thereupon as an unacceptable interference with public law. The penalties imposed by the SKV were therefore unlawful.

With the SKV judgment, the Supreme Court adopted a collision course with all kinds of forms and initiatives of self-regulation. Especially in the Dutch 'polder model'[14] and after the pillarization in the Netherlands,[15] there have been frequent pleas for self-regulation: the willingness of people to comply within their own group would be larger, there is specific expertise and it would relieve the government. Instruments like self-regulation become ineffective or useless if, as in the SKV case, they are tested against the Two Ways Doctrine. It would mean that legally the government has a monopoly on certain tasks and apparently other, private, actors are not allowed to participate in the performance of those tasks. Such a strict monopolistic approach is followed by the Trade and Industry Appeals Tribunal.[16] This court decided that a Product Board cannot leave the certification of a company as prescribed in the regulation to a foundation. The Board argued that this would not be transparent for a company or organization wishing to be certified.

The possibilities for using non-state law in government policy will become increasingly limited if this approach is adopted. With this case law, the balance between non-state law and state law is disrupted, as in the SKV case, in which the non-state law organization was in fact ignored by the court.

7. CONCLUDING REMARKS

The administrative courts have introduced public law elements in the area of non-state law and subjected non-state law organizations to the rules of public law. Is it a problem when a non-state law organization becomes a governmental institution?

For the organization itself, the public law standards are substantively not much different from those under private law. Elements of public law often have a counterpart in private law. However, the pressure on the organization can be increased, for example by the application of the Autonomous Administrative Authorities Framework Act, on the basis of which all kinds of public organizational rules are applied. This Act only became effective on 1 February 2007, so it is not yet clear what its effects will be in practice. Furthermore, there is the question of whether non-state law organizations will be able to understand and apply all these unfamiliar rules. In a worst-case scenario, the organization will lose its private law character to the outside world to the detriment of the effectiveness of non-state law.

As for the government, the legislature should be aware of the impact of public law on non-state law organizations and should realize that this impact is often caused by the legislature or steps taken by authorities. On the other hand, the government is presented with an awkward dilemma: the use of self-regulation and non-state law may be wise and efficient but must also be supervised and this requires substantive and institutional relationships. A court can subsequently react by applying public law to a non-state law organization and, as a possible result, a private law organization can even be taken out of the private law sphere.

The use of self-regulation and non-state law may become incompatible as a result. For some, this is probably more a question of culture and feeling than a legal matter. Is there still room for the use of non-state law as a result of the court judgments? At this moment, the approach of the courts is not 'non-state law minded'. The very strict legal approach will definitely have consequences for the use and effectiveness of non-state law and its important role in Dutch society. In my opinion, this is something that the courts, with their strict, legal approach, should reflect on.

NOTES

1. For a translation of the Government Information (Public Access) Act, see <http://www.minbzk.nl/actueel?ActItmIdt=9070>, accessed 1 June 2008.
2. AR 11 February 1991, *AB* 1991, 598.
3. For a translation of the General Administrative Law Act, see http://www.justitie.nl/images/Wettekst%20Awb%20Engelse%20Versie_tcm34-2121.pdf, accessed 1 June 2008.
4. Autonomous Administrative Authorities are administrative authorities as referred to in Article 1:1 General Administrative Law Act. These organizations perform governmental functions, often with government funding or other support, without (full) ministerial responsibility because the organization does not form part of the hierarchy of a particular ministry but is (more or less) independent of it. That is why the Autonomous Administrative Authorities Framework Act gives general rules for these organizations. In international literature, the term 'quango' is frequently used as an acronym for 'QUasi-Autonomous Non-Governmental Organization'.
5. See Article 92, second paragraph, of the General Guidelines for Legislative Drafting.
6. ABRvS 24 January 2007, *AB* 2007, 166.
7. ABRvS 24 December 2003, *JB* 2004/82.
8. CBb 9 February 2005, *AB* 2005, 305.
9. ABRvS 30 November 1995, *AB* 1995, 136.
10. ABRvS 11 October 2006, *AB* 2007, 81.
11. HR 20 December 2002, *AB* 2003, 344.
12. HR 26 January 1990, *AB* 1990, 408.
13. Letter of 27 June 1991, *Parliamentary Papers* II 21 800 XIV.
14. The 'polder model' is a consultation model. It is a popular name for the Dutch practice of policymaking by consensus between the government and its citizens, especially between the government, employers and trade unions.
15. As a result of denominational segregation, before World War II, Dutch society was vertically divided into 'pillars', with all kinds of organizations, associations, clubs and institutions representing the different denominations and ideologies. The religious

context has mainly disappeared but the high degree of organization has remained, so there is a strongly organized field between the government and the citizens that offers possibilities for self-regulation.

16. CBb 10 February 2006, *AB* 2006, 271.

REFERENCES

Black, Julia (2001), 'Decentring Regulation: Understanding the Role of Regulation and Self-regulation in a "Post-regulatory" World', in Michael Freeman (ed.), *Current Legal Problems*, Volume 54, Oxford: Oxford University Press, pp. 103–146.

Pitlo, A. (1988), *Het systeem van het Nederlandse privaatrecht*, Arnhem: Gouda Quint.

Van Zutphen, A.H. (1991), *De rechtspositie van de Rijksambtenaar*, Den Haag: Vuga.

13. Conclusions and challenges: towards a fruitful relationship between state regulation and non-state law

Hanneke van Schooten and Jonathan Verschuuren

1. QUESTIONS

In recent decades, non-state law has boomed. The national state legislature's power is generally thought to be diminishing given the shift in focus of various topics, such as trade, and the environment, to the global level. It is not just other states or supranational organizations that influence national law. Non-governmental organizations (NGOs) such as human rights organizations, environmental organizations and religious groups, as well as business organizations and multinational corporations, have also become important players in the field of law-making. It is hardly conceivable that regulation in such fields as the environment, the Internet or world security should be developed without these non-state actors. They play a part in a globalizing world that cannot be ignored by the state legislature and by regulators. This development sheds new light on the role of the state and thus on the role of state regulation. The state no longer has the monopoly of setting rules and regulations on topics that are considered to be in the public realm. In a world where non-state actors become increasingly important, so do the rules they make.

However, the fact that globalization will continue to change the role of the state as the main producer and enforcer of rules and regulations is not the end of the state legislature. It remains important, not just for the allocation of collective resources, but also for (political) decision-making on the basis of evidence and reason and designing an appropriate legal framework. In the situation of legal pluralism that has developed together with the rise of non-state law, it may very well be only the state, or a state-like entity, that can offer at least some coordination between the various rules, as well as sufficient capacity for monitoring, enforcement and judicial review.

The questions that arise, and that formed the starting point for the journey that led to this book, focus on the (remaining) role of the state; more specifically, of the regulatory state, i.e., on the interaction between state regulation (legislative and regulatory acts) and regulatory activity by non-state actors. What does the decreasing role of the legislature and regulators mean for the concept of the rule of law and, vice versa, what does the rule of law mean for non-state law? Should the legislature and regulators keep an eye on the development of non-state law in a certain policy field, should they take it into account when drafting new legislation, or should they integrate non-state law in laws and regulations? The overarching question addressed in this book, therefore, is the following:

To what extent does non-state law currently influence state regulation, and what should be the consequences of non-state law for state regulation?

2. ANSWERS: A THEORETICAL PERSPECTIVE

This question requires a sharp definition of both non-state law and state law. To this end, the phenomenon of non-state law, and its contrast with state law, must be explored, categorized and analysed. This will shed more light on this complex issue which, as was indicated in the introduction to this volume, is closely related to issues of legitimacy and effectiveness of rules and regulations, and to the rule of law. The wide variety of forms of non-state law, and their specific position in a specific field of law with its underlying principles, make it difficult to sharply distinguish between non-state and state law in general. Instead, it may even be more useful to put non-state law and state law at two ends of the same scale, with less or more state involvement as the determining factor.

When analysing existing studies on the variety of different forms of non-state law, it is useful, however, for methodological/analytical reasons, to distinguish between non-state law within and without the state, as Hertogh shows in Chapter 2. When defined as a body of norms produced and enforced by non-state actors, local rules and customs without state involvement can be the subject of study. Although it is recognized that primitive societies lack a 'definite machinery of enactment, administration, and enforcement of law' typically associated with the state, law is still an important aspect of tribal life. This 'primitive' law – or 'tribal', 'customary', 'religious' law – of indigenous peoples was not only discussed among social scientists, but also became integrated within different systems of colonial law.

'New legal pluralism' or 'legal pluralism at home' study these phenomena wherever they are found, in social groups and associations *within* the state. This 'living law' is seen as the law which dominates life itself even though it has no role in state law. People experience justice and injustice not only in forums sponsored by the state but at 'the primary institutional locations of their activity': home, neighbourhood, workplace, business, and so on.

With the evolution of globalization, a new form of non-state law stemming from non-state actors came into being: an autonomous non-state legal order with special rules and special adjudicating, in particular arbitral, bodies. Internet rules and sports law are examples of this kind of non-state law.

From the various forms of non-state law, Hertogh concludes that non-state law can be categorized as follows: (1) non-state law in the form of rules of conduct; (2) non-state law in the form of norms for decision-making. Within each of these two categories, the rules of conduct and norms for decision-making can either function within the state or without the state, i.e., without a clear recognition by the state or a state entity of the legal value of these rules or norms. Empirical research presented in the second part of this volume shows that the most common form of non-state law consists of rules of conduct, and that it is often recognized by the state in one way or another. This finding will be further discussed below.

Globalization is only one of the factors that stimulated the rise of non-state law. Economic aspects, such as costs involved in the implementation and enforcement of state law, as well as rapidly advancing technologies, have been a stimulus too. In this respect, state law has failed to meet standards of effectiveness and efficiency, especially in so far as state law is aimed at steering (parts of) society or individuals' behaviour in a certain direction. It is generally accepted that non-state actors, through non-state law, can, at least partly, compensate for the ineffectiveness of state law. This, however, raises questions as to the legitimacy of both non-state law and non-state actors in their role as 'regulators'. Do they possess a legitimacy that is somehow comparable to that of the legislature within a democratic state?

In one way or another, all chapters in the theoretical part of this volume deal with the tension between the relevance and usefulness of non-state law, with rules of conduct and norms for decision-making, on the one hand, and with the (monopolistic) claim of legitimacy of state law, on the other. The rule of law is identified with state law. This leads to the question of whether it is possible to generate a rule of law with non-state actors, for instance in such well-regulated domains of life as that of industrial relations. In Chapter 3, Krygier shows that non-state organizations can and do apply the rule of law, thus bringing non-state law into a position to claim legitimacy. The absence of a rule of law and the principle of legality is associated with arbitrariness with traits such as capriciousness, wilfulness and, most of all, with the absence of reasoned justification. The rule of law leads to the 'progressive' reduction of arbitrariness in law and its administration, so the extension of the rule of law to and within non-state organizations is needed 'to infuse [the] mode of governance of those organizations with the aspirations and constraints of a legal order'.

Krygier shows that this approach of law is concentrated on function, not on location. In this way, it is possible to distinguish a number of sources of convergence between what are conventionally understood as 'public' and 'private' domains. Correspondences come to blur differences, both in the sense that 'governmental' powers can be found, and that 'non-governmental' activities occur, in both state and non-state organizations.

If that is the case, to what extent, and in what respect, is state law needed to fulfil important functions, claimed to be legal, in society? And to what extent, and by virtue of what characteristics, can non-state regulation fulfil these functions? In what way do state and non-state regulation interact in the performance of these functions?

It is interesting to search for an answer to these questions in a way that abstracts away from the typical opposites legal/illegal and state law/non-state law.

The 'juristic method', developed by Taekema in Chapter 4, offers opportunities to that end. The juristic method encompasses particular forms of persuasive reasoning, making use of formal rules and institutions, developing a specialized language, and a special focus on correct procedure. As a particular way of handling tasks to be done, the juristic method is best seen as a gradual concept. The more specialized, formal, rule- and procedure-oriented a practice becomes, the more legal it is. The idea that legal character is a matter of degree may seem counterintuitive because we are used to regarding law as a binary concept: something is either legal or it is not. There are many important phenomena, however, that are not fully law in the traditional sense, i.e., modelled on state law, but that share many of its characteristics, known by such names as soft law, emergent law and implicit law. For the purposes of this book, it is important to note that some non-state regulation resembles state law more closely than other non-state regulation. If something has all the characteristics of the juristic method, except that it was not made and is not enforced by state agencies, it can be stated that there is no reason not to call it 'law'.

This implies that (groups of) non-state actors can, to a greater or lesser extent, fulfil those functions of a state that legitimize state legislation. Such a concept of law offers the opportunity for non-state law to be considered 'legal'. This is different from the binary concept of law, according to which all law is state law, leaving little or no room for non-state law. It is worthwhile to juxtapose the positions of state law and non-state law (closely interwoven with legal/illegal), since they seem to represent two extremes on a sliding scale in a continuing debate about the meaning and significance of non-state law: at the one end, the pluralist and decentralized position in which society takes precedence over the state in the process of law creation and, at the other end, the monolithic and state-centred view in which law always has to originate from the state. A state-centred concept of law places an important restraint on the creation and modification of legal norms. This means a significant limitation of arbitrariness in the exertion of power and gives some prospect that such values as equality of citizens before the law, legality and legal security are being protected, as argued by van Klink in Chapter 5. The state (or a functional equivalent of the state) has to fulfil several tasks which can, according to van Klink, be labelled as follows:

1. identification, or the 'imaginative construction of identity';
2. resource mobilization and allocation of collective resources;
3. deliberation, or decision-making on the basis of evidence and reasoning;
4. regulation, or designing an appropriate legal framework, and
5. commitment, or ensuring that people have confidence in the state's actions.

These functions can partly be transferred to non-state organizations. Going back to Taekema's 'juristic method', in so far as a non-state organization fulfils one or more of these functions of the state, and does so in a way that is in line with the basic requirements of the rule of law, its product, i.e., non-state law, can be considered legal and legitimate. The sharp distinction between state law and non-state law as being legal and illegal, respectively, should therefore be rejected. As a consequence, the superiority of either form of law should be rejected as well. Advocates of either non-state law or state law often argue that one form is better than the other. The well-known argument, often used in literature on non-state law, that Roman law was non-state law, thus creating the image that non-state law was the basis of state law in the first place and granting it a status of superiority over state law, was shown to be false by Tellegen-Couperus in Chapter 6.

3. MORE ANSWERS: AN EMPIRICAL POINT OF VIEW

Although more is now known about what non-state law is and how it should be valued in the context of state law, it is still not clear what the influence of non-state law on state law is. This problem is addressed in the empirical research that is presented in the second part of this volume.

In the field of environmental law, non-state law became important in the 1980s and 1990s with the resurgence of the free-market ideology and as a consequence of globalization. National regulators are confronted with severe limitations when it comes to regulating global environmental issues, or companies that operate on a global scale. There is a worldwide trend towards deregulation and self-regulation. As Gunningham demonstrates in Chapter 7, government regulators have been losing their powers and resources, while at the same time NGOs, often together with individual corporations, commercial third parties, business groups and the financial sector, have begun to fill the regulatory gap. Gunningham also shows that this has not led to a total retreat of state law. Instead, the state 'almost invariably retains a supporting role, underpinning alternative solutions and providing a backdrop without which other, more flexible options, would lack credibility, and stepping in where they fail'. Instead of devising command and control instruments, the state seeks to encourage and reward enterprises for going beyond compliance with existing regulation and, generally, to adopt a cooperative approach. Although this development clearly has not come to an end yet, and 'regulatory reconfiguration' is still in full swing, Gunningham does come up with specific suggestions for state regulators and politicians. They should:

- harness the capacities of second and third parties (such as corporations and NGOs, respectively) to more effectively develop non-state law;
- empower the institutions of civil society to make corporations more accountable, for instance through informational regulation;
- strengthen the capability of enterprises for internal reflection and self-control, for instance through focusing more on process-based strategies such as environmental management systems;
- facilitate partnerships between NGOs and industry;
- encourage and reward environmental leaders, and shame laggards;
- encourage best practice rather than merely achieving minimum standards and compliance.

It must be acknowledged, though, that there are not many experiences with such a new regulatory approach, and there is some well-founded criticism as well. Furthermore, research shows that the single most important motivator of improved environmental performance is regulation, as Gunningham indicates. Therefore, Gunningham concludes that a command and control type of regulation by the state will remain important, at least as a complement to a range of next-generation policies and increasingly influential non-state law.

Another policy field where non-state law is rapidly developing is that of nanotechnology. Standardization at the international level, the promotion of codes of conduct, research, and development funding, are instruments applied, rather than the command and control type of instruments in state law. The authors of the chapter on nanotechnology focus on the legal status of the instruments used and, thus, speak of soft law versus hard law, rather than of non-state law versus state law, although their contribution shows that most soft law instruments are in fact non-state law. Their conclusion as to the role of state law in this field is very similar to that of Gunningham. State law should support the effectiveness of non-state law, for instance by providing predictability and a reliable framework for action. This is important not only from a rule of law perspective, but also from a business perspective: investments and technological innovation need stability. In addition, Dorbeck-Jung and Van Amerom conclude that, for non-state law to be taken seriously, it would have to be subjected to a 'surrogate' political process. Only then can it be legitimate. A similar conclusion was reached above when discussing the theoretical chapters of this book.

The potential negative effects of relying too much on non-state law are shown in the chapter on the Australian tax law case. Job shows that the state should not build on the social status of a certain professional group (in this case, the barristers organized through the Bar Association) and think self-regulation and voluntary compliance will do the trick. If there is no voluntarism or self-regulation, the state has to step in. Self-regulation has to be backed up by legal sanctions (although, in this case, there was another complicating factor: the courts were reluctant to enforce the sanctions that existed). An issue not yet addressed is the role of non-state law in the enforcement of state law. Interestingly, the case presented by Job also shows that non-state law can be applied to achieve compliance with existing legislation, even in such a heavily regulated field as tax law. Job shows that the state reacted to illegal activities by the barristers through tightening state legislation and simultaneously urging the Bar Association to strengthen its self-regulatory system. Public exposure (through the media) of the Bar Association's failure to address the problems did the rest. Job concludes that state and non-state actors can work together effectively to achieve compliance with both state and non-state law.

Australia also provides interesting case law on one of the oldest existing categories of non-state law, i.e., aboriginal law. An extensive discussion of case law on native title to land shows that, in the Australian legal system, native law is considered to be non-state law, and even foreign law. The courts are reluctant to open the legal system to native law. Dominello shows that this is not necessarily only due to the existing legal system, but that it may very well be a consequence of a lack of respect for cultural difference in Australia. She argues that this attitude has to change before a more fruitful integration of state law and non-state law can take place. This conclusion may very well be true for 'modern' non-state law on such issues as nanotechnology or the environment that we discussed above: society has to accept non-state law as a valuable and legitimate source of law. The application of elements of the rule of law as a prerequisite for legitimacy was discussed. The conclusion found in the Australian aboriginal case law adds another prerequisite: a social and cultural acceptance of non-state law that goes far beyond the mere concept of the rule of law.

The topic of passive euthanasia, as presented by Lembcke, offers an example of a clash between state law and non-state law, as well as a clash of norms within non-state law. Criminal law, as well as the Hippocratic Oath, an early form of non-state law, prohibit the killing of a patient, while that same Hippocratic Oath and guidelines of medical associations stress the importance of the patient's will as a determining factor for medical decisions. Lembcke shows, through studying the German, Dutch and US euthanasia cases, that this conflict cannot be solved by state law alone, be it legislation or judge-made law. Instead, the actors involved have to interact in a procedural context, establishing a self-regulatory system in which both governmental actors (lawmakers, courts, experts) and social actors (doctors, patients, family members, attendants) are not too demanding. Since state law lacks the instruments to steer this process, its role here is very limited.

In the final empirical chapter, Peters shows that courts can draw non-state law into the realm of state law. Dutch laws and regulations sometimes explicitly refer to non-state law, or even charge a private actor, such as a business organization, with a certain public task. Once there are such references to non-state law in state laws and regulations, courts react by applying public law to private actors. Courts thus fail to appreciate the special position of non-state law. This may have negative consequences for the use of non-state law, as actors may be deterred from developing and applying non-state law.

4. THE FUTURE RELATIONSHIP BETWEEN STATE REGULATION AND NON-STATE LAW

Looking at the future, what should be the consequences of non-state law for state regulation?

From the above discussion of the results of this project, the following lessons for the state legislature and state regulators can be drawn. In those policy fields where strong non-state law exists, that is considered to have a great deal of legitimacy because it has some of the characteristics that are also typical of state law (e.g., the application of elements of the rule of law), state regulation should no longer be the focus of the policy. Instead, state regulation should support the development and application of non-state law. State regulation can do so in a great number of ways. In general, it should provide predictability and a reliable framework, and focus on processes rather than on targets, without omitting to develop command and control type instruments and sanctions that can be applied in those cases where non-state law does not work (for instance, to combat free riders). In addition, state law should harness the capacities of the parties involved to more effectively develop non-state law, which includes empowering the institutions of civil society (for instance, through informational regulation).

At this stage, where only the first experiments of a closer interaction between state regulation and non-state law are being tested, it is difficult to go further than the general views expressed above. It is likely that each situation, depending on the specific traits of the policy field concerned, the social and cultural conditions, the legal culture, and of the organizations involved, requires a different set of tools that must be part of the state regulation that is going to be the legal framework within which non-state law has to be developed and applied. Future research monitoring the results of such modern laws and regulations will have to show what equipment is needed in what situation. What is certain, however, is that more and more state laws and regulations will have to be intertwined with non-state law.

Index